إهداء إلى أختي

من أختك

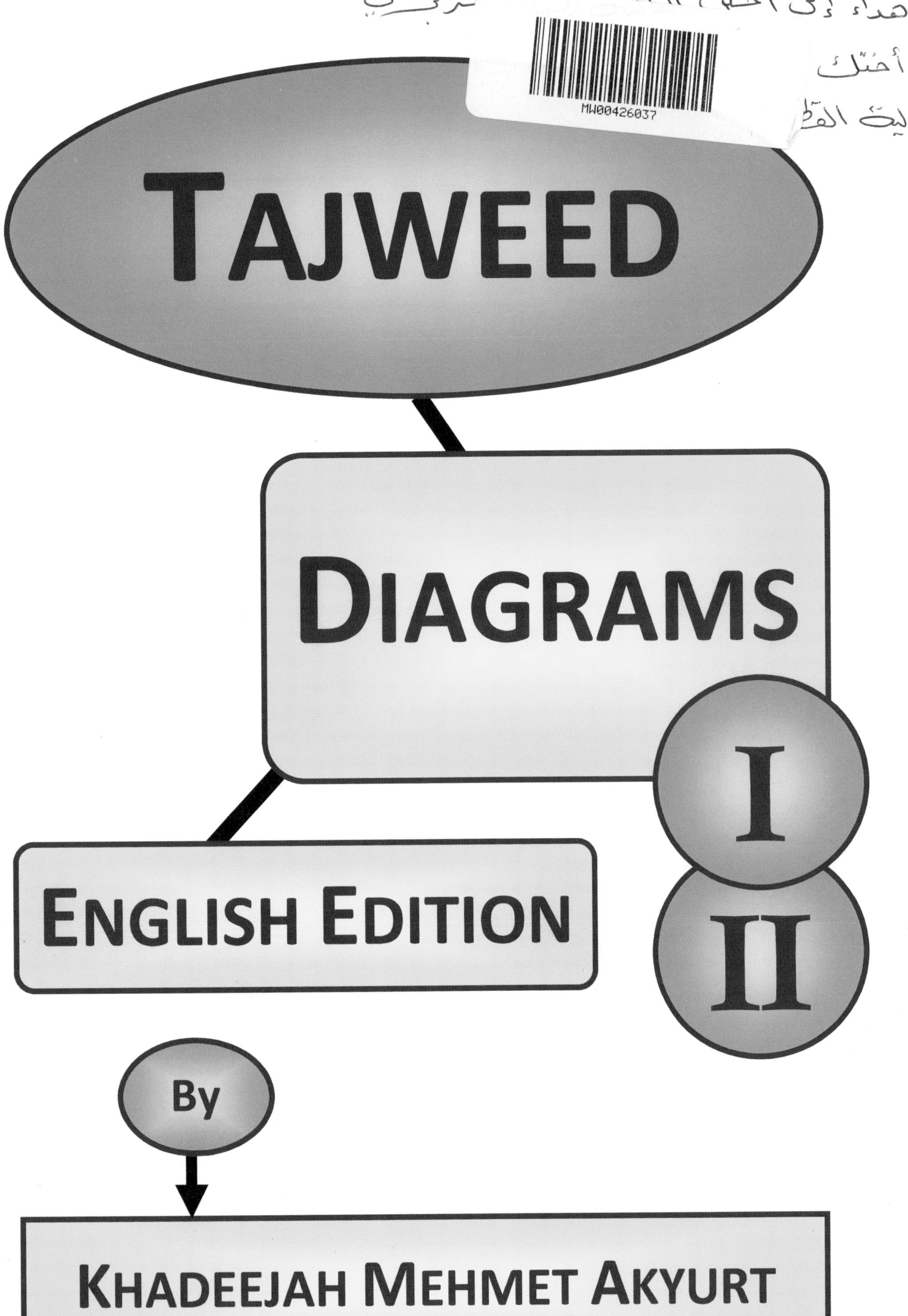

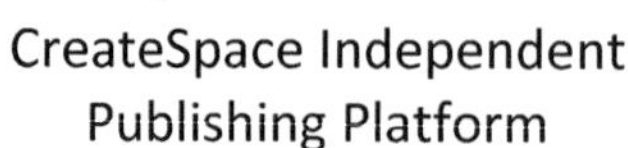

CreateSpace Independent
Publishing Platform

Copies may be purchased from:
www.amazon.com

To contact the author:
P.O. Box 7232
McLean, VA 22106
USA

ISBN-13: 978-1497336582
ISBN-10: 1497336589

بسم الله الرحمن الرحيم

الحَمْدُ للهِ الَّذِي هَدَانَا
لِهَذَا وَمَا كُنَّا لِنَهْتَدِيَ
لَوْلاَ أَنْ هَدَانَا الله

Introduction

What

Detailed, yet concise diagrams of both foundational and advanced tajweed lessons along with related tajweed poems, as narrated by Hafs from 'Asim by the way of *Shatibiyyah*

Why

Lessons are visually appealing, unlike most text books, which can be visually repulsing

There is less text per page, and the information is boiled down to the essentials, which helps students focus and recall

This edition eliminates the lined pages which were intended for note taking, allowing for a full tajweed text book and more information per copy

History

Ustathah Aishah Seriou, the author's mentor and inspiration, is a brilliant teacher who breaks down difficult lessons into easy chunks

By the end of a lesson with Ustathah Aishah, one can see the whole overview in addition to the details, all spread out in a single, appealing diagram

There are no tajweed books modeled in Ustathah Aishah's concise and much needed method, thus the idea for *Tajweed Diagrams* was born

Tajweed Diagrams I, published in 2013, and *Tajweed Diagrams II*, published in 2014, are combined in this edition

Who

Students of tajweed can see difficult, complicated lessons laid out in a single, clear diagram

Teachers have an easy resource when preparing lessons, and a clear layout for their presentations

ACKNOWLEDGEMENTS

My Teachers

Shaikh **Dr. Adel Ibrahim Abushaar** for listening to me and testing me for five months and giving me an ijazah, then continuing to answer my questions through his Facebook page

Shaikhah **Asma Sakka** for joining my 5:30 AM recitation sessions with her husband, Shaikh Adel

Ustathah **Aishah Seriou** for teaching me tajweed and making the impossible become easy through her diagramming methods

My Family

My youngest daughter, **Safiyah,** for helping me edit this book and giving me important pointers on how to improve it

My husband**, Tammam**, for joining me so early each day while I recited to my shaikh

My older daughter, **Fatimah**, for reviewing this book

My parents, who continue to encourage me to be what I want to be

My dear sister, **Asiya**, for editing both the Arabic and English editions of this book

My sisters-in-law, **Fatma** and **Huda,** for yummy food and a comfy second home

My Friends

My halaqah sisters and lifelong friends for their continuous encouragement and advice

My dear friends and students this year for celebrating my previous books and encouraging me to publish again

Thank you!

TABLE OF CONTENTS

LAYING THE FOUNDATIONS 1

- Isti'athah and Basmalah 3
- Points of Articulation 4
- Characteristics of Letters 5
- Letters of Tafkheem 6
  - Levels of Tafkheem 7
  - Light and Heavy Raa 9

FOUNDATIONS OF ELONGATED GHUNNAH 9

- Noon Sakinah 11
  - Ith-haar 12
  - Idghaam 13
  - Iqlaab 14
  - Ikhfaa 15
- Meem Sakinah 16
- Laam Sakinah 18
- Levels of Ghunnah 19

FOUNDATIONS OF ELONGATED VOWELS 21

- Medd 23
  - When two or more medds meet 24
  - Nabr 26
  - Hamzah Al-Wasl 27
  - Hamzat Al-Wasl and Al-Qat' 28

LETTER INTERACTIONS 29

- When Two Letters Meet 31
  - Identical 32
  - Similar 33
  - Close 34
  - Far 35

STOPPING TO TAKE A BREATH 37

- Stopping and Starting 39
- Stopping by Choice 40
  - Complete Stop 41
  - Sufficient Stop 42
  - Good Stop 43
  - Disliked Stop 44

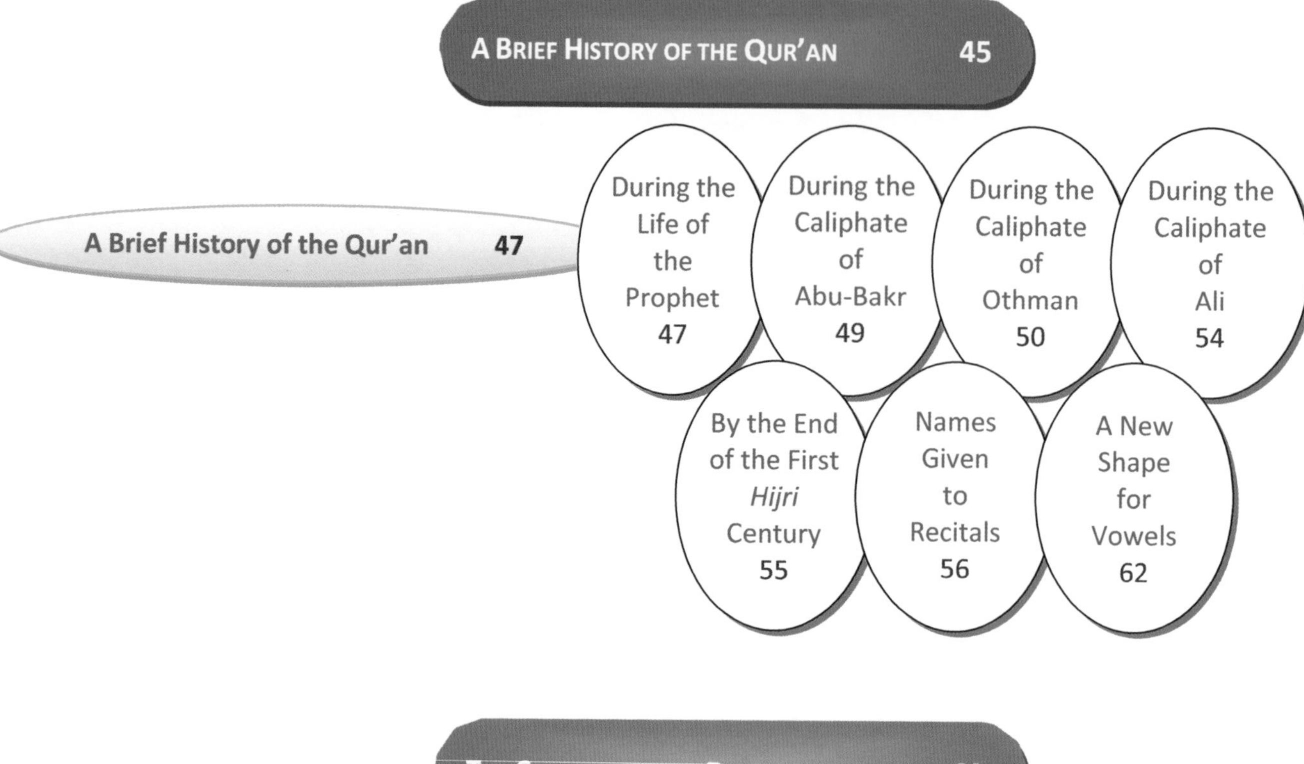

A BRIEF HISTORY OF THE QUR'AN 45

A Brief History of the Qur'an 47

During the Life of the Prophet 47
During the Caliphate of Abu-Bakr 49
During the Caliphate of Othman 50
During the Caliphate of Ali 54
By the End of the First *Hijri* Century 55
Names Given to Recitals 56
A New Shape for Vowels 62

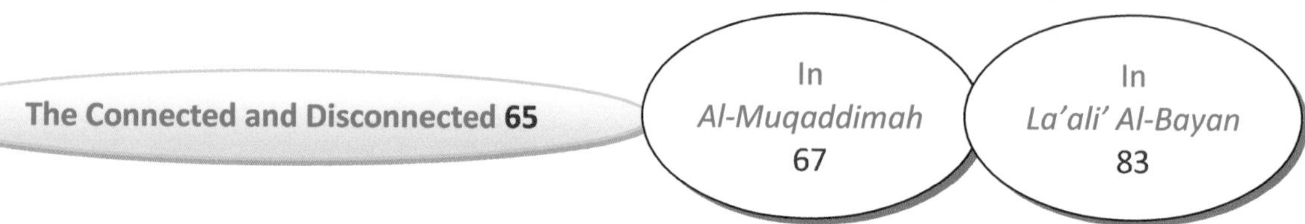

THE CONNECTED AND DISCONNECTED 63

The Connected and Disconnected 65

In *Al-Muqaddimah* 67
In *La'ali' Al-Bayan* 83

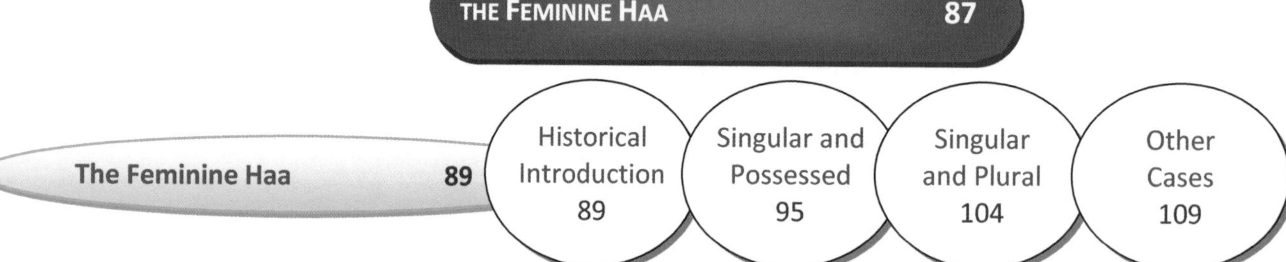

THE FEMININE HAA 87

The Feminine Haa 89

Historical Introduction 89
Singular and Possessed 95
Singular and Plural 104
Other Cases 109

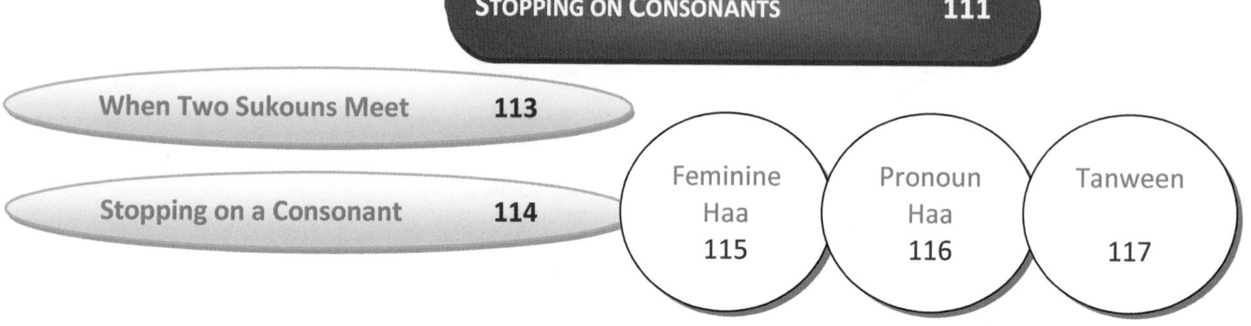

STOPPING ON CONSONANTS 111

When Two Sukouns Meet 113
Stopping on a Consonant 114

Feminine Haa 115
Pronoun Haa 116
Tanween 117

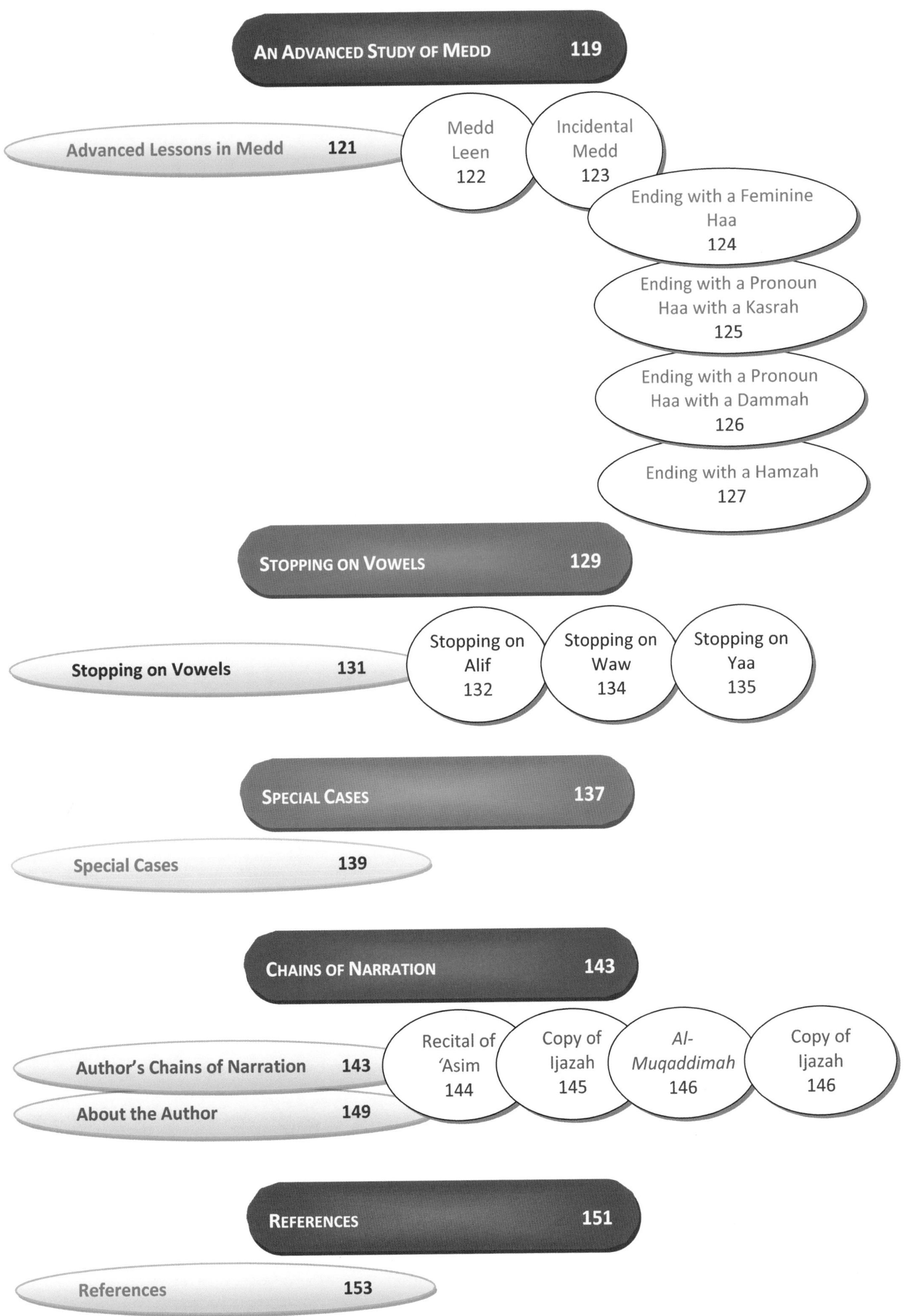

An Advanced Study of Medd 119
Advanced Lessons in Medd 121
Medd Leen 122
Incidental Medd 123
Ending with a Feminine Haa 124
Ending with a Pronoun Haa with a Kasrah 125
Ending with a Pronoun Haa with a Dammah 126
Ending with a Hamzah 127
Stopping on Vowels 129
Stopping on Vowels 131
Stopping on Alif 132
Stopping on Waw 134
Stopping on Yaa 135
Special Cases 137
Special Cases 139
Chains of Narration 143
Author's Chains of Narration 143
Recital of 'Asim 144
Copy of Ijazah 145
Al-Muqaddimah 146
Copy of Ijazah 146
About the Author 149
References 151
References 153

Laying the Foundations

Levels of Tafkheem

Tafkheem of the Laam and Raa

Tafkheem and Tarqeeq

Isti'athah and Basmalah

Articulation Points

Characteristics of letters

Rules of Seeking Refuge and Basmalah

Seeking Refuge

Wording:

1. أَعُوذُ بِاللهِ مِنَ الشَّيْطَانِ الرَّجِيمِ
A'outhu billahi minash-shaitani arrajeem
2. أَعُوذُ بِاللهِ مِنَ الشَّيْطَانِ
A'outhu billahi minash-shaitan
3. أَعُوذُ بِاللهِ السَّمِيعِ العَلِيمِ مِنَ الشَّيْطَانِ الرَّجِيمِ
A'outhu billahi Assamee'i Al'aleem minash-shaitani arrajeem

Ruling:

1. **The Majority**: recommended at beginning of recitation.
2. **Some Scholars**: obligatory at beginning of recitation.

The Basmalah

Wording:

بِسْمِ اللهِ الرَّحْمَـٰنِ الرَّحِيمِ
Bismillahi Arrahmani Arraheem

Ruling:

1. **Beginning of Surahs:** Obligatory, except at the beginning of Surat At-Tawbah
2. **Within Surahs:** Recommended, except within Surat At-Tawbah.

Ways of Seeking Refuge, Basmalah, and Starting a Surah

1. **Cutting all three off from each other:**
أَعُوذُ بِاللهِ مِنَ الشَّيْطَانِ الرَّجِيمْ | بِسْمِ اللهِ الرَّحْمَـٰنِ الرَّحِيمْ | وَالْعَصْرْ

2. **Joining all three with each other:**
أَعُوذُ بِاللهِ مِنَ الشَّيْطَانِ الرَّجِيمِ بِسْمِ اللهِ الرَّحْمَـٰنِ الرَّحِيمِ وَالْعَصْرْ

3. **Joining the basmalah and the beginning of the surah:**
أَعُوذُ بِاللهِ مِنَ الشَّيْطَانِ الرَّجِيمْ | بِسْمِ اللهِ الرَّحْمَـٰنِ الرَّحِيمِ وَالْعَصْرْ

4. **Joining seeking refuge with the basmalah:**
أَعُوذُ بِاللهِ مِنَ الشَّيْطَانِ الرَّجِيمِ بِسْمِ اللهِ الرَّحْمَـٰنِ الرَّحِيمْ | وَالْعَصْرْ

Ways of Basmalah between Two Surahs

1. **Separating all of them:**
فِي عَمَدٍ مُمَدَّدَةْ | بِسْمِ اللهِ الرَّحْمَـٰنِ الرَّحِيمْ | أَلَمْ تَرَ ...

2. **Joining all of them:**
فِي عَمَدٍ مُمَدَّدَةٍ بِسْمِ اللهِ الرَّحْمَـٰنِ الرَّحِيمِ أَلَمْ تَرَ ...

3. **Joining the basmalah with the beginning of the surah:**
فِي عَمَدٍ مُمَدَّدَةْ | بِسْمِ اللهِ الرَّحْمَـٰنِ الرَّحِيمِ أَلَمْ تَرَ ...

4. **Not allowed:** Joining the end of the surah with the basmalah:
فِي عَمَدٍ مُمَدَّدَةٍ بِسْمِ اللهِ الرَّحْمَـٰنِ الرَّحِيمْ | أَلَمْ تَرَ ...

Ways of Connecting Al-Anfal with At-Tawbah

1. **Separating:** (with taking a breath)
إِنَّ اللهَ بِكُلِّ شَيْءٍ عَلِيمْ | بَرَاءَةٌ ...

2. **Joining:** (with applying Iqlaab)
إِنَّ اللهَ بِكُلِّ شَيْءٍ عَلِيمٌ بَرَاءَةٌ ...

3. **Pausing السكت:** (without taking a breath)
إِنَّ اللهَ بِكُلِّ شَيْءٍ عَلِيمْ ۜ بَرَاءَةٌ ...

The Articulation Points of Letters

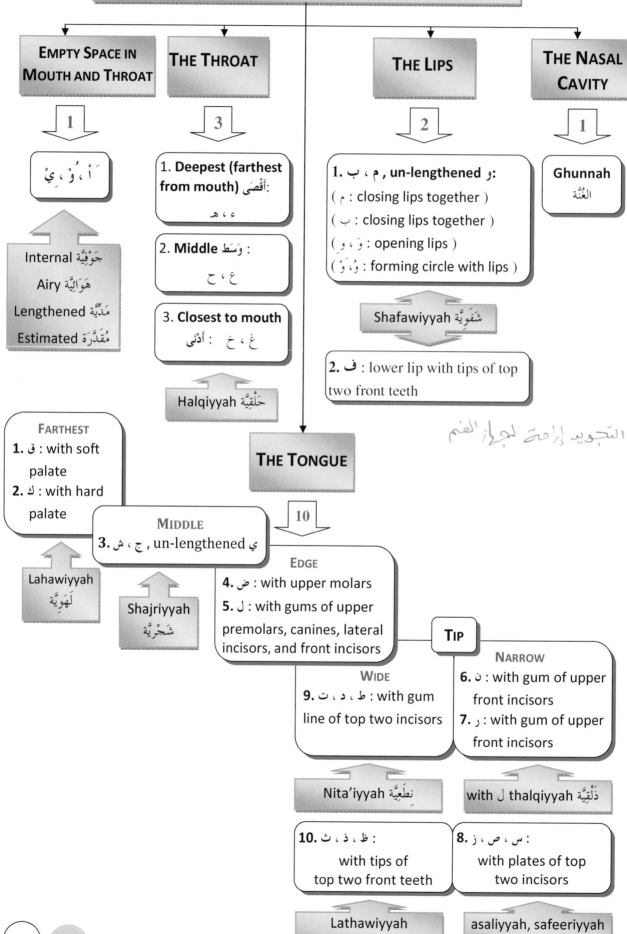

Empty Space in Mouth and Throat

1

اَ ، وْ ، يِ

Internal جَوْفِيَّة
Airy هَوَائِيَّة
Lengthened مَدِّيَّة
Estimated مُقَدَّرَة

The Throat

3

1. **Deepest (farthest from mouth)** أَقْصَى: ء ، هـ
2. **Middle** وَسَط : ع ، ح
3. **Closest to mouth** أَدْنَى : غ ، خ

Halqiyyah حَلْقِيَّة

The Lips

2

1. ب ، م , un-lengthened و:
(م : closing lips together)
(ب : closing lips together)
(وَ ، و : opening lips)
(وُ ، وْ : forming circle with lips)

Shafawiyyah شَفَوِيَّة

2. ف : lower lip with tips of top two front teeth

The Nasal Cavity

1

Ghunnah
الغُنَّة

التجويد إراحة لجهاز الفم

The Tongue

10

Farthest
1. ق : with soft palate
2. ك : with hard palate

Lahawiyyah لَهَوِيَّة

Middle
3. ش ، ج , un-lengthened ي

Shajriyyah شَجْرِيَّة

Edge
4. ض : with upper molars
5. ل : with gums of upper premolars, canines, lateral incisors, and front incisors

Tip

Narrow
6. ن : with gum of upper front incisors
7. ر : with gum of upper front incisors

with ل thalqiyyah ذَلْقِيَّة

Wide
9. ت ، د ، ط : with gum line of top two incisors

Nita'iyyah نِطَعِيَّة

10. ث ، ذ ، ظ : with tips of top two front teeth

Lathawiyyah لَثَوِيَّة

8. ز ، ص ، س : with plates of top two incisors

asaliyyah, safeeriyyah أَسَلِيَّة ، صَفِيرِيَّة

THE CHARACTERISTICS OF LETTERS

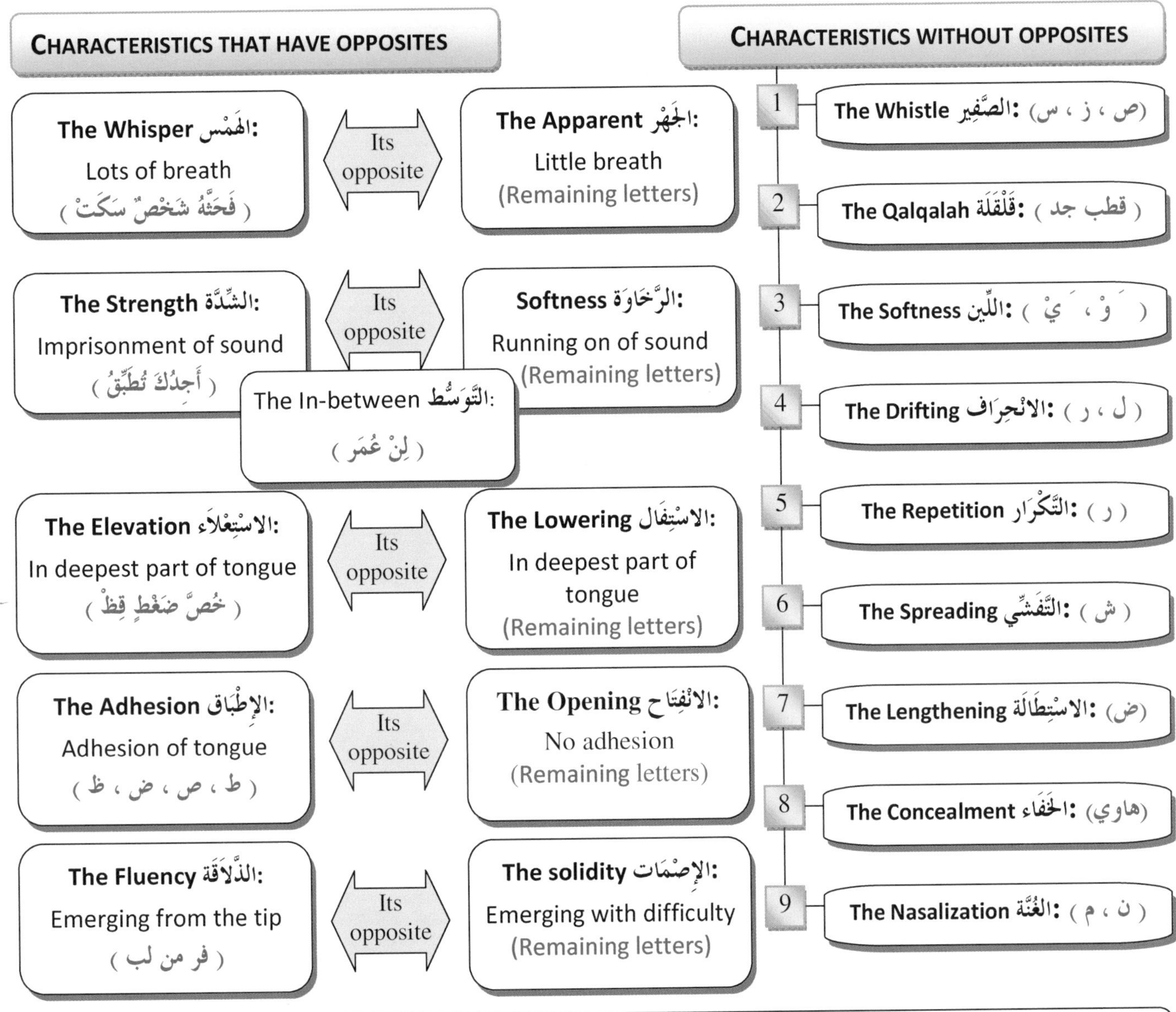

FROM IBN AL-JAZARI'S *AL-MUQADDIMAH*

Their characteristics are: Apparent, Softness, Lowered, Opened, Solid, and the opposite say,
Its Whispered [are] فحثه شخص سكت, its Strengthened أجد قط بكت
And Between Soft and Strong [are] لن عمر and the seven Elevated gathered [in] خص ضغط قظ
And صاد، ضاد، طاء، ظاء [are] Adhered, and فر من لب [are the] letters of Fluency
Their Whistled [are] صاد، زاي، سين , the Qalqalah قطب جد , and the [letters of] Softness [are] واو and ياء with a sukoon preceded by a fat-hah and the Drifting is correct on the lam and the raa', and [on the raa'] the Repetition, and the Spreading for the شين , and Lengthen the ضاد

صِفاتُها جَهْرٌ و رِخْوٌ مُسْتَفِلْ   مُنْفَتِحٌ مُصْمَتَةٌ و الضِدَّ قُلْ
مَهْمُوسُها فَحَثَّهُ شَخْصٌ سَكَتْ   شَدِيدُها لَفْظُ أَجِدْ قَطٍ بَكَتْ
و بَيْنَ رِخْوٍ و الشَّدِيدِ لِنْ عُمَر   و سَبْعُ عُلْوٍ خُصَّ ضَغْطٍ قِظْ حَصَرْ
و صَادُ ضَادٌ طَاءُ ظَاءٌ مُطْبَقَةْ   و فَرَّ مِنْ لُبِّ الحروفُ المُذْلَقَةْ
صَفِيرُها صَادٌ وَ زَايٌ سِينُ   قَلْقَلَةٌ قُطْبُ جَدٍ وَ اللِّينُ
وَاوٌ وَ يَاءٌ سُكِّنا وَ انْفتحا   قَبْلَهُمَا و الانْحِرَافُ صُحِّحَا
فِي اللامِ وَ الرَّا وَ بِتَكْرِيرٍ جُعِلْ   وَ لِلتَّفَشِّي الشِّينُ ضَاداً اسْتَطِلْ

The Letters According to Tafkheem and Tarqeeq

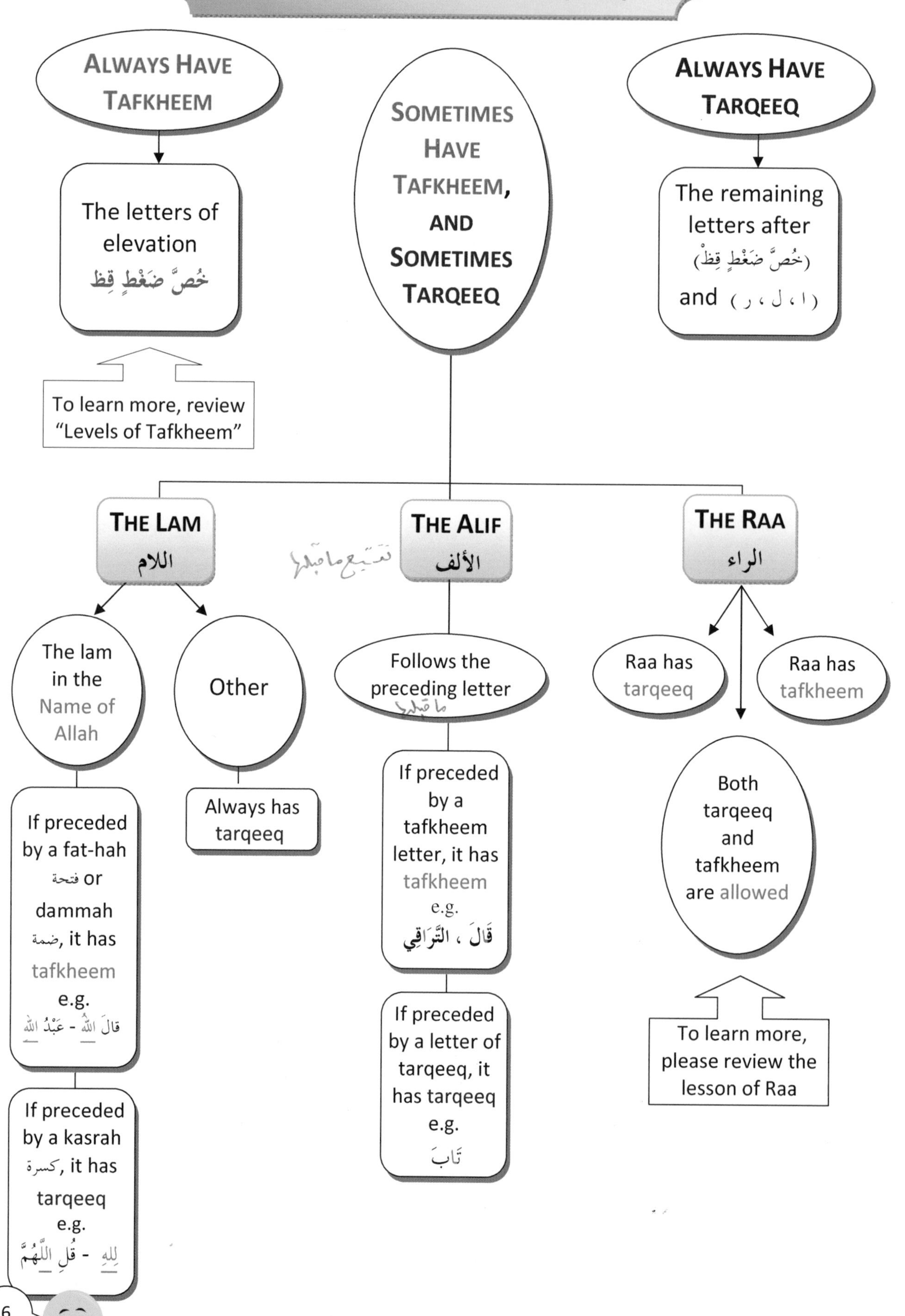

Always Have Tafkheem
The letters of elevation
خُصَّ ضَغْطٍ قِظ
To learn more, review "Levels of Tafkheem"
Sometimes Have Tafkheem, and Sometimes Tarqeeq
Always Have Tarqeeq
The remaining letters after (خُصَّ ضَغْطٍ قِظْ) and (ا ، ل ، ر)
The Lam
اللام
The lam in the Name of Allah
If preceded by a fat-hah فتحة or dammah ضمة, it has tafkheem
e.g.
قالَ اللهُ - عَبْدُ الله
If preceded by a kasrah كسرة, it has tarqeeq
e.g.
لِلهِ - قُلِ اللَّهُمَّ
Other
Always has tarqeeq
The Alif
الألف
Follows the preceding letter
If preceded by a tafkheem letter, it has tafkheem
e.g.
قَالَ ، التَّرَاقِي
If preceded by a letter of tarqeeq, it has tarqeeq
e.g.
تَابَ
The Raa
الراء
Raa has tarqeeq
Raa has tafkheem
Both tarqeeq and tafkheem are allowed
To learn more, please review the lesson of Raa

Levels of Tafkheem for the Letters of Elevation

(خُصَّ ضَغْطٍ قِظْ)

School of Thought of Mohamed Ibn Al-Jazari

1. The letter with a fat-hah followed by an Alif:
e.g.: خَابَ ، أَصَابَ ، ضَاقَتْ ، غَائِبَة ، طَائِفَة ، قَالَ ، يُظَاهِرُونَ

2. The letter with a fat-hah with no Alif following it:
e.g.: خَلَتْ ، صَدَقَ ، ضَرَبَ ، غَفَرَ ، طَبَعَ ، قَتَلَ ، ظَنَّ

3. The letter with a dammah:
e.g.: خُلِقَ ، صُرِفَتْ ، ضُرِبَتْ ، غُلِبَتْ ، طُبِعَ ، قُتِلَ ، يَظُنُّونَ

4. The letter with a sukoon:
e.g.: إِخْوَانًا ، أَصْبَرَهُمْ ، يَضْرِب ، أَفْرِغْ ، يَطْبَع ، نُذِقْهُ ، يَظْلِم

5. The letter with a kasrah:
e.g.: يَتَّخِذ ، الصِّرَاط ، يُضِلّ ، غِلّ ، يُطِع ، قِيلَ ، ظِلاًّ

School of Thought of Ibn At-Tahhan Al-Andalusi

1. The letter with a fat-hah, and the letter with a sukoon preceded by a fat-hah:
e.g.: خَابَ ، أَصَابَ ، ضَاقَتْ ، غَائِبَة ، طَائِفَة ، قَالَ ، يُظَاهِرُونَ
e.g.: خَلَتْ ، صَدَقَ ، ضَرَبَ ، غَفَرَ ، طَبَعَ ، قَتَلَ ، ظَنَّ
e.g.: أَخْرَجْنَا ، أَصْبَرَهُم ، يَضْرِبُ ، مَغْفِرَة ، يَطْبَعُ ، يَقْتُل ، يَظْلِم

2. The letter with a dammah, and the letter with a sukoon preceded by a dammah:
e.g.: خُلِقَ ، صُرِفَتْ ، ضُرِبَتْ ، غُلِبَتْ ، طُبِعَ ، قُتِلَ ، يَظُنُّونَ
e.g.: يُخْلَقُونَ ، يُقْتَل ، يُطْعِمُونَ ، يُظْلَمُونَ
e.g.: لُوط (when stopping)

3. The letter with a kasrah, and the letter with a sukoon preceded by a kasrah:
e.g.: يَتَّخِذ ، الصِّرَاط ، يُضِلّ ، غِلّ ، يُطِع ، قِيلَ ، ظِلاًّ
e.g.: إِخْوَانًا ، مِصْرَ ، أَفْرِغْ ، إِطْعَام ، نُذِقْهُ
e.g.: مَحِيصْ ، مُحِيطْ ، سَحِيقْ (when stopping)

Al-Mutawalli – May Allah have mercy on him – said:

ثُم المفخَّماتُ عنهم آتية — على مَراتِبٍ ثلاثٍ وَ هِيَهْ
مفتوحُها مضمومُها مكسورُها — و تابعٌ ما قبلَهُ ساكنُها
فما أتى مِن قبلِهِ من حَرَكَةْ — فَافْرِضْهُ مُشْكَلاً بتلكَ الحركةْ
و قِيلَ بل مفتوحُها معَ الألِفْ — وبَعدَهُ المفتوحُ مِنْ دونِ أَلِفْ
مضمومُها ساكنُها مكسورُها — فهذهِ خَمسٌ أتاكَ ذِكْرُها
فَهِيَ و إنْ تَكُنْ بأدنى مَنْزِلَةْ — فَخيمةٌ قطْعاً مِن المُستَفِلَةْ
فَلا يُقالُ إنَّها رَقِيقَةْ — كَضِدِّها تلكَ هِيَ الحَقيقَةْ

And then the letters of tafkheem are coming; In three levels, and they are: With a fat-hah, a dammah, a kasrah And with a sukoon following what precedes it; So whichever vowel precedes it Suppose it [the saakin] is voweled with it And it is said, "No, they are [the ranks]: The fat-hah followed by an alif And after it a fat-hah without an alif The one with the dammah, the saakin, the one with the kasrah; So that is five, its mention came to you." And if it is in the lowest level, it has *tafkheem*, cut off from the *Istifaal* (lowering of the tongue); So it cannot be said it has *tarqeeq*, like its opposite, that is the truth

The Cases of Tarqeeq and Tafkheem for the Raa الراء

Raa is Always Muraqqaqah

The raa' has a **kasrah**
e.g. رِجَال

The raa' has a **sukoon**, preceded by a **kasrah**, not followed by an **Elevation** letter in the same word
e.g. فِــرْعَوْن

The raa' has a **sukoon**, preceded by a Lowered letter with a **sukoon** which is preceded by a **kasrah**
e.g. الذِّكْــرْ

The raa' has a **sukoon**, preceded by a **Lengthened** مدية or **Softened** لينية yaa'
e.g. خَبِيْــرْ ، خَيْــرْ

Both Tarqeeq and Tafkheem are Allowed

The raa' has a **sukoon**, preceded by a **kasrah**, followed by an **Elevation letter** with a kasrah

Only Example:
فِرْقٍ

The raa' has a **sukoon**, preceded by an Elevated letter with a **sukoon** which is preceded by a **kasrah**
Only Two Examples:
1. مِصْرْ
tafkheem is prevalent
2. القِطْرْ
tarqeeq is prevalent

Raa is Always Mufakhamah

The raa' has a **fat-hah** or **dammah**
e.g. رَحْمَة ، رُبَمَا

The raa' has a **sukoon**, preceded by a **fat-hah** or **dammah** or **alif** or **waw madiyyah**
e.g. مَرْيَم ، الفُرْقَان ، النَّارْ، نُورْ

The raa' has a **sukoon**, preceded by a **sukoon** (not a yaa') which is preceded by a **fat-hah** or **dammah**
e.g. العَصْــرْ ، خُسْــرْ

The raa' has a **sukoon**, preceded by an **incidental kasrah** (hamzat wasl)
e.g. اِرْجِعِي

The raa' has a **sukoon**, preceded by a **kasrah**, followed by an **Elevation letter** without a kasrah in the same word, and they are:
إِرْصَادًا ، مِرْصَادًا ، لَبِالْمِرْصَاد ، قِرْطَاسًا ، فِرْقَــة ، فِرْقْ

The Foundations of Elongated Ghunnah

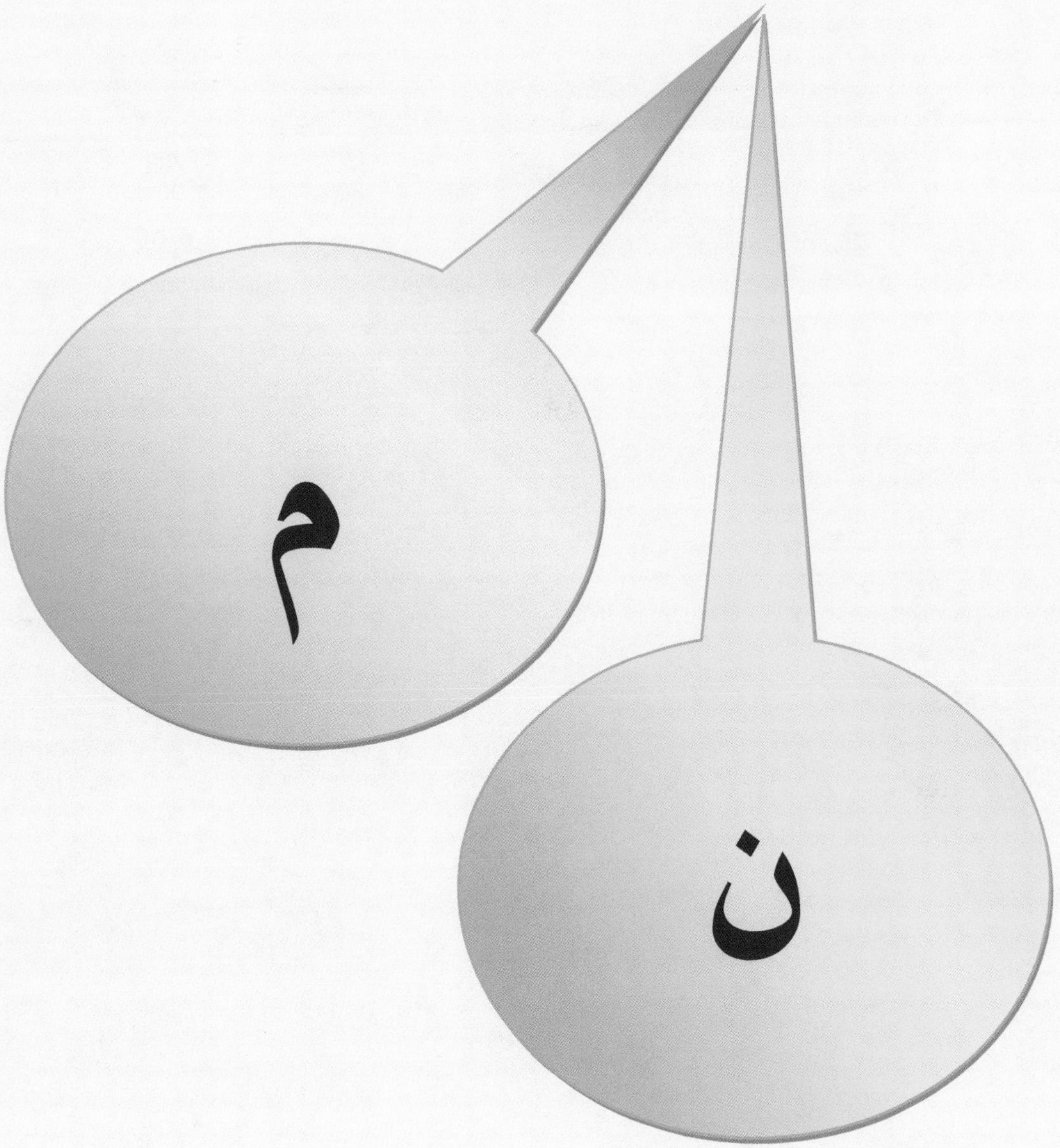

م

ن

NOON SAKINAH AND TANWEEN RULES

نْ ـً ـٌ ـٍ

AL-ITH-HAAR الإِظْهَار

Clarifying نْ ـً ـٌ ـٍ at the throat letters, without lengthening the ghunnah

ITS LETTERS

ء هـ ، ع ح ، غ خ

EXAMPLES

ء : يَنْئَوْنَ ، مَنْ أَعْطَى ، كُفُواً أَحَد

هـ : يَنْهَوْنَ ، مَنْ هَاجَرَ ، سَلَامٌ هِيَ

ع : الأَنْعَام ، مَنْ عَمِلَ ، وَاسِعٌ عَلِيم

ح : وَانْحَرْ ، مِنْ حَيْثُ ، عَزِيزٌ حَكِيم

غ : فَسَيُنْغِضُونَ ، مِنْ غَيْرِ قَوْلاً غَيْرَ

خ : الْمُنْخَنِقَة ، مَنْ خَلَقَ ، لَطِيفٌ خَبِير

ITS NAMES

Ith-haar Halqi
إِظْهَار حَلْقِيّ

AL-IDGHAAM الإِدْغَام

إدخال الحرف مع الحرف — دمج

Merging نْ ـً ـٌ ـٍ into the idghaam letters, partially or completely

ITS LETTERS

يَرْمَلُون

ITS GROUPS

Ghunnah	No Ghunnah
Its letters: ينمو	ل ، ر
Accompanied by an elongated ghunnah	Not accompanied by a ghunnah

EXAMPLES

With Ghunnah

ي : مَن يُطِع ، وُجُوهٌ يَوْمَئِذ

ن : مِن نِّعْمَة ، مَلِكاً نُّقَاتِل

م : مِن مَّاء ، ماءٍ مَّهِين

و : مِن وَلِيّ ، وَلِيٍّ وَلاَ

Without Ghunnah

ل : أَن لَّن ، مَالاً لُّبَدَا

ر : مِن رِّزْق ، رَؤُوفٌ رَّحِيم

EXCEPTIONS

1. Absolute Ith-haar إظهار مطلق is compulsory in: دُنْيَا ، بُنْيَان ، قِنْوَان ، صِنْوَان
2. Ith-haar is compulsory in*: (يسٓ وَالْقُرْءَانِ) ، (نٓ وَالْقَلَمِ)

1. Pausing without taking a breath سكت is compulsory in*: (وَقِيلَ مَنْ ~س رَاقٍ)

AL-IQLAAB الإِقْلَاب

Changing نْ ـً ـٌ ـٍ into a hidden meem at the baa', with an elongated

ITS LETTERS

ب

EXAMPLES

أَنبِئُونِي
مِن بَـعْدِ
سَمِيعٌ بَصِير

AL-IKHFAA الإِخْفَاء

15 letters

Hiding نْ ـً ـٌ ـٍ at the letters of ikhfaa', with an elongated ghunnah

عارٍ عن التشديد

ITS LETTERS

The rest of the alphabet, which are the first letters of the following words:

صِفْ ذَا ثَنَا كَمْ جَادَ شَخْصٌ قَدْ سَمَا دُمْ طَيِّباً زِدْ فِي تُقًى ضَعْ ظَالِماً

EXAMPLES

ذ : مُنذِر ، مَن ذَا ، سِرَاعاً ذَلِك

ش : أَنشَرَه ، إِن شَآء ، عَذَابٌ شَدِيد

ق : مَنقَلَبًا، مِن قَبْلِهِم، كُتُبٌ قَـيِّمَة

ITS NAMES

Ikhfaa' Haqeeqee
إِخْفَاء حَقِيقِيّ

* In the reading of Hafs from 'Asim, by the way of *Shatibiyyah*

ITH-HAAR

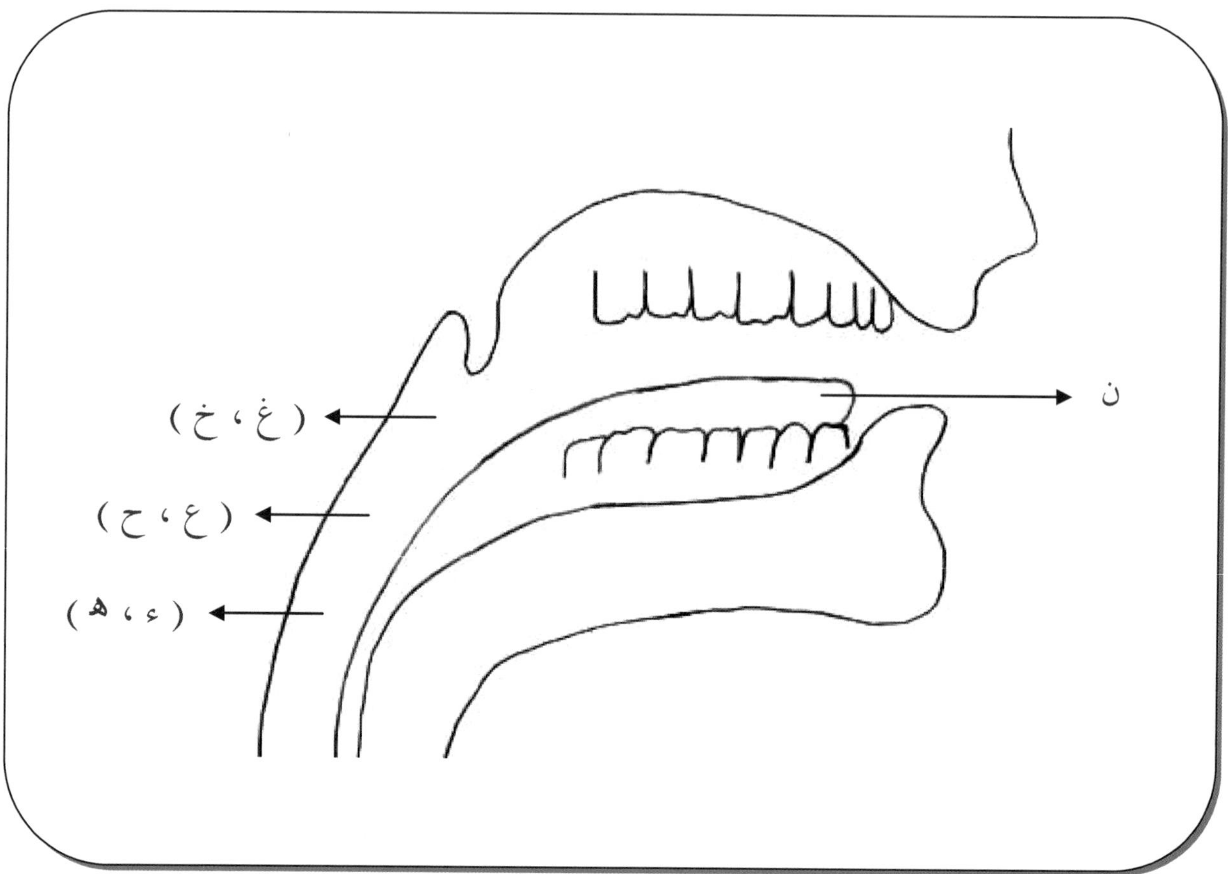

ن is far from all the letters of Ith-haar, in both points of articulation as well as in their characteristics.

This detachment results in the impossibility of any level of merging

We are thus left with Ith-haar

Ith-haar implies a **quick** and **clear** pronunciation of both letters: ن and any of the six letters خ ، غ ، ح ، ع ، هـ ، ء

IDGHAAM

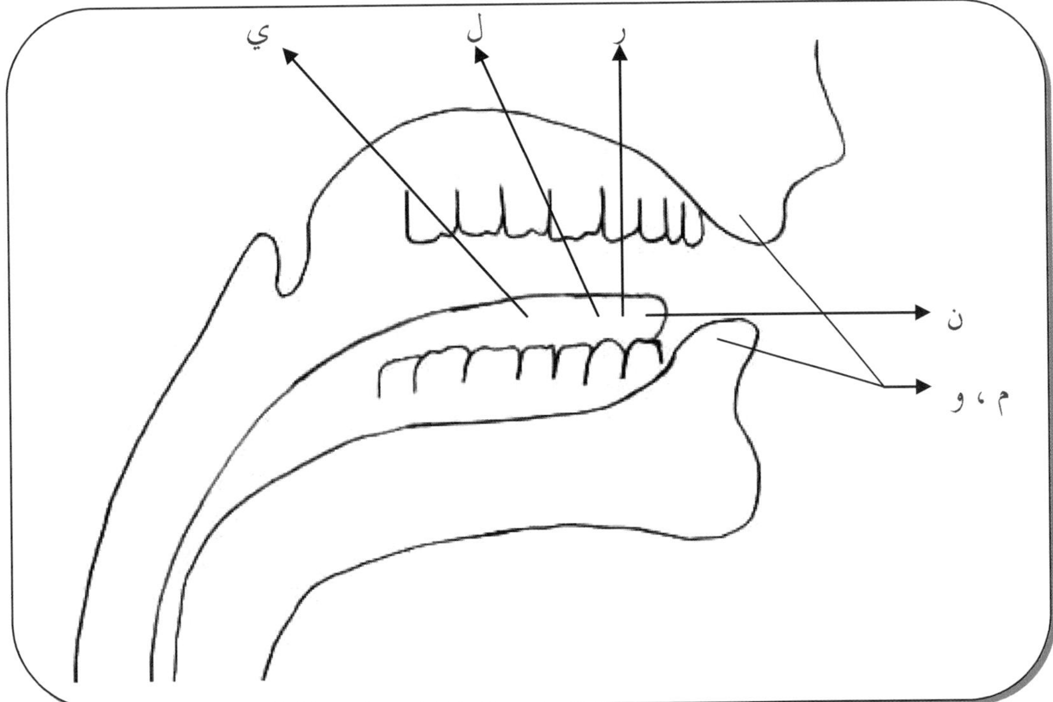

Partial Merging: The first letter mostly disappears, and only its most prominent characteristic remains, such as ghunnah

Something Remains ← Second Letter × First Letter

Complete Merging: The first letter disappears entirely

First disappears ← Second Letter × First Letter

IDGHAAM

- **Without Ghunnah**
  - (Complete) ل ، ر

    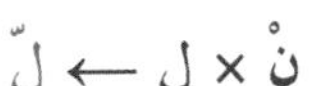

    نْ × ل ← لّ

    The ن disappears completely

    نْ × ر ← رّ

    The ن disappears completely

- **With Ghunnah**
  - (Partial) ي ، و

    نْ × ي ← ي

    The ي is pronounced with a ghunnah, which is left over from the ن

    نْ × و ← و

    The و is pronounced with a ghunnah, which is left over from the ن

  - (Complete) ن ، م

    نْ × ن ← نّ

    The first ن disappears completely and the remaining ghunnah is that of the second ن

    نْ × م ← مّ

    The ن disappears completely and the remaining ghunnah is that of م

IQLAAB

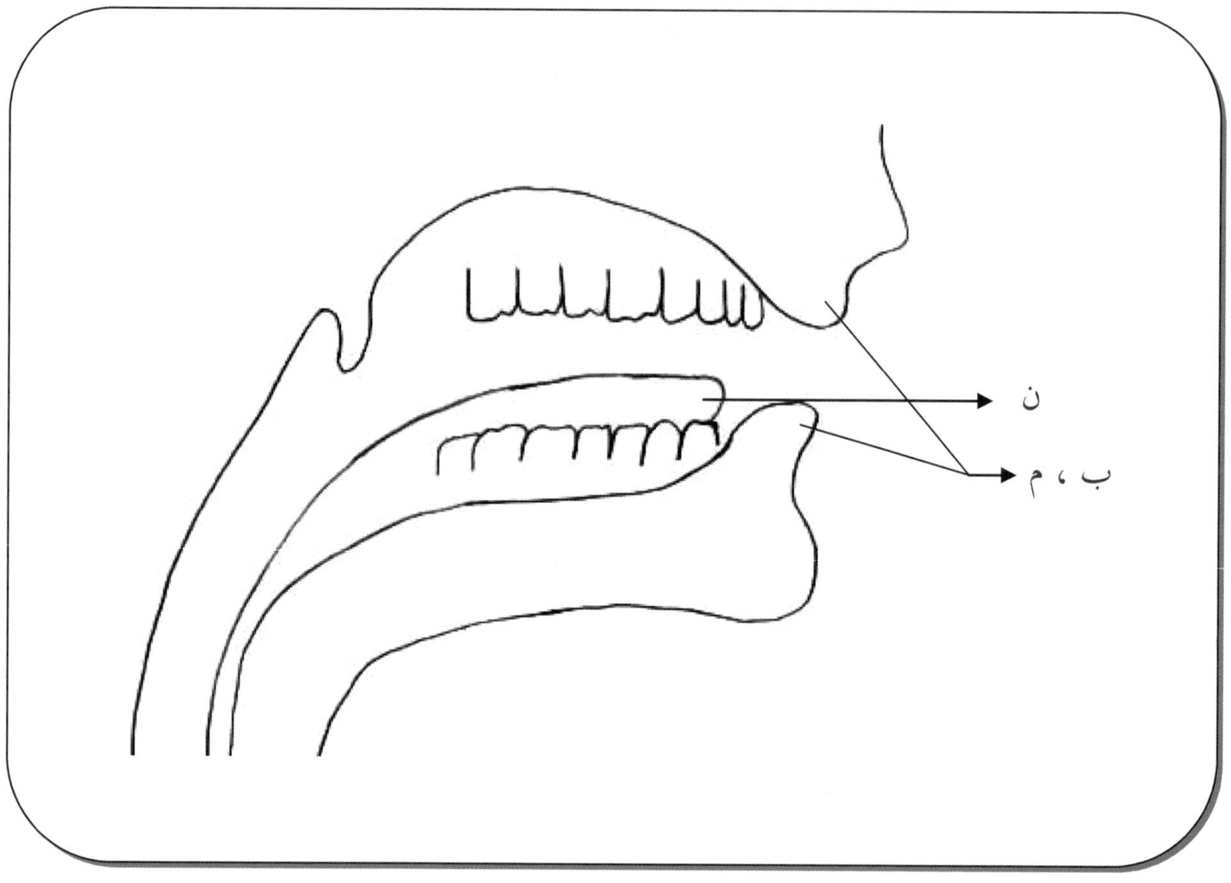

ن and ب are **remote** in their characteristics, and are articulated from different points

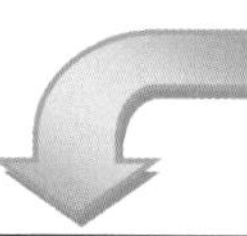

ن and م have identical characteristics
(They are **close** letters)

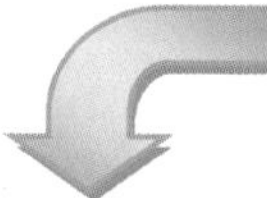

ب and م share the same detailed point of articulation
(They are **similar** letters)

Since م shares ب's articulation point, and ن's characteristics, it is a "mediating" letter that helps the tongue transition to pronouncing the ب, thus we **turn** the ن into a م

IKHFAA

حروف الاخفاء

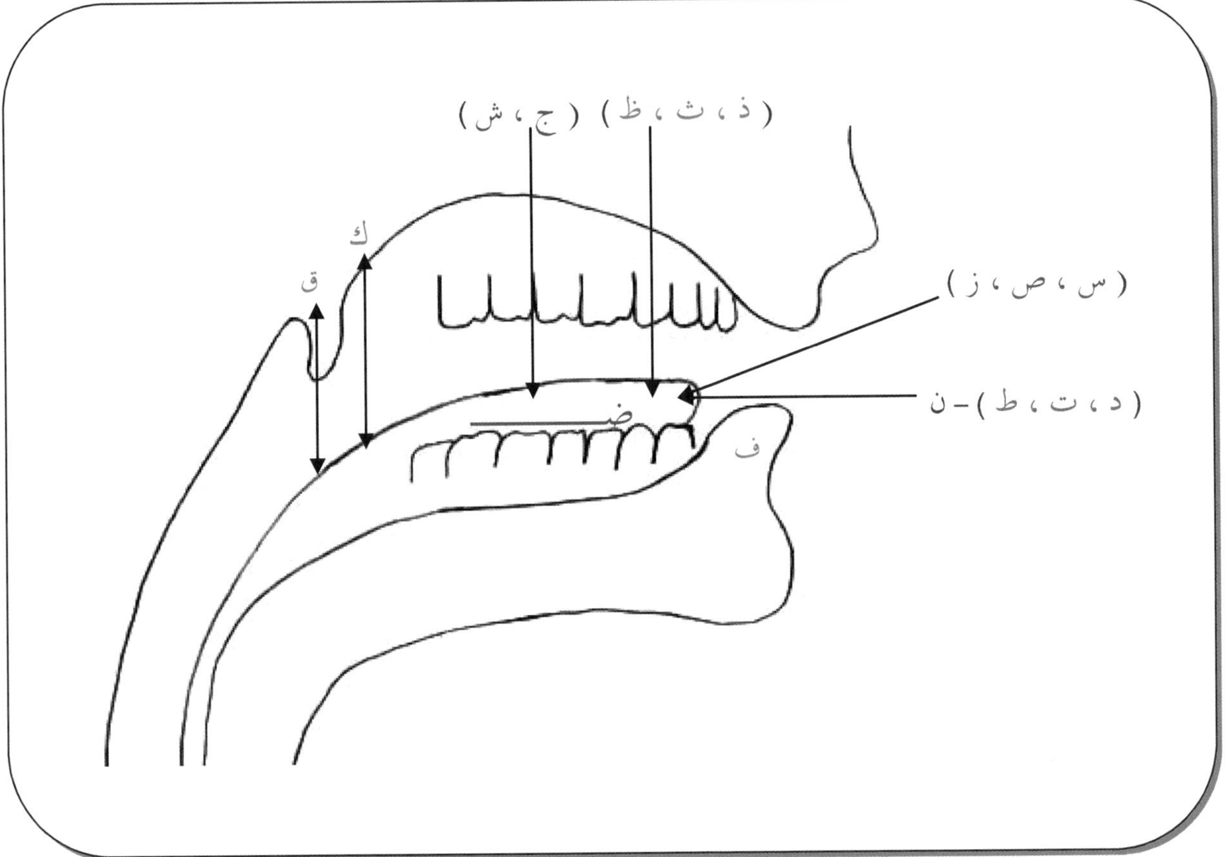

Ikhfaa occurs at a letter: The mouth readies itself for the letter following the ن

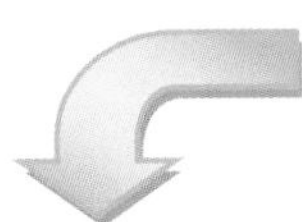

Ghunnah can be heavy or light: Depending on the letter following ن

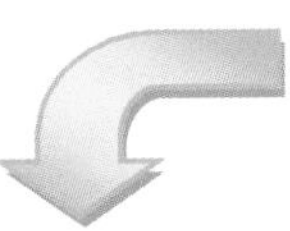

There are three letters whose articulation points are adjacent to that of ن , and the tongue must avoid their region of the mouth so as not to pronounce the ن too clearly. These letters are:

(د ، ت ، ط)

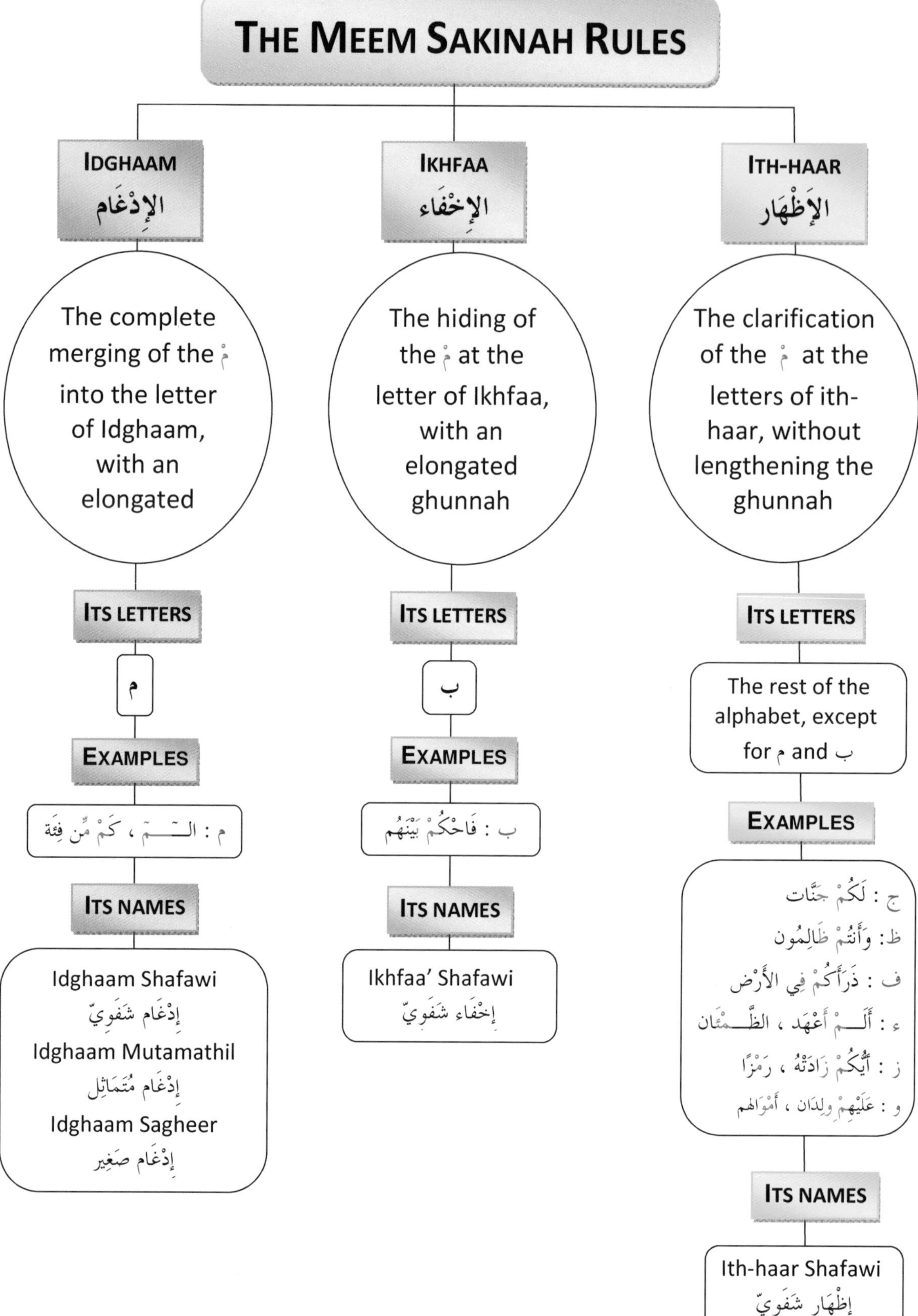

THE MEEM SAKINAH RULES
IDGHAAM
الإِدْغام
IKHFAA
الإِخْفَاء
ITH-HAAR
الإِظْهَار
The complete merging of the مْ into the letter of Idghaam, with an elongated
The hiding of the مْ at the letter of Ikhfaa, with an elongated ghunnah
The clarification of the مْ at the letters of ith-haar, without lengthening the ghunnah
ITS LETTERS
م
ITS LETTERS
ب
ITS LETTERS
The rest of the alphabet, except for م and ب
EXAMPLES
م : الــــمّ ، كَمْ مِّن فِئَة
EXAMPLES
ب : فَاحْكُمْ بَيْنَهُم
EXAMPLES
ج : لَكُمْ جَنَّات
ظ: وَأَنتُمْ ظَالِمُون
ف : ذَرَأَكُمْ فِي الأَرْض
ء : أَلَــمْ أَعْهَد ، الظَّــمْئَان
ز : أَيُّكُمْ زَادَتْهُ ، رَمْزًا
و : عَلَيْهِمْ وِلدَان ، أَمْوَالهم
ITS NAMES
Idghaam Shafawi
إِدْغَام شَفَوِيّ
Idghaam Mutamathil
إِدْغَام مُتَمَاثِل
Idghaam Sagheer
إِدْغَام صَغِير
ITS NAMES
Ikhfaa' Shafawi
إِخْفَاء شَفَوِيّ
ITS NAMES
Ith-haar Shafawi
إِظْهَار شَفَوِيّ

Meem Sakinah

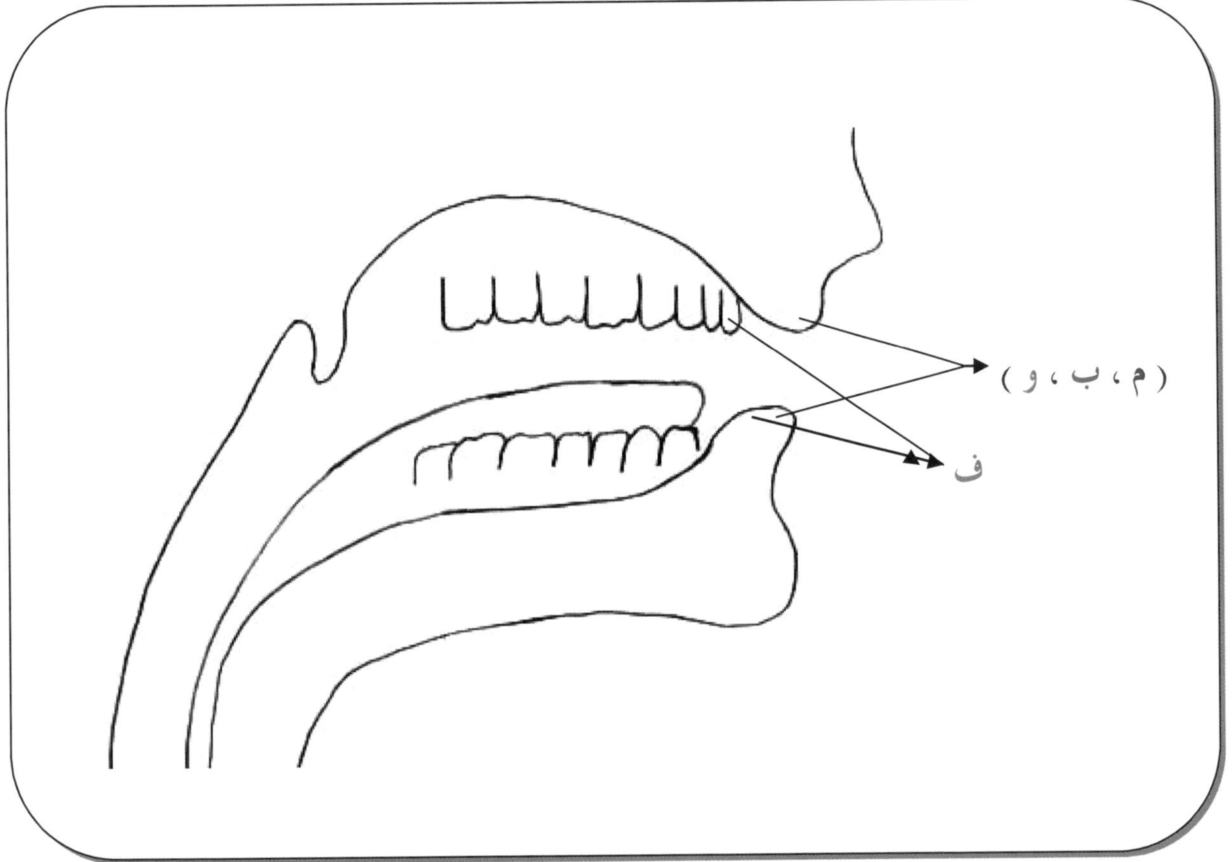

The م sakinah **merges** with another م since they are **identical** letters

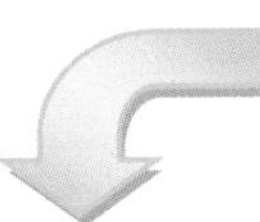

The م sakinah is **hidden** at a ب since they are **similar** letters which share points of articulation

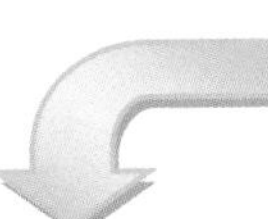

The م sakinah does **not** merge with nor hide at و or ف although they share points of articulation

THE RULES OF LAM SAKINAH

BEGINNING OF WORD

Lam of the definite article لَامَ التَّعْرِيف (اَلْ)

ITS RULING

Ith-haar الإِظْهَار
With the 14 letters in the group: اِبْغِ حَجَّكَ وخَفْ عَقِيمَهُ
e.g.: اَلْقَمَر

Id-ghaam الإدغام
With the remaining 14 letters: (in red)
طِبْ ثُمّ صِلْ رَحِماً تَفُزْ ضِفْ ذَا نِعَمْ
دَعْ سُوءَ ظَنٍّ زُرْ شَرِيفاً لِلْكَرَمْ
e.g.: اَلشَّمْس

MIDDLE OF WORD

In a noun لام الاسم
e.g. سُلْطَان

In a verb لام الفعل
e.g. الْتَقَى
يَلْتَقِطْهُ ، أَلْقِ

In an order لام الأمر
e.g. فَلْيَمْدُدْ

THEIR RULING: Ith-haar الإظهار

END OF WORD

In a verb
e.g.
قُلْ يَجْعَلْ

In a particle لام الحرف
e.g. هَلْ ، بَلْ

THEIR RULING

Idghaam الإدغام
with ل and ر
e.g. قُل لَّكُم ، قُل رَّبِّ ، يَجْعَل
لَّكُمْ ، بَل لاَّ ، بَل رَّفَعَهُ ، هَل لَّكُمْ

Ith-haar الإظهار
with the rest of the letters
e.g. قُلْ تَعَالَوْا ، فَاجْعَلْ أَفْئِدَةً
بَلْ نَحْنُ ، هَلْ تَعْلَمُ

EXCEPTION

Pausing (without taking a breath) is obligatory in:
(كَلاَّ بَلْ ۜ رَانَ)

In the reading of Hafs from 'Asim, by the way of *Shatibiyyah*

Levels of Ghunnah

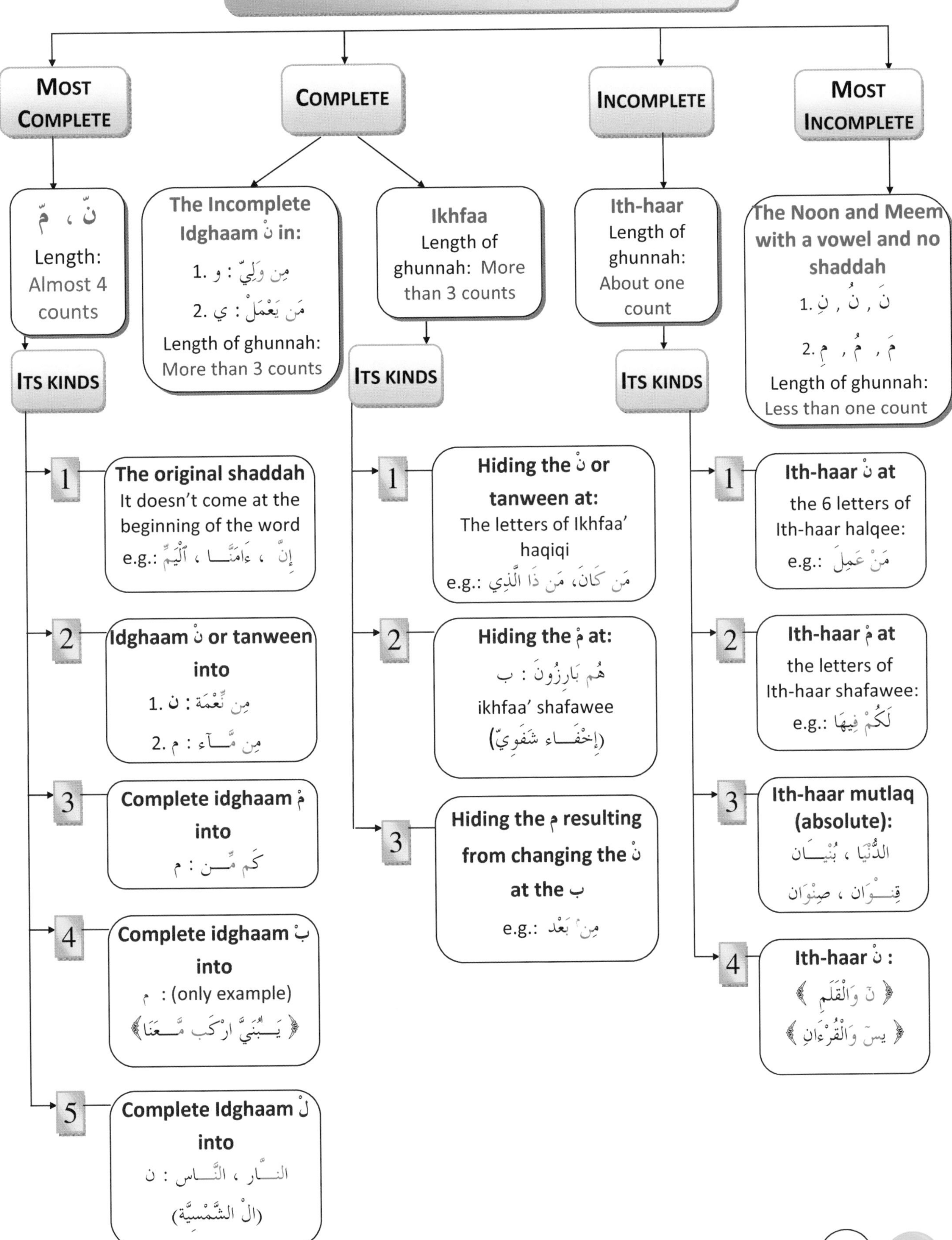

Most Complete
Complete
Incomplete
Most Incomplete
نّ ، مّ
Length: Almost 4 counts
The Incomplete Idghaam نْ in:
1. و : مِن وَلِيّ
2. ي : مَن يَعْمَلْ
Length of ghunnah: More than 3 counts
Ikhfaa
Length of ghunnah: More than 3 counts
Ith-haar
Length of ghunnah: About one count
The Noon and Meem with a vowel and no shaddah
1. نِ , نُ , نَ
2. مِ , مُ , مَ
Length of ghunnah: Less than one count
Its kinds
1 The original shaddah
It doesn't come at the beginning of the word
e.g.: إِنَّ ، ءَامَنَّا ، ٱلْيَمِّ
2 Idghaam نْ or tanween into
1. ن : مِن نِّعْمَةَ
2. م : مِن مَّآءِ
3 Complete idghaam مْ into
م : كَم مِّن
4 Complete idghaam بْ into
م : (only example)
﴿ يَـبُنَيَّ ارْكَب مَّعَنَا ﴾
5 Complete Idghaam لْ into
ن : النَّار ، النَّاس
(الْ الشَّمْسِيَّة)
Its kinds
1 Hiding the نْ or tanween at:
The letters of Ikhfaa' haqiqi
e.g.: مَن كَانَ، مَن ذَا الَّذِي
2 Hiding the مْ at:
ب : هُم بَارِزُونَ
ikhfaa' shafawee
(إِخْفَاء شَفَوِيّ)
3 Hiding the م resulting from changing the نْ at the ب
e.g.: مِنۢ بَعْد
Its kinds
1 Ith-haar نْ at the 6 letters of Ith-haar halqee:
e.g.: مَنْ عَمِلَ
2 Ith-haar مْ at the letters of Ith-haar shafawee:
e.g.: لَكُمْ فِيهَا
3 Ith-haar mutlaq (absolute):
الدُّنْيَا ، بُنْيَان
قِنْوَان ، صِنْوَان
4 Ith-haar نْ :
﴿ نٓ وَالْقَلَمِ ﴾
﴿ يسٓ وَالْقُرْءَانِ ﴾

THE FOUNDATIONS OF ELONGATED VOWELS

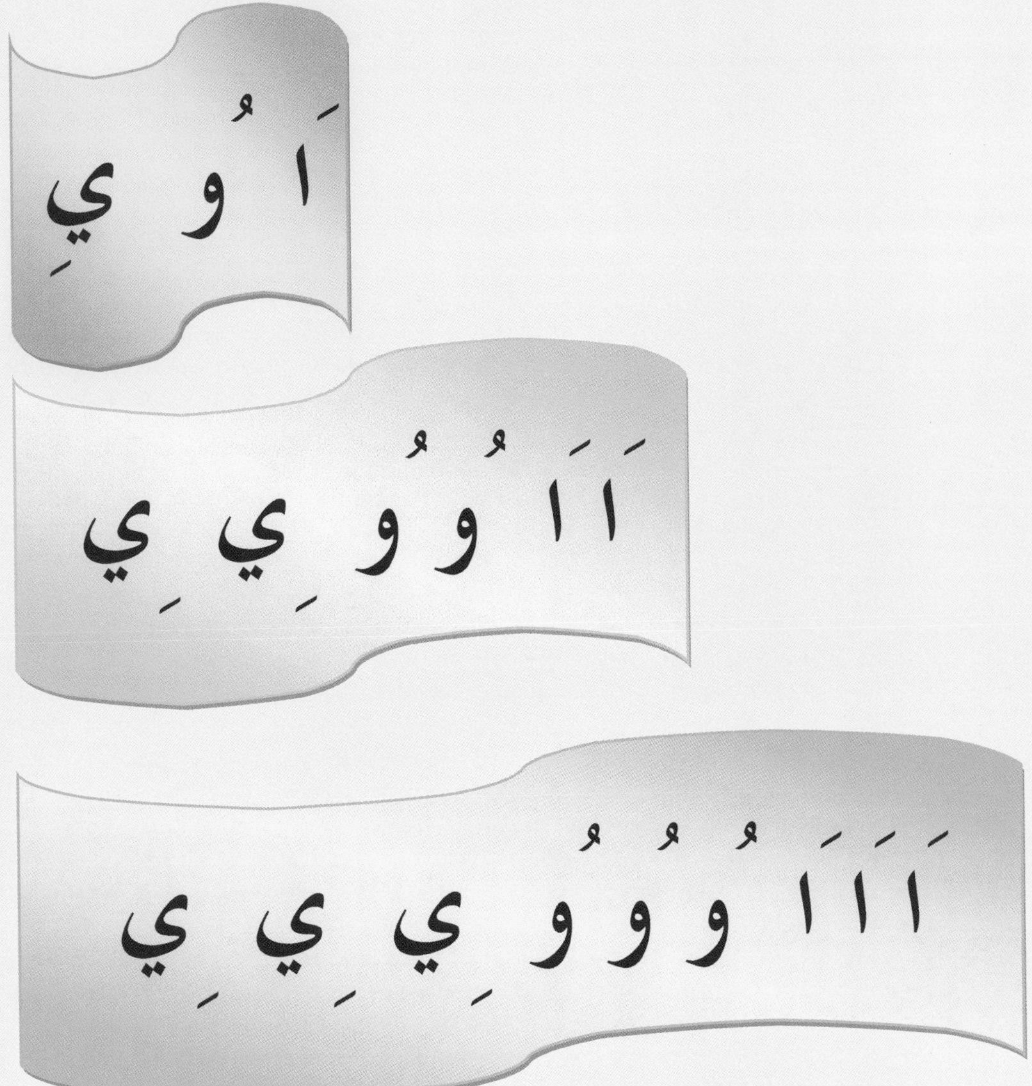

THE MEDD

In the reading of Hafs from 'Asim, by the way of *Shatibiyyah*

NATURAL LENGTHENING
Lengthened **two counts**, and **can appear as:**

The Lesser Connecting Medd مد الصلة الصغرى
(مِن رَّبِّهِ ـ) (وَالْمُؤْمِنُون) (لَهُ فِيهَا) with the condition that:
1. There is a pronoun هاء representing the singular male in third person, or the pronoun هاء of the female noun هذه
2. The هاء is voweled between two voweled letters
3. There is no همزة after the هاء

The Strengthening Medd مد التمكين:
1. In one word: e.g. ﴿النَّبِيِّـــــــــنَ﴾
2. In two words: e.g. ﴿قَالُوا وَهُمْ﴾ ﴿فِــي يَوْمٍ﴾

The Substitute Medd مد العوض (عِوَجاً) (مَآءً) with the condition that:
1. There is a tanween fat'h تنوين فتح on the end of the word.
2. We stop on this word.
3. The last letter is not a (ة) هاء التأنيث

The Natural Lengthening in Letters المد الطبيعي الحرفي:
The lengthening of the Alif in (حَيٌّ طَهُرَ) in the opening of some surahs.
e.g. ﴿الــمـّـر﴾ , ﴿طــه﴾ , ﴿يـــسَ﴾ , ﴿حمَ﴾

SECONDARY MEDD
DUE TO HAMZAH OR SUKOON

HAMZAH

TWO WORDS

ONE WORD

The Greater Connecting Medd مد الصلة الكبرى lengthened 4 or 5 counts:
(عِلْمِهِ ـ إلاَّ) (عِندَهُ ـ إلاَّ)

The Separate Allowed Medd مد جائز منفصل (both kinds) lengthened 4 or 5 counts: (يَاۤأَيُّهَا) (لاَ تُؤَاخِذْنَاۤ إِن)

SUKOON

INCIDENTAL DUE TO STOPPING

HAMZAH BEFORE THE MEDD LETTER: The Exchange Medd مد البدل lengthened 2 counts
(ءَادَم)
(بَآءُوا)

HAMZAH AFTER THE MEDD LETTER: Required Attached Medd المد الواجب المتصل lengthened 4 or 5 counts:
(الْمَلَاۤئِكَة)

Incidental Medd المد العارض للسكون:
The medd letter comes before the last letter in the word, and is lengthened 2, 4, or 6 counts: (غَفُورٌ) (عَلِيمٌ)

The Leen Medd مد اللين :
Leen letter comes before the last letter in the word, and is lengthened less than 2, 4, or 6 counts: (خَوْف) (شَيْءٌ)

ORIGINAL OR COMPULSORY 6 COUNTS

IN A WORD

HEAVY
Due to Idghaam:
e.g. ﴿الْحَآقَّــة﴾
﴿وَلاَ الضَّآلِّين﴾

LIGHT
No Idghaam: only example:
﴿ءَآلْــئَـــنَ﴾

IN A LETTER

HEAVY
Due to Idghaam:
e.g. ﴿الــمَّ﴾
﴿طســمَّ﴾

LIGHT
No Idghaam,
e.g. ﴿الــرَ﴾
﴿كــهيـعــصَ﴾

23

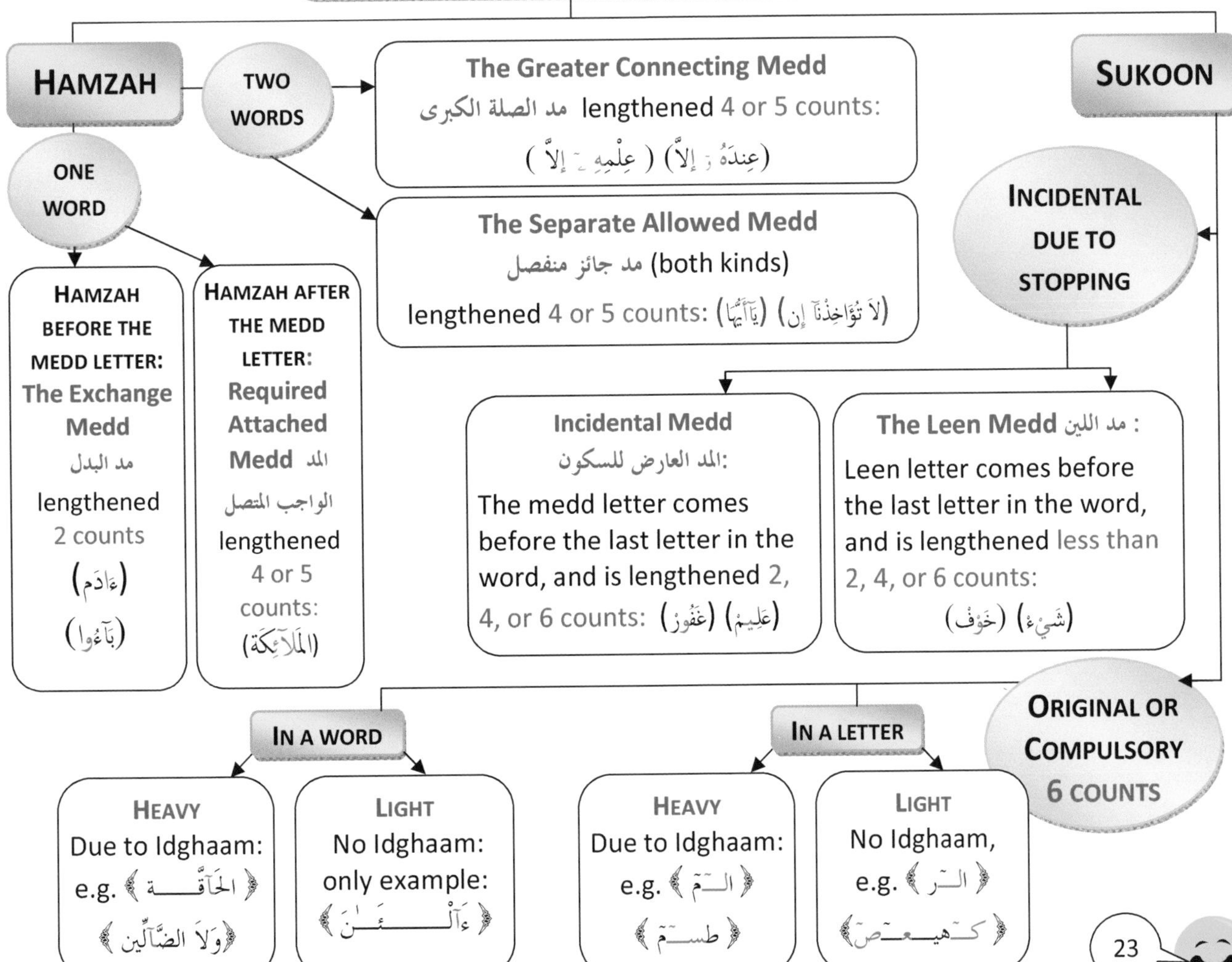

ADJUSTING THE MUDOOD

In the reading of Hafs from 'Asim, by the way of *Shatibiyyah*
The scholar, Ibrahim Shahatah As-Samannoudi, said:

أَقْوَى الْمُدُودِ لازِمٌ فَمَا اتَّصَلْ فَعَارِضٌ فَذُو انْفِصَالٍ فَبَدَلْ

The strongest Medd is the Compulsory then the Connected
Then the Incidental, then the Separate, then the Exchanged

MORE THAN ONE CAUSE FOR THE SAME LETTER OF MEDD

بدل with عارض:
Allowed to lengthen:
2 considered بدل and عارض
4, 6 considered عارض only.
e.g.: ﴿ الْمَئَاب ﴾ ﴿ الظَّمْئَان ﴾

بدل with لازم : بدل is canceled because it is weaker than لازم
Held for 6 counts,
e.g.: ﴿ ءَآللَّه ﴾ ﴿ ءَآمِّـــينَ ﴾

بدل with متصل: بدل is canceled because it is weaker than متصل
Held for 4 or 5 counts,
e.g.: ﴿ بُرَءَآءُ ﴾ and ﴿ رِءَآءَ ﴾

بدل with منفصل : بدل is canceled because it is weaker than منفصل
Held for 4 or 5 counts,
e.g.: ﴿ وَجَاءُوٓ أَبَاهُم ﴾﴿ رَءَآ أَيْدِيَهُم ﴾

عارض with متصل
or عارض with متصل with بدل :
Allowed to lengthen:
4 considered متصل & عارض
5 considered متصل only
6 considered عارض only
بدل canceled due to weakness,
e.g.: ﴿ السَّمَآءْ ﴾
﴿ الدُّعَآءْ ﴾ ﴿ رِءَآءْ ﴾ ﴿ بُرَءَآءْ ﴾

SIMILAR MUDOOD IN ONE RECITATION

WE MUST EQUALIZE:
1. All Connected medds (متصل)
2. All Separate medds (منفصل)
3. All صلة كبرى medds
4. The متصل with the منفصل with the صلة كبرى
5. All Incidental medds (عارض)
6- All لين medds

DIFFERENT MUDOOD IN ONE RECITATION

IF THE WEAK MEDD PRECEDES THE STRONG:
The strong equals the weak or surpasses it,
e.g.: لين before عارض

لين	عارض
2	2 or 4 or 6
4	4 or 6
6	6

IF THE STRONG MEDD PRECEDES THE WEAK:
The weak equals the strong or falls short of it,
e.g.: عارض before لين

عارض	لين
2	2
4	2 or 4
6	2 or 4 or 6

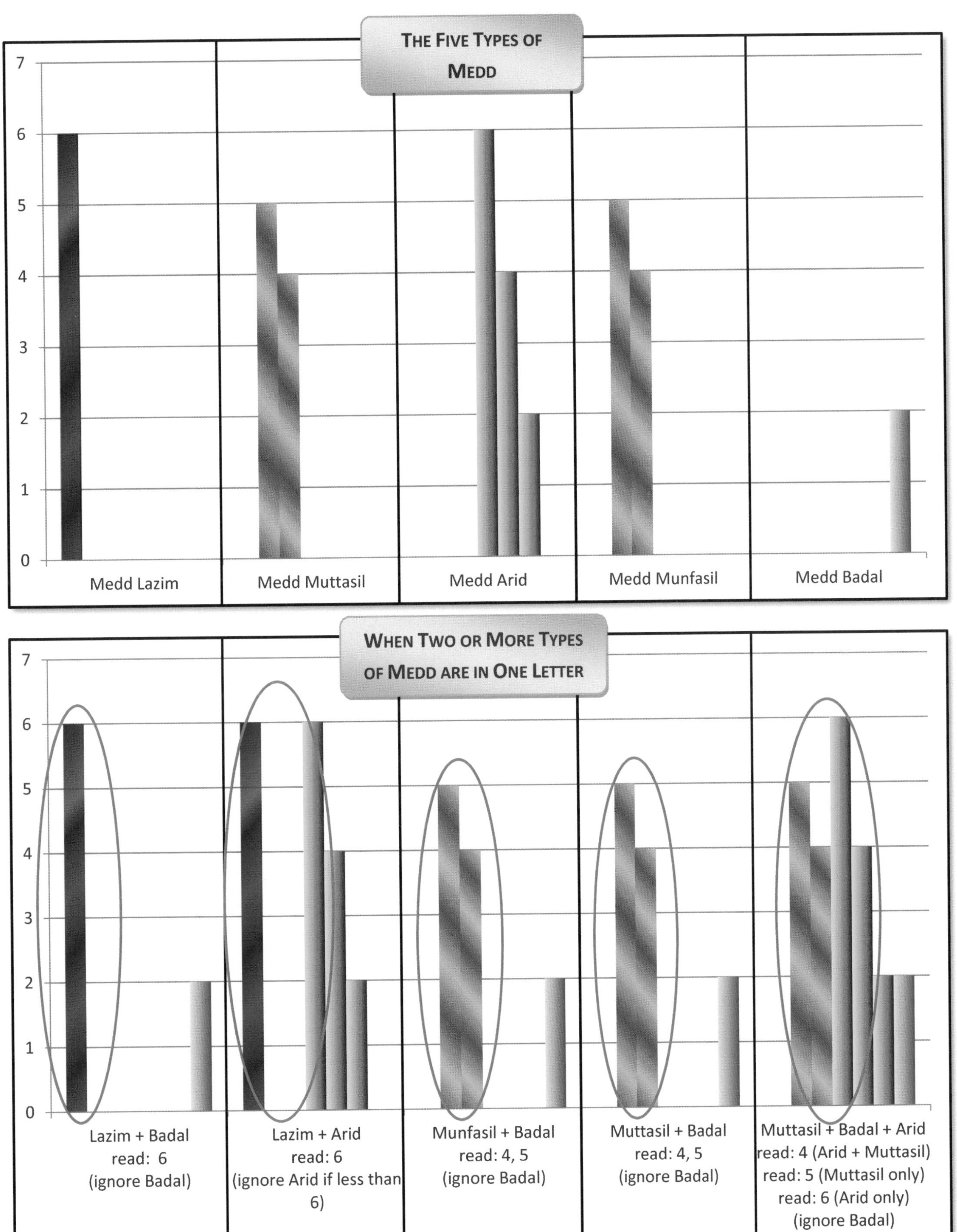
THE FIVE TYPES OF MEDD
7
6
5
4
3
2
1
0
Medd Lazim
Medd Muttasil
Medd Arid
Medd Munfasil
Medd Badal
WHEN TWO OR MORE TYPES OF MEDD ARE IN ONE LETTER
7
6
5
4
3
2
1
0
Lazim + Badal
read: 6
(ignore Badal)
Lazim + Arid
read: 6
(ignore Arid if less than 6)
Munfasil + Badal
read: 4, 5
(ignore Badal)
Muttasil + Badal
read: 4, 5
(ignore Badal)
Muttasil + Badal + Arid
read: 4 (Arid + Muttasil)
read: 5 (Muttasil only)
read: 6 (Arid only)
(ignore Badal)
(Ignore Arid that is 2)

Circumstances of Nabr النَّبْر in the Glorious Qur'an

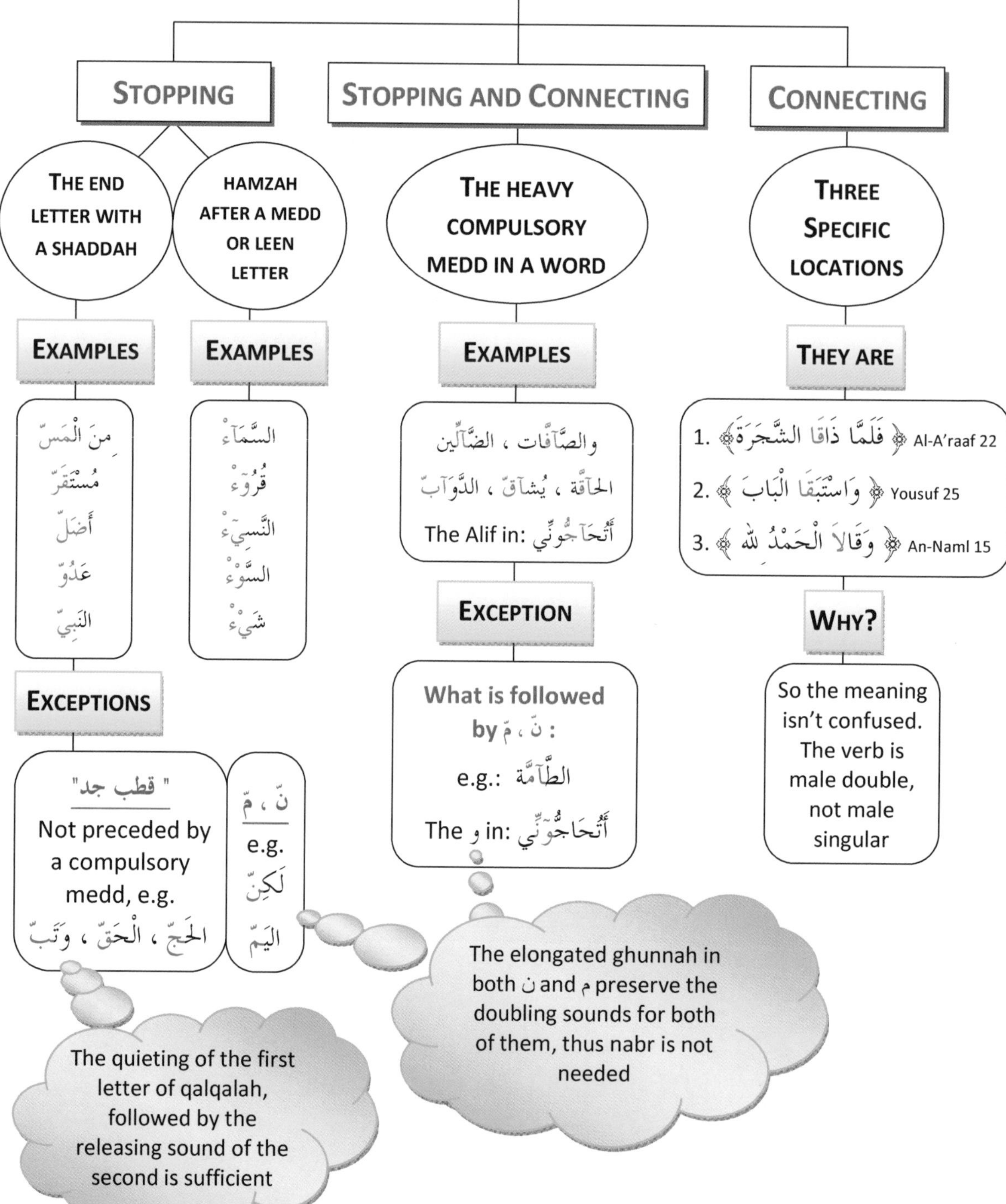

The Accent النَّبْر: making the sound of a letter louder than the surrounding letters

The Vowel for Beginning a Word with Hamzat Al-Wasl

هَمزةُ الوَصْلِ

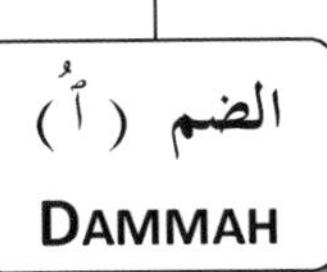

الضم (اُ) Dammah

In verbs only

If the third letter:
Has an **original dammah** on it (i.e. it is part of the original verb)
e.g.
﴿ اُجْتُثَّتْ ﴾
﴿ اُسْتُحْفِظُوا ﴾
﴿ اُقْتُلُوا ﴾

الكسر (اِ) Kasrah

In Verbs

If the 3rd letter:
Has a **fat-hah**
e.g.
﴿ اِرْتَضَى ﴾ ﴿ اِذْهَب ﴾

If the 3rd letter:
Has a **kasrah**
e.g.
﴿ اِصْبِر ﴾ ﴿ اِكْشِف ﴾

If the 3rd letter:
Has an **incidental dammah**
There are only four examples
﴿ اِقْضُوا ﴾ ﴿ اِبْنُوا ﴾
﴿ اِمْشُوا ﴾ ﴿ اِئْتُوا ﴾

In Nouns

Always starts with a kasrah:
The regular **nouns**, e.g.
﴿ اِفْتِرَاءً ﴾ ﴿ اِسْتِغْفَارُ ﴾
The irregular **nouns**, which are:
﴿ اِبْن ﴾ ﴿ اِبْنَت ﴾
﴿ اِمْرُؤ ﴾ ﴿ اِثْنَيْن ﴾
﴿ اِمْرَأَت ﴾
﴿ اِسْم ﴾ ﴿ اِثْنَتَيْن ﴾

Note: in Al-Hujurat, in
﴿ بِئْسَ الاِسْمُ الْفُسُوقُ ﴾
When starting with الِاسم
two ways are allowed:
" اَلِسْمُ " and " لِسْمُ "

الفتح (اَ) Fat-hah

In Particles

In the defining " ال ":
e.g.
﴿ اَلرَّحْمَـٰن ﴾
﴿ اَلْقُرْءَان ﴾

(اِئْتُوا) is pronounced "اِيتوا" when you begin with it.
For more details, review the lesson "When Hamzah Al-Wasl and Al-Qat' Meet"

From Ibn Al-Jazari's *Al-Muqaddimah*

وَ ابدَأْ بِهَمْزِ الوَصْلِ مِنْ فِعْلٍ بِضَمْ ... إِنْ كانَ ثالِثٌ مِنَ الفِعْلِ يُضَم
وَاكْسِرْهُ حالَ الكَسْرِ والفَتْحِ وفِي ... الأَسماءِ غيرِ اللامِ كَسْرُها وَفِيّ
ابنٍ مَعَ ابْنَتِ امْرِئٍ واثْنَين ... وَامْرَأَةٍ وَاسْمٍ مَعَ اثْنَتَينِ

Begin the Hamzah Al-Wasl in a verb with a dammah
If the third letter has a dammah,
Give it a kasrah if the third has a kasrah or fat-hah,
And in nouns, except for the defining Laam, the kasrah is complete, and in
ابن with ابنت , امرئ and اثنين and امرأة and اسم with اثنتين

The Meeting of Hamzah Al-Qat' and Hamzah Al-Wasl in One Word

When Hamzah Al-Wasl همزة الوصل Precedes Hamzah Al-Qat' همزة القطع

In verbs

Examples:

﴿ فَلْيُؤَدِّ الَّذِي ٱؤْتُمِنَ أَمَانَتَهُ ﴾

﴿ يَقُولُ ٱئْذَن لِّي ﴾

﴿ ثُمَّ ٱئْتُوا صَفًّا ﴾

﴿ يَا صَالِحُ ٱئْتِنَا بِمَا تَعِدُنَا ﴾

Pronunciation When Connecting

Hamzah Al-Wasl is dropped, and Hamzah Al-Qat' remains

الَّذِ ؤْتُمِنَ

يَقُولُ ئْذَن

ثُمَّ ئْتُوا

يَا صَالِحُ ئْتِنَا

Pronunciation When Starting

Hamzah Al-Wasl stays fixed, and Hamzah Al-Qat' is changed to a medd letter matching the vowel on Hamzah Al-Wasl:

اُوتُمِنَ

إيـــذَن

إيـــتُوا

إيـــتِنَا

When Hamzah Al-Qat' همزة القطع Precedes Hamzah Al-Wasl همزة الوصل

In verbs

Hamzah Al-Wasl is dropped, and the questioning Hamzah Al-Qat' remains

Only Seven Examples:

﴿ قُلْ أَتَّخَذْتُمْ ؟ ﴾ → أَٱتَّخَذْتُمْ

﴿ أَطَّلَعَ الْغَيْبَ ؟ ﴾ → أَٱطَّلَعَ

﴿ أَفْتَرَى عَلَى اللهِ ؟ ﴾ → أَٱفْتَرَى

﴿ أَسْتَكْبَرْتَ ؟ ﴾ → أَٱسْتَكْبَرْتَ

﴿ أَتَّخَذْنَاهُمْ سِخْرِيًّا ؟ ﴾ → أَٱتَّخَذْنَاهُمْ

﴿ أَصْطَفَى الْبَنَاتِ ؟ ﴾ → أَٱصْطَفَى

﴿ أَسْتَغْفَرْتَ لَهُمْ ؟ ﴾ → أَٱسْتَغْفَرْتَ

In nouns

Hamzah Al-Qat' remains

Either

Changing الإبدال:

Hamzah Al-Wasl is changed into an Alif that is lengthened six harakahs

Or

Easing التسهيل:

Hamzah Al-Wasl is "eased", with no medd, by pronouncing it between a Hamzah and an Alif.

Only Three Words in Six Ayahs:

﴿ قُلْ ءَاۤلذَّكَرَيْنِ حَرَّمَ ؟ ﴾ or ﴿ قُلْ ءَآلذَّكَرَيْنِ حَرَّمَ ؟ ﴾ → أَٱلذَّكَرَيْنِ

﴿ قُلْ ءَاۤللهُ أَذِنَ لَكُمْ ؟ ﴾ or ﴿ ءَآللهُ خَيْرٌ أَمَّا يُشْرِكُونَ ؟ ﴾ → أَٱللهُ

﴿ ءَاۤلْــئَـــٰنَ وَقَدْ كُنتُمْ ؟ ﴾ or ﴿ ءَآلْــئَـــٰنَ وَقَدْ عَصَيْتَ ؟ ﴾ → أَٱلآنَ

The medd resulting from "changing" is called by some "Medd Al-Farq" or the distinguishing medd

INTERACTIONS AMONG LETTERS

The Two Meeting Letters

With Hafs from 'Asim, by the way of *Shatibiyyah*

Big

(ـَـ ـُـ ـَـ ـُـ)

Rule: Required **Ith-haar** إِظْهَار

Except

Two Words:

تَـأْمَـنَّـا

Originally: تَأْمَـنُـنَـا

Rule:

May be read two ways

1. Clarifying the first Noon with rowm

Or

2. Merging the first Noon with ishmaam

مَكَّـنِّي

Originally: مَكَّـنَـنِي

Rule:

The first Noon must be purely merged into the second one

Small

(ـَـ ـُـ ـْـ)

Rule:

Required **Ith-haar** إِظْهَار generally

- **Similar** مُتَجَانِسَان
- **Close** مُتَقَارِبَان
- **Far** مُتَبَاعِدَان

Required **merging** إِدْغَام generally

- **Identical** مُتَمَاثِلَان

Absolute

(ـْـ ـُـ ـَـ)

Rule: Required **Ith-haar** إِظْهَار

IDENTICAL LETTERS

الْمُتَمَاثِلاَنِ

United in name, form, articulation point, and characteristics

WHEN MEETING*:
Required **Complete Merging** إِدْغَام كَامِل

EXCEPT

IF THE FIRST LETTER IS:

1. THE و ، ي OF MEDD

Example: فِـــي يَوْمٍ ، قَالُوا وَهُم

Rule: Ith-haar إظهار , also known as the strengthening medd مد التمكين

Reason:

1. Non-matching: The point of articulation for the first letter is the empty space in the mouth and throat الجوف, but for the second it is the lips (و) or middle of tongue (ي)
2. Or Preservation of letter of medd: for those who believe in the unity of the articulation points of the letter of medd and the normal letter

2. THE HAA هاء OF PAUSE السكت

Single example: ﴿ مَالِيَهْ ۞ هَّلَكَ ﴾

Rule:

Either
1. Ith-haar with pausing
Or
2. Idghaam without pausing

* In the reading of Hafs from 'Asim, by the way of *Shatibiyyah*

SIMILAR LETTERS

الْمُتَجَانِسَانِ

United articulation point, different characteristics

WHEN MEETING*:
REQUIRED **ITH-HAAR**
إظْهَار

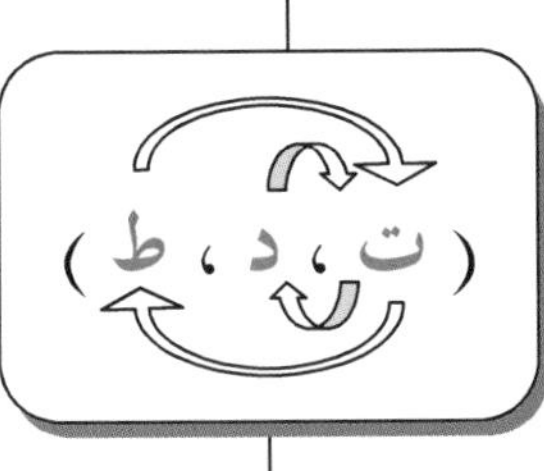

(ث ، ذ ، ظ)

(ب ، م ، و ، ف)

ت × د : required **complete idghaam** إدغام كامل

Only 2 examples:

1. ﴿ أَثْقَلَت دَّعَوَا اللهَ ﴾
2. ﴿ قَدْ أُجِيبَت دَّعْوَتُكُمَا ﴾

د × ت : required **complete idghaam** إدغام كامل

Example: ﴿ قَد تَّبَيَّنَ ، مَهَّدتُّ ﴾

ت × ط : required **complete idghaam** إدغام كامل

Example: ﴿ قَالَت طَّائِفَة ﴾

ط × ت : required **incomplete idghaam** إدغام ناقص due to remaining adhesion إطباق characteristic of the طاء

Example: ﴿ بَسَطتَ ، فَرَّطتُ ﴾

ث × ذ : required **complete idghaam** إدغام كامل

Only example: ﴿ يَلْهَث ذَّلِكَ ﴾

ذ × ظ : required **complete idghaam** إدغام كامل

Example: ﴿ إِذ ظَّلَمْتُمْ ﴾

ب × م : required **complete idghaam** إدغام كامل

Only example: ﴿ ارْكَب مَّعَنَا ﴾

م + ب : required **ikhfaa'** إخفاء

Example: ﴿ تَرْمِيهِم بِحِجَارَة ﴾

* In the reading of Hafs from 'Asim, by the way of *Shatibiyyah*

CLOSE LETTERS الْمُتَقَارِبَانِ

Close articulation points and characteristics, or close articulation points not characteristics, or close characteristics not articulation points

WHEN MEETING:

REQUIRED ITH-HAAR إِظْهَار

WHAT MUST BE MERGED إِدْغَام

يرملو × نْ :

1. نْ × (ي ، و): incomplete idghaam due to remaining ghunnah
2. نْ × (م): complete idghaam with ghunnah
3. نْ× (ل ، ر): complete idghaam without ghunnah

Except: ﴿ يسٓ وَالْقُرْءَانِ ﴾ ﴿ نٓ وَالْقَلَمِ ﴾ here is absolute ith-haar, and ﴿ مَنْ ۜ رَاقٍ ﴾ is with a pause سكت

WHAT MUST BE CHANGED إِقْلَاب

نْ + ب :

Must change Noon into a hidden Meem

e.g.: ﴿ مِنۢ بَعْدِ ﴾

WHAT MUST BE HIDDEN إِخْفَاء

نْ+ letters of ikhfaa' except (ق ، ك):

صِفْ ذَا ثَنَا كَمْ جَادَ شَخْصٌ قَدْ سَمَا

دُمْ طَيِّباً زِدْ فِـــي تُقًى ضَعْ ظَالِمًا

Required ikhfaa', e.g.: ﴿ مَن ذَا الَّذِي ﴾

ال × the شمسية letters except " ل ":

طِبْ ثُـــمَّ صِلْ رَحِمًا تَفُزْ ضِفْ ذَا نِعَمْ دَعْ سُوءَ ظَنٍّ زُرْ شَرِيفًا لِلْكَرَمْ

Required complete idghaam, example: ﴿ الرَّحْمَة ﴾

لْ × ر:

Required complete idghaam, e.g.: ﴿ قُل رَّبِّ ﴾ except: ﴿ بَلْ ۜ رَانَ ﴾, must clarify إظهار with a pause سكت

قْ × ك : only example: ﴿ أَلَمْ نَخْلُقكُّم ﴾

1. Complete idghaam: (نَخْلُكُّم), which is the predominant method among recitals
2. Or incomplete idghaam: (نَخْلُقكُّم) with remaining Elevation استعلاء in ق

Hafs read this word with only **complete idghaam**

FAR-APART LETTERS

الْمُتَبَاعِدَانِ

Far apart articulation points and different characteristics

WHEN MEETING *:
REQUIRED **ITH-HAAR**
إظْهَار

1. نْ + ق :

Example: ﴿ مِن قَبْلِ ﴾

Rule: ikhfaa' إخفاء

Except: ﴿ عِوَجاً س قَيِّمًا ﴾,

must pause سكت

2. نْ + ك :

Example: ﴿ مَن كَانَ ﴾

Rule: ikhfaa' إخفاء

* In the reading of Hafs from 'Asim, by the way of *Shatibiyyah*

STOPPING TO TAKE A BREATH

Stopping

Cutting the reading for a time, in which a breath is usually taken, with the intention of resuming

Tested

It is stopping on a word which is not a usual place of stopping, for testing or teaching, to clarify the rule of the word stopped on.

Example

﴿ امْرَأَتَ نُوحٍ ﴾

Stopping with a Taa Maftouhah تاء مفتوحة ,

﴿ وَإِنِ امْرَأَةٌ خَافَتْ ﴾

Stopping with a Taa Marbootah تاء مربوطة

Rule

Allowed stopping on any word, but must return to it and connect it to following words if suitable, or previous words suitable for starting with

Forced

It is stopping on a word, not usually a place of stopping, because of what befalls the reader forcing a stop

Example

Sneezing, shortness of breath, forgetting, or overwhelming crying

Rule

Allowed stopping on any word until urgency ends, then must return to it and connect it with following words if suitable, or previous words suitable for starting with

Waiting

It is stopping on a word with the intention of fulfilling all different ways of reading, by combining narrations when presenting or learning

Example

﴿ فَمَا ءَاتَانِ ـےَ اللَّهُ ﴾

Stopping to include the Yaa or to omit it

Rule

Allowed stopping on any word, but must return to it and connect it to following words if suitable, or previous words suitable for starting with

Voluntary

The reader **chooses** to stop on a word with no need, test, or waiting

Categories

- **Complete** تَامٌّ
- **Sufficient** كَافٍ
- **Good** حَسَنٌ
- **Ugly** قَبِيحٌ

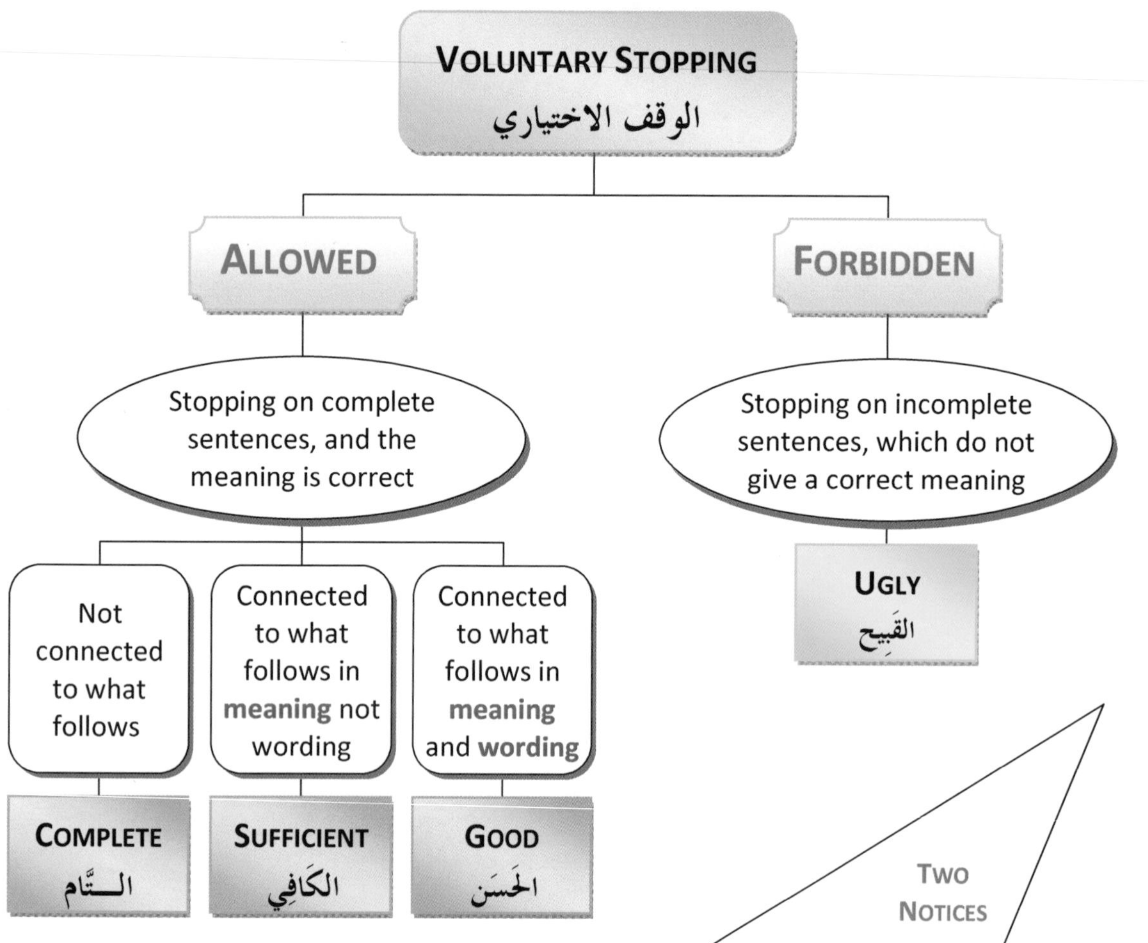

1. Knowing the allowed stopping from the forbidden depends on the meaning that stopping conveys, and because the interpretation and the grammatical dissertation of the verses could differ from scholar to scholar, so might the stopping differ in ruling from person to person.
2. The signs of stopping like لا ، صلى ، ج ، قلى ، م were established by the scholars after the era of Prophethood, and thus differ from one mus-haf to another.

From Ibn Al-Jazari's *Al-Muqaddimah*

وَبَعْدَ تَجْوِيدِكَ للحُروفِ   لابُدَّ مِنْ مَعْرِفَةِ الوُقوفِ
والاِبْتِداءِ وَهْيَ تُقْسَمُ إذَنْ   ثلاثَةٌ تامٌ وكافٍ وحَسَنْ
وَهْيَ لِما تَمَّ فَإنْ لَمْ يُوجَدِ   تَعَلُّقٌ أوْ كان مَعْنىً فَابْتَدي
فَالتامُ فالكافي ولَفْظاً فَامْنَعَنْ   إلا رُؤوسَ الآيِ جَوِّزْ فَالحَسَنْ
وغَيْرُ ما تَمَّ قَبيحٌ ولَهُ   الوَقْفُ مُضْطَرّاً وَيَبْدا قَبْلَهُ
ولَيْسَ في القرآنِ مِنْ وَقْفٍ يَجِبْ   ولا حَرامٌ غَيْرُ ما لَهُ سَبَبْ

And after you have perfected the letters you must know the stoppings;
And the startings, and they are divided into three: **Complete**, **Sufficient**, and **Good**;
And they are for what is complete in meaning, so if there is no connection, or there is in meaning not wording; then start, and they are:
The **Complete**, and the **Sufficient**. If the connection is in wording, prevent (beginning), except beginnings of verses are allowed, it is the **Good**;
What is not complete is **Ugly**, and one may stop if forced, then one must begin before it;
And there is no stopping in the Qur'an that is a must, or forbidden, except for a reason.

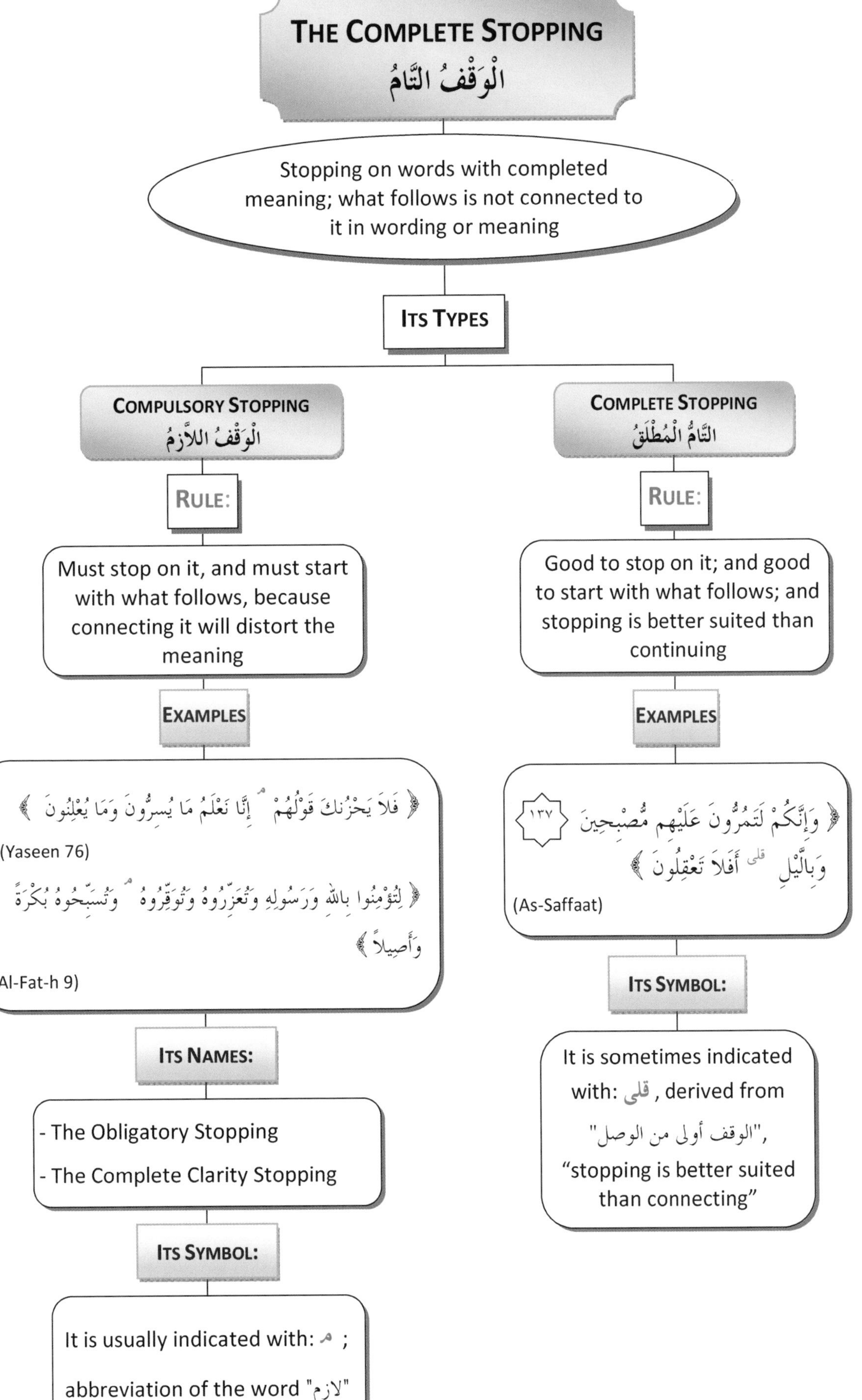

THE COMPLETE STOPPING
الْوَقْفُ التَّامُ
Stopping on words with completed meaning; what follows is not connected to it in wording or meaning
ITS TYPES
COMPULSORY STOPPING
الْوَقْفُ اللاَّزِمُ
RULE:
Must stop on it, and must start with what follows, because connecting it will distort the meaning
EXAMPLES
﴿ فَلاَ يَحْزُنكَ قَوْلُهُمْ ۘ إِنَّا نَعْلَمُ مَا يُسِرُّونَ وَمَا يُعْلِنُونَ ﴾
(Yaseen 76)
﴿ لِتُؤْمِنُوا بِاللَّهِ وَرَسُولِهِ وَتُعَزِّرُوهُ وَتُوَقِّرُوهُ ۚ وَتُسَبِّحُوهُ بُكْرَةً وَأَصِيلاً ﴾
(Al-Fat-h 9)
ITS NAMES:
- The Obligatory Stopping
- The Complete Clarity Stopping
ITS SYMBOL:
It is usually indicated with: م ;
abbreviation of the word "لازم"
COMPLETE STOPPING
التَّامُ الْمُطْلَق
RULE:
Good to stop on it; and good to start with what follows; and stopping is better suited than continuing
EXAMPLES
﴿ وَإِنَّكُمْ لَتَمُرُّونَ عَلَيْهِم مُّصْبِحِينَ ١٣٧ وَبِالَّيْلِ ۗ أَفَلاَ تَعْقِلُونَ ﴾
(As-Saffaat)
ITS SYMBOL:
It is sometimes indicated with: قلى , derived from "الوقف أولى من الوصل", "stopping is better suited than connecting"

Sufficient Stopping
الْوَقْفُ الْكَافِي

Stopping on words with completed meaning, and what follows is connected to it in meaning not wording

Rule

It is good to stop, and good to begin with what is after it, as with the Complete Stopping, except that stopping on the Complete is better

Example

﴿ رَبَّنَا تَقَبَّلْ مِنَّا صلى إِنَّكَ أَنتَ السَّمِيعُ الْعَلِيمُ ج ﴾ (Al-Baqara 127)

﴿ فِي قُلُوبِهِم مَّرَضٌ فَزَادَهُمُ اللَّهُ مَرَضاً صلى وَلَهُمْ عَذَابٌ أَلِيمٌ بِمَا كَانُوا يَكْذِبُونَ ج ﴾ (Al-Baqara 10)

Its sign:

- Sometimes it is indicated with: ج , an abbreviation of the word "جائز" “allowed”
- And sometimes with: صلى , derived from "الوصل أولى من الوقف", which means continuing is better suited than stopping

GOOD STOPPING
الْوَقْفُ الْحَسَنُ

Stopping on words with acceptable meanings, but what follows is connected to it in both wording and meaning

ITS TYPES

DURING THE VERSE

RULE

It is good to stop, but not good to start with what follows

EXAMPLES

﴿الْحَمْدُ لله * رَبِّ الْعَالَمِين﴾ (Al-Fatihah 2)

﴿خَتَمَ اللهُ عَلَى قُلُوبِهِمْ * وَعَلَى سَمْعِهِمْ﴾
(Al-Baqarah 7)

﴿يُخْرِجُونَ الرَّسُولَ لا وَإِيَّاكُمْ أَن تُؤْمِنُوا بِاللهِ رَبِّكُمْ﴾
(Al-Mumtahanah 1)

ITS SIGN

It is sometimes indicated with: لا , for the repulsiveness of starting with what follows

ENDING OF VERSE

RULE

THREE APPROACHES

1. **The majority**:
   Good to stop on it, and good to start with what follows, because that is sunnah.
2. **Some**:
   Good to stop on it and good to start with what follows, on condition of continuing reading. Otherwise it is not good to start after it.
3. **Others**:
   Good to stop on it but *not* good to start with what follows.

EXAMPLE

﴿لَعَلَّكُمْ تَتَفَكَّرُونَ ٢١٩ فِي الدُّنْيَا وَالآخِرَةِ﴾
(Al-Baqara)

Ugly Stopping
الْوَقْفُ الْقَبِيحُ

Stopping on words which are incomplete or do not give the right meaning, because what follows is strongly connected with the previous words, in both wording and meaning

Its Types

Not Understood

Rule

It is forbidden to stop on it, except in need. You must go back and connect it with following words if suitable, or previous words suitable for starting

Example

(بِسْمِ * اللهِ) (Al-Fatiha 1)

(الحَمْدُ * لله) (Al-Fatiha 2)

Its Sign

It is sometimes indicated with: لا

Gives Meanings Other than What Allah Meant

During a Verse

Rule

This stopping is uglier and more repulsive. It is forbidden to stop on it except in need. You must go back and connect it with following words if suitable, or previous words suitable for starting

Example

﴿ إِنَّ اللهَ لاَ يَسْتَحْيِي * أَن يَضْرِبَ مَثَلاً ﴾ (Al-Baqara 26)

﴿ فَاعْلَمْ أَنَّهُ لاَ إِلَهَ * إِلاَّ اللهُ ﴾ (Muhammad 19)

Its Sign

It is sometimes indicated with: لا

Ending of a Verse

Rule

Three Approaches

1. **Ibn Al-Jazari**: Forbidden to stop on it unless forced to. You must connect it.
2. **Others**: Allowed to stop on it, allowed to begin with what follows, on condition of continuing reading, because that is sunnah.
3. **Some**: Allowed to stop on it, forbidden to start with what follows. Must go back and connect with following words.

Example

﴿ فَوَيْلٌ لِّلْمُصَلِّينَ ۙ ﴿٤﴾ الَّذِينَ هُمْ عَن صَلاَتِهِمْ سَاهُونَ ﴾ (Al-Ma'oon)

Its Sign

It is sometimes indicated with: لا

A Brief History of the Oral and Written Qur'an

A Brief History of the Oral and Written Qur'an

During the Life of the Prophet

Whenever some verses of the Qur'an were revealed to Prophet Mohamed ﷺ, he would recite these verses exactly how they were revealed to the scribes of the Qur'an and to the rest of his companions

The companions of the Prophet memorized the Qur'an verbatim, letter by letter, vowel sound by vowel sound, not missing a single utterance from the Prophet without repeating it and storing it in their memory

There were also at least forty scribes dedicated to writing the Qur'an as it was revealed, who would rotate the times and days they spent with the Prophet ﷺ so that he would always have a number of scribes by his side

Some of these scribes were Abu-Bakr, Omar Ibn Al-Khattab, Othman Ibn Affan, Ali Ibn Abi-Talib, Ubay Ibn Ka'b, Zaid Ibn Thabit, Al-Arqam Ibn Abi-Al-Arqam, Thabit Ibn Qais, and Aban Ibn Sa'eed

They would write the Qur'an on the materials that were available to them at the time such as palm leaves, flat bones, smooth stones, and skins

After scribing the verses, they would take turns reciting to the Prophet what they had written and making corrections if there were any

Once approved by the Prophet ﷺ, these scriptures, along with the oral recitations and memorizations, were the basis of teaching the Qur'an to all the companions

A Brief History of the Oral and Written Qur'an

Near the End of the Prophet's Life

Some scribes spent more time with the Prophet and memorized more Qur'an than others, such as Zaid Ibn Thabit and Mu'awiah Ibn Abi-Sufyan رضي الله عنه

During the final year of the Prophet's life, Angel Jibreel reviewed the entire Qur'an in its final version with the Prophet, and Zaid Bin Thabit was present during these final reviews

Since the Qur'an was revealed in various accents of the Arabian tribes, some companions were taught, and had memorized, slightly differing versions of pronouncing the Qur'an than others

After the Prophet's death, hundreds of companions had memorized the Qur'an entirely, and all the verses were written down, but these scribed verses were scattered among the companions

The Prophet had prohibited his companions from scribing from him anything other than the Qur'an, keeping the written verses purely the words of Allah, without any explanations or alterations

Some of the written verses were abrogated in the final review, but they were still studied amongst the companions who had not yet been informed of their removal from the Qur'an

A Brief History of the Oral and Written Qur'an

During the Caliphate of Abu-Bakr

After the Battle of Yamamah, in which hundreds of those who had memorized the Qur'an were martyred, Omar رضي الله عنه was terrified of losing any of the Qur'an

He convinced Abu-Bakr رضي الله عنه who in turn summoned Zaid Ibn Thabit رضي الله عنه and convinced him as well to be in charge of the task of collecting the Qur'an from all the scattered scriptures, and binding what he writes into one book

The project was announced and anyone who had written a verse or more of the Qur'an in the presence of the Prophet and had been approved by him was called upon to come forth with that scripture

In addition, Zaid accepted only scriptures that two of the companions could attest to being scribed in the presence of the Prophet and had been approved by him, and that were taught by Jibreel in the final review

Zaid scribed all these scattered verses into a single book, which the companions called a *mus-haf*, with the verses in the order in which they were presented in the final review

This mus-haf was approved by the companions and was kept in the house of Abu-Bakr, then in the house of Omar, and then in his daughter, Hafsah's, house رضي الله عنهم

A Brief History of the Oral and Written Qur'an

During the Caliphate of Othman

By the time Othman ﷺ was the caliphate, Islam had spread outside the Arabian Peninsula, and people from all regions were embracing Islam and reciting Qur'an to the best of their abilities

Huthayfah Ibn Al-Yaman ﷺ was in Armenia and witnessed the Muslims quarreling amongst each other over differences in the ways they were reciting the Qur'an

Huthayfah hurried to Othman ﷺ and conveyed the problem, after which the decision was taken to make multiple copies of the Qur'an and send these copies to the major areas within and surrounding Arabia

Each copy of the Qur'an would be accompanied by several of the best reciters who read the specific recital with which the scripture was written to be compatible

A committee was formed to carry out this massive project, and leading this committee was Zaid Ibn Thabit who had the help of Abdullah Ibn Az-Zubair, Sa'eed Ibn Al-'As, and Abdul-Rahman Ibn Al-Harith Ibn Hisham

Before writing the Qur'an in all its different recitals, they requested the mus-haf from Hafsah ﷺ, and used it to make copies that differed in the slight variations found in the different recitals taught by the Prophet ﷺ

A Brief History of the Oral and Written Qur'an

During the Caliphate of Othman

The copies of the mus-haf are called *Al-Masahif Al-Othmaniah*, and collectively preserve all the different recitals taught to the Prophet ﷺ by Jibreel in which the Qur'an can be read

In order to accommodate the recitals, the scribes wrote these copies by voiding their writing from vowel symbols and from all markings

These markings included dots, Hamzahs, numberings, surah names, juz' indicators, sajdah signs, and some vowel letters which Arabs used to deem as unnecessary to scribe, all of which were added over the next centuries

If two recitals could be scribed using one word, then that is how all the copies were written, such as ﴿ ملك ﴾ which could be read as (مَلِكِ) or (مَالِكِ)

If a single word could not accommodate different recitals, one or more copies were written in one form and the others in a different way, such as ﴿ سارعوا ﴾ which was scribed in three copies and ﴿ وسارعوا ﴾ in the other copies

If some recitals used uncommon pronunciations, such as pronouncing (سراط) with a Saad instead of a Seen, then the committee scribed these words using the uncommon form

This way the common pronunciation in the other recitals would be included by default, such as ﴿ الصراط ﴾ which could be read as (الصِّرَاط) or (السِّرَاط)

A Brief History of the Oral and Written Qur'an

During the Caliphate of Othman

In addition to scribing the Qur'an so that all recitals could be read from it, the companions also scribed some words in special forms

Some examples include phrases that are usually written as two separate words but were scribed as one combined word such as ﴿ إلم ﴾ which is normally written as (إن لم)

Other examples include omitting the Alif, Waw, or Yaa at the end of some words, such as ﴿ أيه ﴾ , ﴿ يمح ﴾ , and ﴿ الداع ﴾ which normally would be written as (أيها), (يمحو), and (الداعي)

Further examples are the added letters that aid in pronouncing words that are void of *tashkeel* or vowel accents, such as ﴿ تلقاءى ﴾ indicating that the Hamzah has a kasrah

Most scholars confirm that seven copies of these masahif were made, four of which are agreed upon by all scholars. These copies were sent to Kufa, Basra, Levant, and one that was kept in Medina

In addition, there was one sent to each of Yemen, Bahrain, and Makkah. Some add a special copy kept in the house of Othman ﷺ

A Brief History of the Oral and Written Qur'an

During the Caliphate of Othman

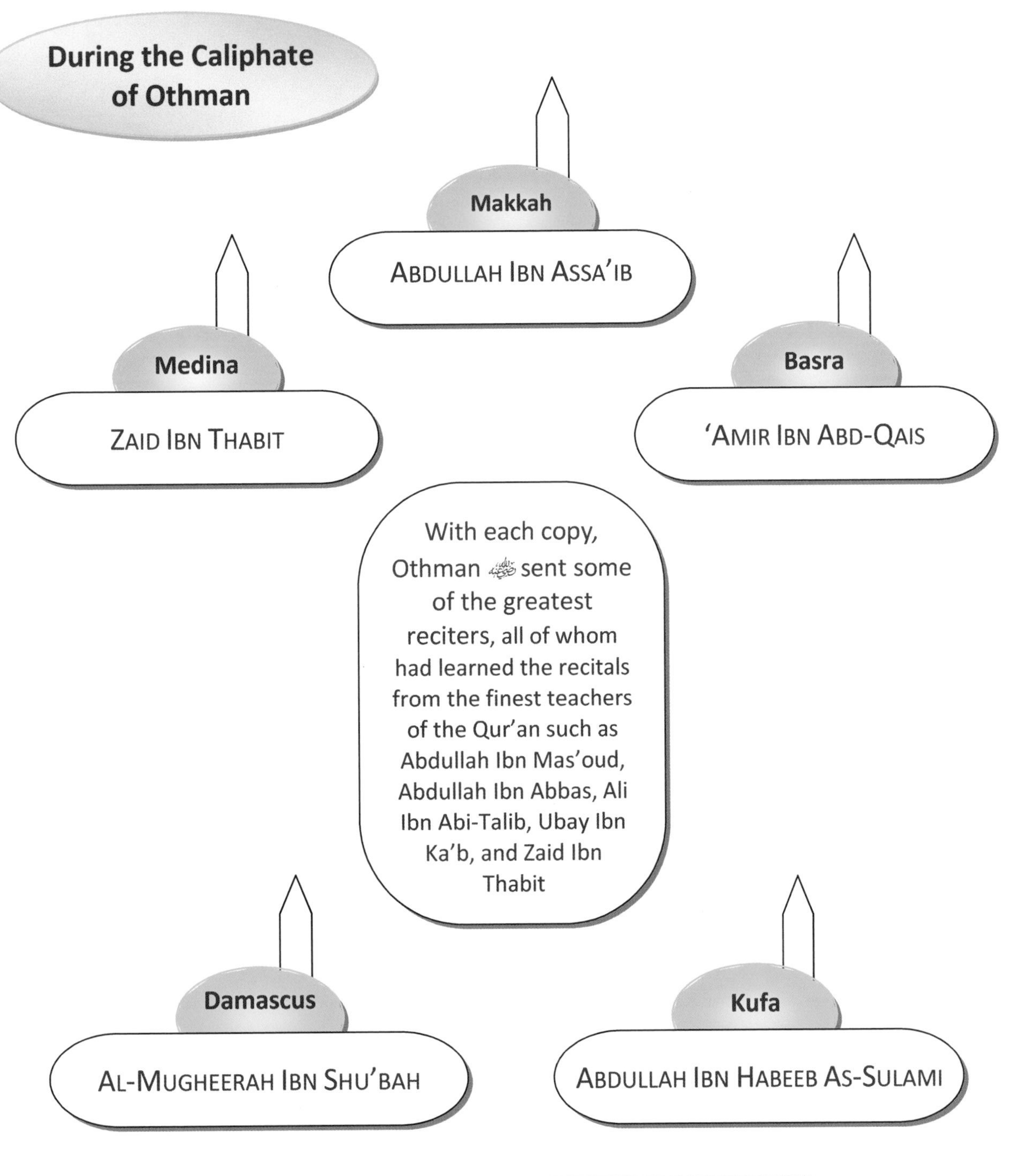
Makkah
Abdullah Ibn Assa'ib
Medina
Zaid Ibn Thabit
Basra
'Amir Ibn Abd-Qais
With each copy, Othman ﷺ sent some of the greatest reciters, all of whom had learned the recitals from the finest teachers of the Qur'an such as Abdullah Ibn Mas'oud, Abdullah Ibn Abbas, Ali Ibn Abi-Talib, Ubay Ibn Ka'b, and Zaid Ibn Thabit
Damascus
Al-Mugheerah Ibn Shu'bah
Kufa
Abdullah Ibn Habeeb As-Sulami

Othman ﷺ also sent other teachers to Bahrain, Yemen, and Egypt to teach the people of those regions the remaining variations and recitals

A Brief History of the Oral and Written Qur'an

During the Caliphate of Ali

Although each region had the best teachers for their specific recital, there remained some problems which were not solved by scribing the Othmani Copies

One such problem was that the majority of Muslims did not speak Arabic, and even those who were born to Arab parents had mixed exposure to the language, resulting in weakening their grammatical abilities

Accenting words with the correct vowels requires high Arabic skills, an ability that was deteriorating amongst most people by the time Ali Ibn Abu-Talib ﷺ was the caliphate

The Qur'an was being recited with incorrect vowels because the Othmani copies had no written vowels to assist the readers, who were by now weak in the Arabic language

Abu Al-Aswad Ad-Du'ali (d. 69 A.H.), the leading scholar in the Arabic language at the time, was asked to find a solution to this problem

Abu Al-Aswad asked his student, Nasr Ibn 'Asim (d. 89 A.H.), to use red ink, to contrast with the black ink by which the words of the Qur'an were written, to add the vowels

Abu Al-Aswad requested that when he pronounced a fat-hah that a red dot be placed atop the letter, a dot below the letter for a kasrah, and a dot after the letter representing a dammah

A Brief History of the Oral and Written Qur'an

By the End of the First *Hijri* Century

Although adding vowels to the letters helped solve the problem of misreading the accents of letters, another problem was apparent, which was the difficulty in distinguishing similarly scribed letters from each other

Such letters were the ح, خ, and ج, as well as all other letters with similar bodies that today differ only by dots, which were not part of the Arabic scripture at the time

اياك نعبد

واياك نستعين

Nasr Ibn Aasim (d. 89 A.H.), one of Abu Al-Aswad's students, was asked by the caliphate to create a method to distinguish such letters

Nasr added the dots we know and use today, keeping their colors in black to match the letters and to remain distinguished from the red vowel dots

This resolved a major problem for learners of the Arabic language as well as for reciters and teachers of the Qur'an

While dots and vowels were being added to the scripture, the recitation and memorization of the Qur'an continued and increased throughout the land

For each recital, and in each city, there emerged outstanding and well known scholars, who were documented and written about in numerous books

A Brief History of the Oral and Written Qur'an

Names Given to the Recitals

By the second century after Hijrah, people began to refer to the recitals by the names of the eminent scholars teaching the recitals taught to them through authentic chains of narration, matching the written copies of the Othmani Masahif

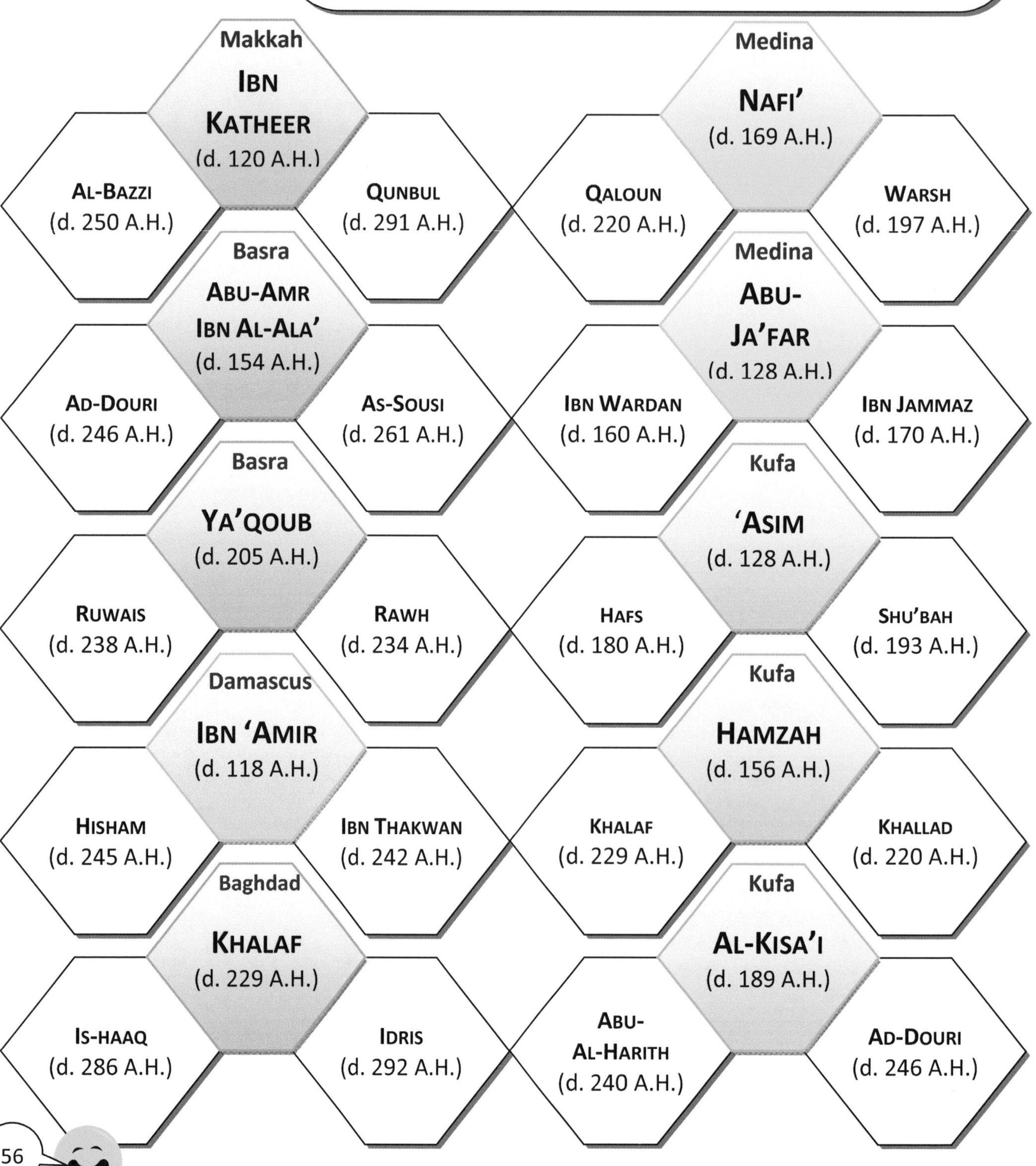

A Brief History of the Oral and Written Qur'an

Names Given to the Recitals

From the Poem *Hirz Al-Amani wa Wajh At-Tahani*

Known as *Ash-Shatibiyyah*, by Al-Qasim Ibn Ferro Al-Andalusi Ash-Shatibi (d. 590 A.H.)

May Allah reward, with abundant good, our teachers who conveyed the Qur'an to us pure and fresh	جَزَى اللّٰهُ بِالْخَيْرَاتِ عَنَّا أَئِمَّةً ‏ لَنَا نَقَلُوا القُرْآنَ عَذْباً وَسَلْسَلاَ
From them are seven moons that centered the high sky of justice, shining with perfection	فَمِنْهُمْ بُدُورٌ سَبْعَةٌ قَدْ تَوَسَّطَتْ ‏ سَمَاءَ الْعُلَى وَالْعَدْلِ زُهْراً وَكُمَّلاَ
These seven have stars that gain their glow from the moons, so they brighten the black darkness until it scatters and reveals what is beneath	لَهَا شُهُبٌ عَنْهَا اسْتَنَارَتْ فَنَوَّرَتْ ‏ سَوَادَ الدُّجَى حَتَّى تَفَرَّق وَانْجَلاَ
And you will see them one after another, each with two of their companions	وَسَوْفَ تَرَاهُمْ وَاحِداً بَعْدَ وَاحِدٍ ‏ مَعَ اثْنَيْنِ مِنْ أَصْحَابِهِ مُتَمَثِّلاَ
They were chosen by critics because of their mastery, and none of them earned their livelihood from teaching Qur'an	تَخَيَّرَهُمْ نُقَّادُهُمْ كُلَّ بَارِعٍ ‏ وَلَيْسَ عَلَى قُرْآنِهِ مُتَأَكِّلاَ
As for the glorious, honored one with perfume, for he is Nafi', the one who chose Medina as a dwelling	فَأَمَّا الْكَرِيمُ السِّرِّ فِي الطِّيِّبِ نَافِعٌ ‏ فَذَاكَ الَّذِي اخْتَارَ الْمَدِينَةَ مَنْزِلاَ
Qaloun Isa then **Othman Warsh**, with his friendship they reached glorious heights	**وَقَالُونُ** عِيسَى ثُمَّ عُثْمانُ **وَرْشُهُمْ** ‏ بِصُحْبَتِهِ المَجْدَ الرَّفِيعَ تَأَثَّلاَ

A Brief History of the Oral and Written Qur'an

And **Makkah** has Abdullah who lived in it, he is Ibn Katheer who dominated and rose above others

وَمَكَّةُ عَبْدُ اللهِ فِيهَا مُقَامُهُ ... هُوَ ابْنُ كَثِيرٍ كاثِرُ الْقَوْمِ مُعْتَلَا

Ahmed **Al-Bazzi** narrated from him, and Mohamed nicknamed **Qunbul**, through others connecting them to him

رَوى أَحْمَدُ **الْبَزِّي** لَهُ وَمُحَمَّدٌ ... عَلَى سَنَدٍ وَهْوَ الْمُلَقَّبُ **قُنْبُلا**

As for the pure Mazini Imam he is Abu Amr from **Basra** and his father is Al-Ala'

وَأَمَّا الإِمَامُ المَازِنِيُّ صَرِيحُهُمْ ... أَبُو عَمْرٍو الْبَصْرِي فَوَالِدُهُ الْعَلاَ

He poured all his knowledge upon Yahya Al-Yazeedi, until he was well nourished by this purity

أَفَاضَ عَلَى يَحْيَى الْيَزِيدِيِّ سَيْبَهُ ... فَأَصْبَحَ بِالْعَذْبِ الْفُرَاتِ مُعَلَّلاَ

From Yahya two students accepted this knowledge, Abu Omar **Ad-Douri** and Salih Abu Shu'aib who is **As-Sousi**

أَبُو عُمَرَ **الدُّورِي** وَصَالِحُهُمْ أَبُو ... شُعَيْبٍ هُوَ **السُّوسِيُّ** عَنْهُ تَقَبَّلاَ

As for **Damascus** of **Levant** the home of Ibn 'Amir, it was a merry abode with Abdullah

وَأَمَّا دِمَشْقُ الشَّامِ دَارُ ابْنِ عَامِرٍ ... فَتِلْكَ بِعَبْدِ اللهِ طَابَتْ مُحَلَّلاَ

Hisham and Abdullah who belongs to the tribe of **Thakwan** both narrated from him though others

هِشَامٌ وَ**عَبْدُ اللهِ** وَهْوَ انْتِسَابُهُ ... لِذَكْوَانَ بِالإِسْنَادِ عَنْهُ تَنَقَّلاَ

And in **Kufa**, the white city of scholars, there were three of them who were celebrated, giving the city an aroma of musk and carnations

وَبِالْكُوفَةِ الْغَرَّاءِ مِنْهُمْ ثَلاَثَةٌ ... أَذَاعُوا فَقَدْ ضَاعَتْ شَذاً وَقَرَنْفُلاَ

A Brief History of the Oral and Written Qur'an

فَأَمَّا أَبُو بَكْرٍ وَعَاصِمٌ اسْمُهُ	**فَشُعْبَةُ** رَاوِيهِ الْمُبَرِّزُ أَفْضَلاَ	As for Abu Bakr his name is 'Asim, **Shu'bah** was his student who was best known to narrate from him
وَذَاكَ ابْنُ عَيَّاشٍ أَبُو بَكْرٍ الرِّضَا	**وَحَفْصٌ** وَبِالْإِتْقَانِ كانَ مُفضَّلاَ	He is Ibn 'Ayyash Abu Bakr the content, and **Hafs** also [narrated from 'Asim] and was preferred for his accuracy
وَحَمْزَةُ مَا أَزْكَاهُ مِنْ مُتَوَرِّعٍ	إِمَاماً صَبُوراً لِلْقُرانِ مُرَتِّلاَ	And Hamza, what a pure, pious, and patient leader in the recitation of Qur'an he was!
رَوَى **خَلَفٌ** عَنْهُ **وَخَلَّادٌ** الَّذِي	رَوَاهُ سُلَيْمٌ مُتْقَناً وَمُحَصَّلاَ	**Khalaf** and **Khallad** narrated from him through Sulaim who was accurate and perfectly informed
وَأَمَّا عَلِيٌّ فَالْكِسَائِيُّ نَعْتُهُ	لِمَا كَانَ فِي الإِحْرَامِ فِيهِ تَسَرْبَلاَ	And as for Ali for he is nicknamed Al-Kisa'i because he wore a robe during his ihram
رَوَى **لَيْثُهُمْ** عَنْهُ أَبُو الْحَارِثِ الرِّضَا	وَحَفْصٌ هُوَ **الدُّورِي** وَفِي الذِّكْرِ قَدْ خَلاَ	Narrating from him were Laith **Abu Al-Harith** the content, and Hafs who is **Ad-Douri** the aforementioned

A Brief History of the Oral and Written Qur'an

Names Given to the Recitals

From *Ad-Durra Al-Mudiyyah fi Al-Qira'at Ath-Thalath Al-Mardiyyah*

By Mohamed Ibn Mohamed Ibn Al-Jazari (d. 833 A.H.)

Say al-hamdulillah Who alone is the High, and glorify Him and ask and beg for His help	وَمَجِّــــدْهُ وَاسْأَلْ عَوْنَـــهُ وَتَوَسَّلاَ	قُلِ الحَمْـــدُ للهِ الذِي وَحْدَهُ عَلاَ
And pray for peace and blessing to be upon the best of creation, Mohamed, and upon his family, friends, and followers	وَسَلِّمْ وَآلٍ وَالصِّـــحَابِ وَمَنْ تَلاَ	وَصَـــلِّ عَلَى خَيْرِ الأَنَامِ مُحَمَّـــدٍ
And thus, take my poem about the three who complete the ten recitals, and pass the poem on	تَتِـــمُّ بِهَا الْعَشْـــرُ الْقِرَاءَاتُ وَانْقُلاَ	وَبَعْدُ، فَخُـــذْ نَظْمِي حُرُوفَ ثَلاَثَةٍ
As the seven are mentioned in my book *Tahbeer At-Tayseer*, I ask my lord His blessings so that it may be complete	فَأَسْـــأَلُ رَبِّي أَنْ يَمُـــنَّ فَتَكْـــمُلاَ	كَمَا هُوَ فِي تَحْبِيـــرِ تَيْسِيرِ سَبْعِهَا
Abu Ja'far's narrator was **Ibn Wardan** as well as **Ibn Jammaz** Sulaiman the great	كَذَاكَ **ابْنُ جَمَّازٍ** سُلَيْمَانُ ذُو الْعُلاَ	أَبُو جَعْـــفَرٍ عَنْهُ **ابْنُ وَرْدَانَ** نَاقِـــلٌ
And Ya'qoub say from him [narrated] **Ruwais** and **Rawh**, also **Is-haaq** with **Idris** narrated from Khalaf	**وَإِسْحَاقُ** مَعْ **إِدْرِيسَ** عَنْ خَلَفٍ تَلاَ	وَيَعْقُوبُ قُلْ عَنْهُ **رُوَيْسٌ** **وَرَوْحُهُمْ**

A Brief History of the Oral and Written Qur'an

Names Given to the Recitals

The Ten Recitals

These ten recitals are the recitals of Abu-'Amr, Ibn Katheer, Nafi', Ibn 'Amir, 'Asim, Hamzah, Al-Kisa'i, Abu-Ja'far, Ya'qoub, and Khalaf

Each of these ten are in use today and taught around the world in large numbers such that they maintain authentic chains of narration

There were also many other recitals taught around the world, but most of these recitals have been lost or have gone extinct and only exist in books and are not recited today

You can find a sample of the author's chain of narration at the end of this book

A Brief History of the Oral and Written Qur'an

A New Shape for Vowels

إِيَّاكَ نَعْبُدُ وَإِيَّاكَ نَسْتَعِينُ

While the ten recitals were being taught and meticulously documented by scholars, **Al-Khaleel Ibn Ahmed Al-Farahidi** (d. 170 A.H.) came up with a better way to represent the vowel sounds in the written form

Instead of using red dots to represent the fat-hah, dammah, and kasrah, Al-Farahidi used a short Alif for a **fat-hah**, a small Waw for a **dammah**, and the head of a Yaa for a **kasrah**

Al-Farahidi's method for voweling Arabic letters eventually became the standard in Iraq, Levant, and the surrounding regions

This system did not become standard in the masahif until a few centuries after that in the regions of Andalusia and Morocco

Al-Farahidi's method is still in use today by all the masahif printed around the world. While the dotting system first laid down by Nasr Bin 'Asim may differ slightly in some regions, this system is also still used today

A Brief History of the Oral and Written Qur'an

The Connected and Disconnected

Just as the scribes followed the spelling methods of Quraish in most of the Qur'an, they would also scribe special words to accommodate the recitals taught to them by our Prophet ﷺ

They also scribed some words in unusual ways, such as writing two words as a single one, or splitting words into two parts, all of which followed the scriptures collected at the time of Abu-Bakr رضي الله عنه, which in turn followed the forms written in the presence of our beloved Prophet and approved by him

The following chapter will detail these specific words that are scribed following the Othmani scriptures, where two words are merged into one, or when one word is written as two separate words, all if which are mentioned in a number of poems by prominent scholars

When recited, words that are scribed as one must be treated as a single word, and thus we are not allowed to stop in the middle of them, while words that are scribed separately can be treated as two, and we are allowed to stop on the first half in the times of necessity or teaching

Some words were scribed in some Othmani copies as connected, but scribed in the remaining Othamni copies as disconnected. In this case, the recital of Hafs allows both stopping on the first part and on the second part, but only when it is necessary or for teaching purposes

The Connected and Disconnected

From *Manthoumah Al-Muqaddimah*

By the imam and scholar Abu-Al-Khair Mohamed Ibn Mohamed Ibn Al-Jazari (d. 833 A.H.)

And know the connected, disconnected, and the Taa, how they were scribed in the original leading mus-haf and that is;	فِي الْمُصْحَفِ الإِمَامِ فِيمَا قَدْ أَتَى	وَاعْرِفْ لِمَقْطُوعٍ وَمَوْصُولٍ وَتَا	79
Disconnect: ten words of (أن لا) with مَـلْـجَـأَ and لاَ إِلَـهَ إِلاَّ;	مَـعْ مَلْـجَأَ وَلاَ إِلَـهَ إِلاَّ	فَاقْـطَعْ بِعَشْرِ كَلِمَاتٍ أَنْ لاَ	80
And with تَعْبُدُوا in Yaseen, and the second location in Houd, and with the words: يُشْرِكْنَ , تُشْرِكْ ,يَدْخُلَنْ, and تَعْلُوا عَلَى;	يُشْرِكْنَ تُشْرِكْ يَدْخُلَنْ تَعْلُوا عَلَى	وَتَعْبُدُوا يَاسِـينَ ثَانِي هُودَ لاَ	81
And with أَنْ لا يَقُولُوا and لاَ أَقُولَ, (إِن مَّا) in Ar-Ra'd [should also be disconnected], and the one with a fat-hah [i.e. أَمَّا] should be connected, and (عن مَّا);	بِالرَّعْدِ وَالْمَفْتُوحَ صِـلْ وَعَن مَّا	أَنْ لا يَقُـولُوا لاَ أَقُولَ إِن مَّا	82
When it is followed by (نُهُوا), then disconnect (من مَّا) that is followed by the word "ملك" in both Ar-Roum and An-Nisa'. As for the location in Al-Munafiqeen, it has been scribed both ways, and (أم مَّن) that is followed by the word "أَسَّسَ";	خُلْـفُ الْمُنَافِقِينَ أَم مَّنْ أَسَّـسَا	نُهُوا اقْطَعُوا مِنْ مَا مَلَكْ رُومِ النِّسَا	83

From *Manthoumah Al-Muqaddimah*

By the imam and scholar Abu-Al-Khair Mohamed Ibn Mohamed Ibn Al-Jazari (d. 833 A.H.)

In Fussilat, An-Nisa', and [the surah with the word] "ذِبح" [which is As-Saffaat], [and always disconnect] (حَيثُ مَا) and (أَن لَّم), also (إِنَّ مَا) with a kasrah [under the Hamzah];

84 فُصِّلَتِ النِّسَا وَذِبْحٍ حَيْثُ مَا　　وَأَنْ لَمِ الْمَفْتُوحَ كَسْرُ إِنَّ مَا

In Al-Anaam, and [disconnect] the one with a fat-hah, both followed by "يدعون", and in Al-Anfaal (أَنَّ مَا) is written both ways, as is (إِنَّ مَا) in An-Nahl;

85 الأَنْعَامَ وَالْمَفْتُوحَ يَدْعُونَ مَعَا　　وَخُلْفُ الأَنْفَالِ وَنَحْلٍ وَقَعَا

[And disconnect] (كُلِّ مَا) that is followed by "سَأَلْتُمُوه", but if it is followed by "رُدُّوا" then it was scribed both ways, and also [scribed both ways is] (بِئْسَمَا) that is preceded by "قُلْ", and connected with the following words;

86 وَكُلِّ مَا سَأَلْتُمُوهُ وَاخْتُلِفْ　　رُدُّوا كَذَا قُلْ بِئْسَمَا وَالْوَصْلَ صِفْ

"خَلَفْتُمُونِي" and "اشْتَرَوْا", and disconnect (فِي مَا) when it is followed by "أُوحِي", "أَفَضْتُم", "اشْتَهَتْ", and both ayahs with "يَبْلُوا";

87 خَلَفْتُمُونِي وَاشْتَرَوْا فِي مَا اقْطَعَا　　أُوحِي أَفَضْتُمُ اشْتَهَتْ يَبْلُوا مَعَا

The second ayah with "فَعَلْنَ", and in Al-Waqi'ah [i.e. وَقَعَتْ], Ar-Roum, both ayahs in Az-Zumar [i.e. تَنْزِيل], and in Ash-Shu'ara', and connect all remaining locations;

88 ثَانِي فَعَلْنَ وَقَعَتْ رُومٌ كِلاَ　　تَنْزِيلُ شُعَرَا وَغَيْرَهَا صِلاَ

FROM *MANTHOUMAH AL-MUQADDIMAH*

By the imam and scholar Abu-Al-Khair Mohamed Ibn Mohamed Ibn Al-Jazari (d. 833 A.H.)

89 فَأَيْنَمَا كَالنَّحْلِ صِلْ وَمُخْتَلِفْ   فِي الشُّعَرَا الأَحْزَابِ وَالنِّسَا وُصِفْ

And connect (أَيْنَ مَا) in the word "فَأَيْنَمَا" and in An-Nahl, and it was described to be both ways in Ash-Shu'ara', Al-Ahzab, and An-Nisa';

90 وَصِــــلْ فَإِلَّمْ هُودَ أَلَّنْ نَجْعَلَ   نَجْمَعَ كَيْلاَ تَحْزَنُوا تَــــأْسَوْا عَلَى

And connect (إِن لَّمْ) in Houd, and connect (أَن لَّن) [when it is followed by] "نَّجْعَلَ" and "نَّجْمَعَ", [also connect] (كَيْ لاَ) [when it is followed by] "تَحْزَنُوا" and "تَأْسَوْا عَلَى";

91 حَجٌّ عَلَيْــــكَ حَرَجٌ وَقَطْعُهُمْ   عَنْ مَنْ يَشَــــاءُ مَنْ تَوَلَّى يَوْمَ هُمْ

And in Al-Hajj as well as [when it is followed by] "عَلَيْكَ حَرَجٌ", and they disconnect (عَن مَّن) that is followed by "يَشَاءُ" and by "تَوَلَّى", [and also disconnect] (يَوْمَ هُمْ);

92 وَمَا لِ هَــــذَا وَالَّذِيــــنَ هَؤُلاَ   تَحِيــــنَ فِي الإِمَامِ صِلْ وَوُهِّــــلاَ

And they disconnect (مَا لِ) that is followed by "هَذَا", "الَّذِينَ", and "هَــؤُلاَ", (تَحِينَ) was found connected in the private copy of Othman ﷺ in Medina, but not all scholars agree with that;

93 وَوَزَنُــــوهُمُ وَكَالُوهُمْ صِــــلِ   كَــــذَا مِنَ الْ وَيَا وَهَا لاَ تَفْــــصِلِ

And connect (وَزَنُوهُمْ) and (كَالُوهُمْ), and also connect (الْ), (يَـ), and (هَـ) to whatever follows them;

The Connected and Disconnected

Ibn Al-Jazari says in his poem, *Al-Muqaddimah*

And know the connected, disconnected, and the Taa, how they were scribed in the original leading mus-haf and that is;
Disconnect ten words of (أن لا) with مَـلْـجَـأ and لاَ إلَـهَ إلاَّ;
And with تَعْبُدُوا in Yaseen, and the second location in Houd, and with the words: يَدْخُلَنْ ,تُشْرِكْ ,يُشْرِكْنَ, and تَعْلُوا عَلَى; And with أنْ لا يَقُولُوا and لاَ أقُولَ

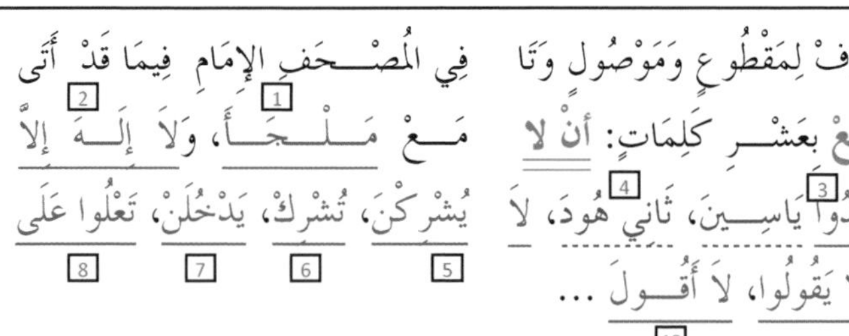

79 وَاعْرِفْ لِمَقْطُوعٍ وَمَوْصُولٍ وَتَا فِي الْمُصْحَفِ الإِمَامِ فِيمَا قَدْ أَتَى
80 فَاقْطَعْ بِعَشْرِ كَلِمَاتٍ: أَنْ لَا مَعْ مَلْجَأ، وَلَا إِلَهَ إِلَّا
81 وَتَعْبُدُوا يَاسِينَ، ثَانِي هُودَ، لَا يُشْرِكْنَ، تُشْرِكْ، يَدْخُلَنْ، تَعْلُوا عَلَى
82 أَنْ لَا يَقُولُوا، لَا أَقُولَ ...

أَن لاَّ

The remaining verses in the Qur'an are scribed in the connected form

أَلاَّ and أَن لاَّ

﴿ أَن لاَّ إِلَـهَ إِلاَّ أَنتَ سُبْحَـانَك ﴾ الأنبياء ٨٧

أَن لاَّ

1. ﴿ أَن لاَّ مَلْجَأَ مِنَ اللهِ إِلاَّ إِلَيْهِ ﴾ التوبة ١١٨
2. ﴿ أَن لاَّ إِلَـهَ إِلاَّ هُو ﴾ هود ١٤
3. ﴿ أَن لاَّ تَعْبُدُوا الشَّيْطَان ﴾ ياسين ٦٠
4. ﴿ أَن لاَّ تَعْبُدُوا إِلاَّ الله ﴾ هود ٢٦ (second location)
5. ﴿ أَن لاَّ يُشْرِكْنَ بِاللهِ شَيْئاً ﴾ الممتحنة ١٢
6. ﴿ أَن لاَّ تُشْرِكْ بِي شَيْئاً ﴾ الحج ٢٦
7. ﴿ أَن لاَّ يَدْخُلَنَّهَا اليوم ﴾ نون ٢٤
8. ﴿ أَن لاَّ تَعْلُوا عَلَى الله ﴾ الدخان ١٩
9. ﴿ أَن لاَّ يَقُولُوا عَلَى اللهِ إِلاَّ الْحَقّ ﴾ الأعراف ١٦٩
10. ﴿ أَن لاَّ أَقُولَ عَلَى اللهِ إِلاَّ الْحَقّ ﴾ الأعراف ١٠٥

As-Samannoudi mentioned this in his poem, *La'ali' Al-Bayan*:

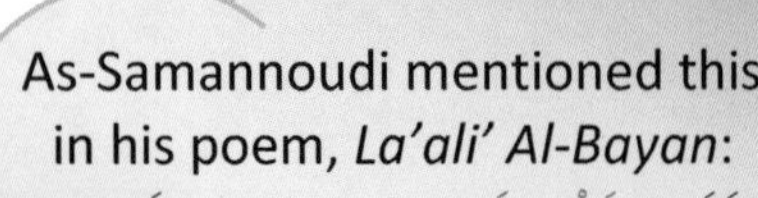

كَذَا بِهَا أَنْ لَا إِلَهَ وَاخْتُلِفْ ** فِي الأَنبِيَا ...

And (أن لا) when found with إِلَـهَ is scribed two ways in Al-Anbiya'

Ibn Al-Jazari says in his poem, *Al-Muqaddimah*

[And] (إِن مَّا) in Ar-Ra'd [should also be disconnected], and the one with a fat-hah [i.e. أَمَّا] should be connected, and (عَن مَّا);

When it is followed by "نُهُوا" then disconnect

إِن مَّا ....بِالرَّعْدِ، وَالْمَفْتُوحَ صِلْ، وَعَنْ مَا   82

نُهُوا اقْطَعُوا ...   83

إِن مَّا

إِمَّا — The remaining verses in the Qur'an are scribed in the connected form

إِن مَّا — ﴿وَإِن مَّا نُرِيَنَّكَ بَعْضَ الَّذِي نَعِدُهُم﴾ الرعد ٤٠

أَمَّا

أَمَّا — All verses in the Qur'an are scribed in the connected form

عَن مَّا

عَمَّا — The remaining verses in the Qur'an are scribed in the connected form

عَن مَّا — ﴿فَلَمَّا عَتَوْا عَن مَّا نُهُوا عَنْه﴾ الأعراف ١٦٦

71

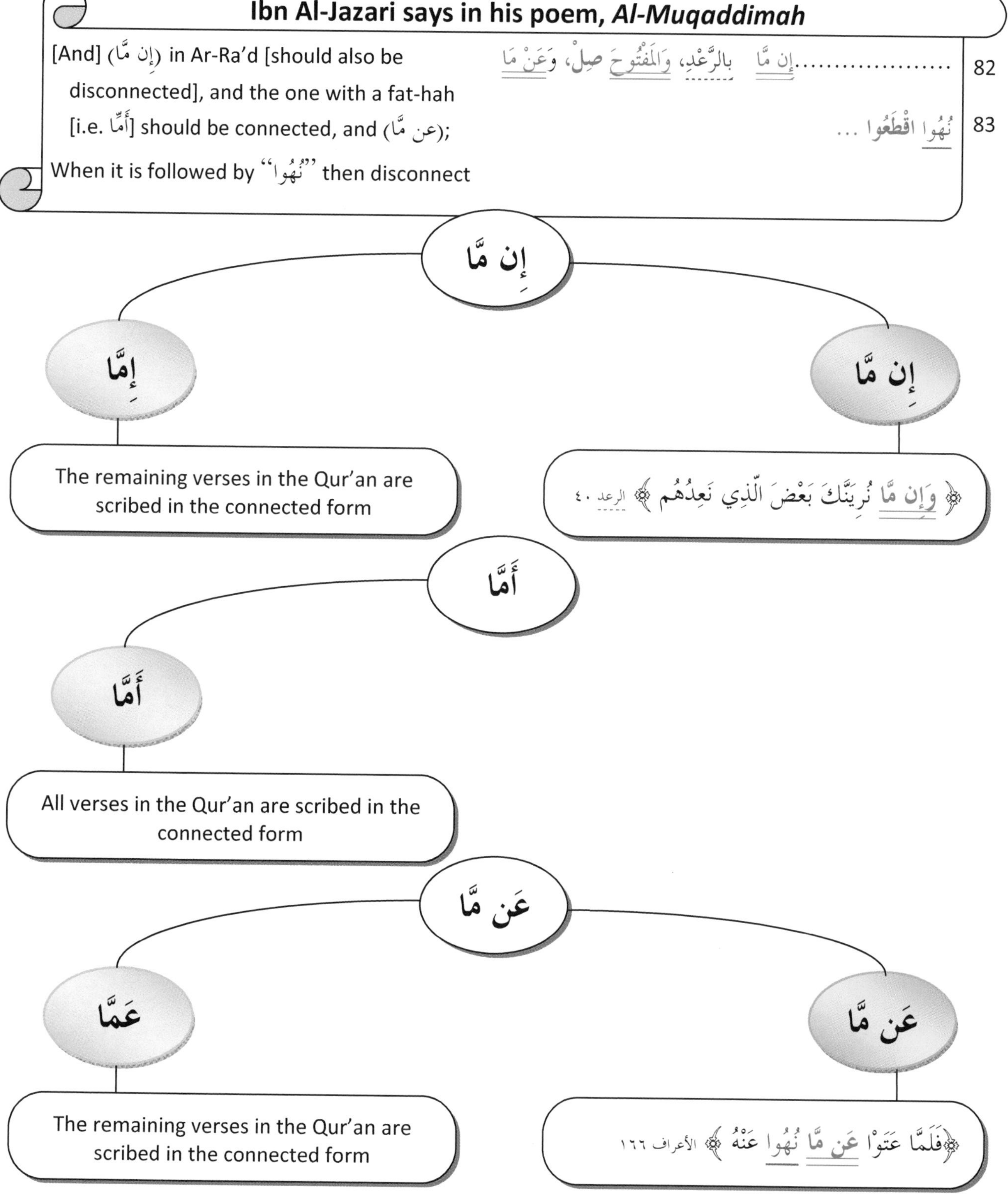

THE CONNECTED AND DISCONNECTED

Ibn Al-Jazari says in his poem, *Al-Muqaddimah*

83 ... اقْطَعُوا مِن مَّا مَلَكْ رُومِ النِّسَا خُلْفُ المُنَافِقِينَ ....

Disconnect (من مَّا) that is followed by the word "ملك" in both Ar-Roum and An-Nisa'. As for the location in Al-Munafiqeen, it has been scribed both ways

Ibn Al-Jazari had originally written this line as "...مِن مَّا بِرُومٍ وَالنِّسَا", but one of his students, Abd Ad-Da'im Al-Azhari, narrated that the line was corrected in later years to reflect the fact that there are multiple ayahs in both surahs containing مما, but the ones with ملك were the only disconnected ones, and this final form is what was then recited to Ibn Al-Jazari and approved by him

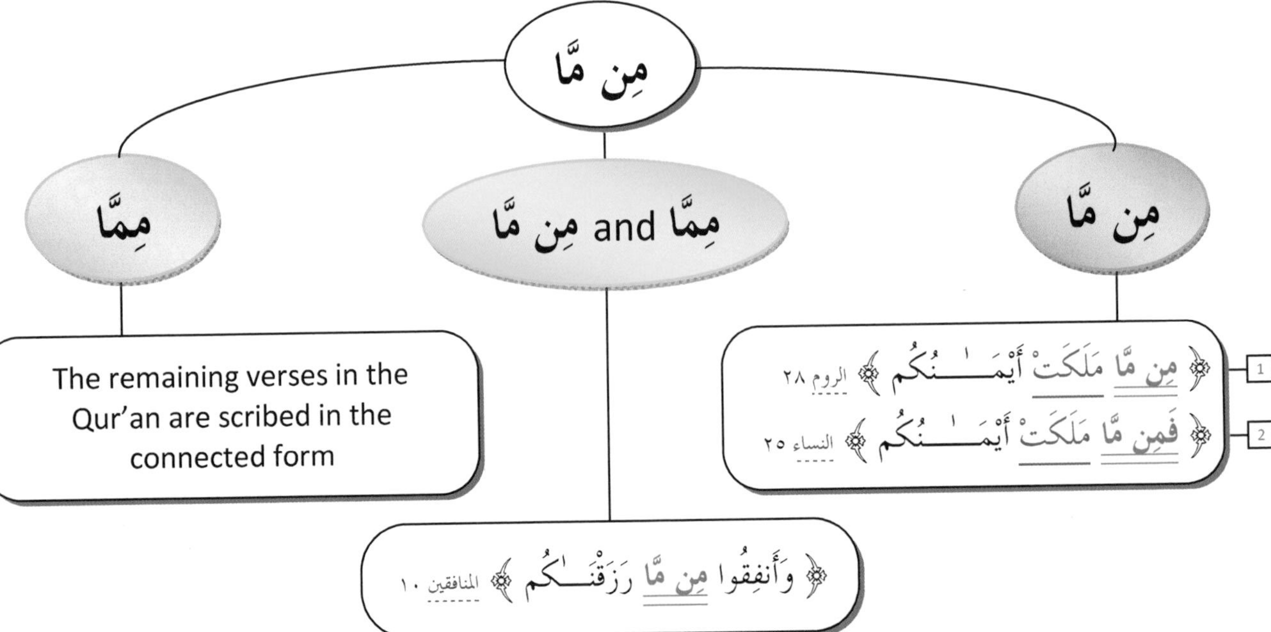

The Connected and Disconnected

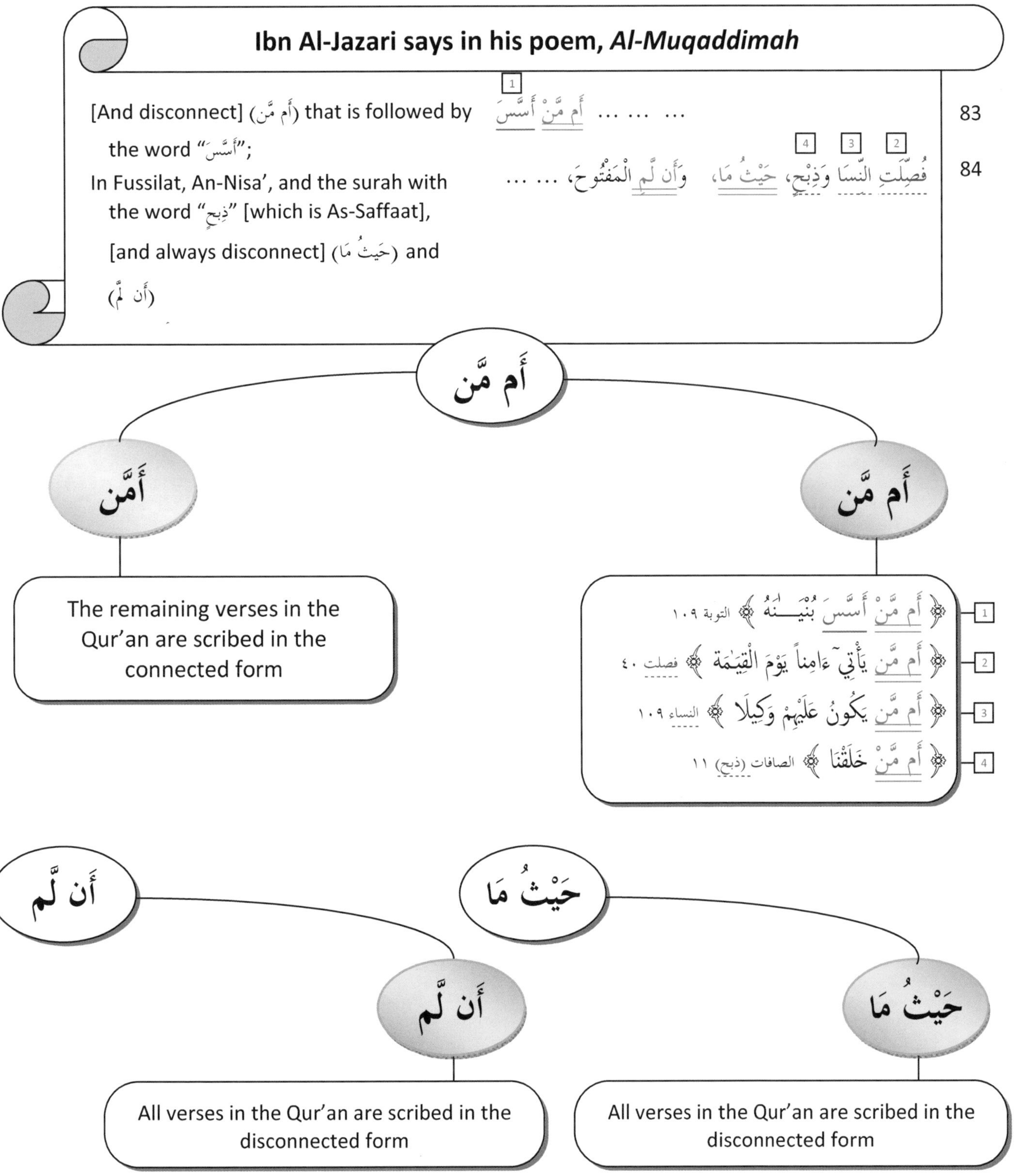

Ibn Al-Jazari says in his poem, *Al-Muqaddimah*
83 ... ... أَم مَّنْ أَسَّسَ
[And disconnect] (أَم مَّن) that is followed by the word "أَسَّسَ";
84 فُصِّلَتِ النِّسَا وَذِبْحِ، حَيْثُ مَا، وَأَن لَّمِ الْمَفْتُوحَ، ... ...
In Fussilat, An-Nisa', and the surah with the word "ذِبحِ" [which is As-Saffaat],
[and always disconnect] (حَيثُ مَا) and (أَن لَّم)
أَم مَّن
أَمَّن
The remaining verses in the Qur'an are scribed in the connected form
أَم مَّن
﴿ أَم مَّنْ أَسَّسَ بُنْيَـٰنَهُۥ ﴾ التوبة ١٠٩
﴿ أَم مَّن يَأْتِيٓ ءَامِناً يَوْمَ الْقِيَـٰمَةِ ﴾ فصلت ٤٠
﴿ أَم مَّن يَكُونُ عَلَيْهِمْ وَكِيلًا ﴾ النساء ١٠٩
﴿ أَم مَّنْ خَلَقْنَا ﴾ الصافات (ذبح) ١١
أَن لَّم
حَيْثُ مَا
أَن لَّم
All verses in the Qur'an are scribed in the disconnected form
حَيْثُ مَا
All verses in the Qur'an are scribed in the disconnected form

The Connected and Disconnected

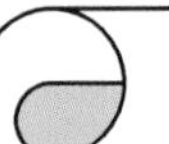

Ibn Al-Jazari says in his poem, *Al-Muqaddimah*

[And disconnect] (إِنَّ مَا) with a kasrah [under the Hamzah];	... ... كَسْرُ إِنَّ مَا	84
In Al-An'aam, and [disconnect] the one with a fat-hah, both followed by "يدعون", and in Al-Anfaal (أَنَّ مَا) is written both ways, as is (إِنَّ مَا) in An-Nahl	الأَنْعَامِ، وَالْمَفْتُوحَ يَدْعُونَ مَعَا ¹ ² وَخُلْفُ الأَنْفَالِ، وَنَحْلٍ وَقَعَا	85

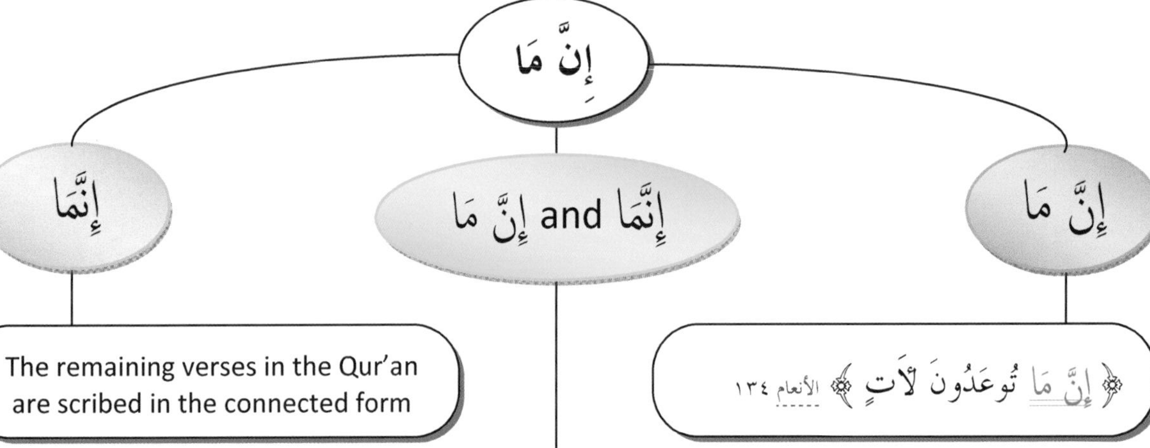

إِنَّ مَا

- **إِنَّ مَا**: ﴿إِنَّ مَا تُوعَدُونَ لَآتٍ﴾ الأنعام ١٣٤
- **إِنَّمَا and إِنَّ مَا**: ﴿إِنَّمَا عِندَ اللهِ هُوَ خَيْرٌ لَّكُمْ﴾ النحل ٩٥
- **إِنَّمَا**: The remaining verses in the Qur'an are scribed in the connected form

أَنَّ مَا

- **أَنَّ مَا**:
  1. ﴿وَأَنَّ مَا يَدْعُونَ مِن دُونِهِ هُوَ الْبَاطِلُ﴾ الحج ٦٢
  2. ﴿وَأَنَّ مَا يَدْعُونَ مِن دُونِهِ الْبَاطِلُ﴾ لقمان ٣٠
- **أَنَّمَا and أَنَّ مَا**: ﴿وَاعْلَمُوٓا أَنَّمَا غَنِمْتُم مِّن شَيْءٍ﴾ الأنفال ٤١
- **أَنَّمَا**: The remaining verses in the Qur'an are scribed in the connected form

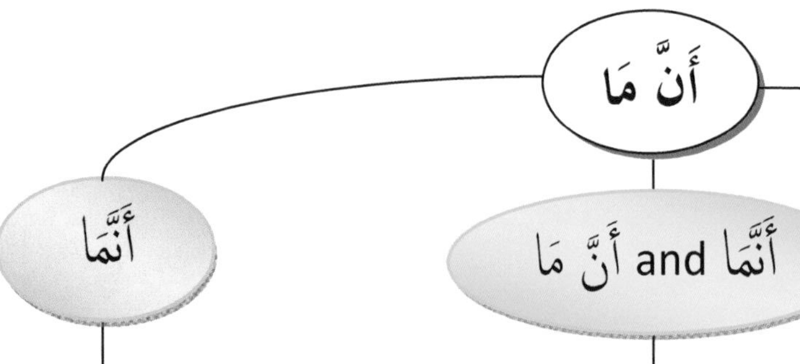

The Connected and Disconnected

Ibn Al-Jazari says in his poem, *Al-Muqaddimah*

وَكُلِّ مَا سَأَلْتُمُوهُ، وَاخْتُلِفْ رُدُّوا، … … … 86

[And disconnect] (كُلِّ مَا) that is followed by "سَأَلْتُمُوهُ", but if it is followed by "رُدُّوا" then it was scribed both ways [in the Othmani copies]

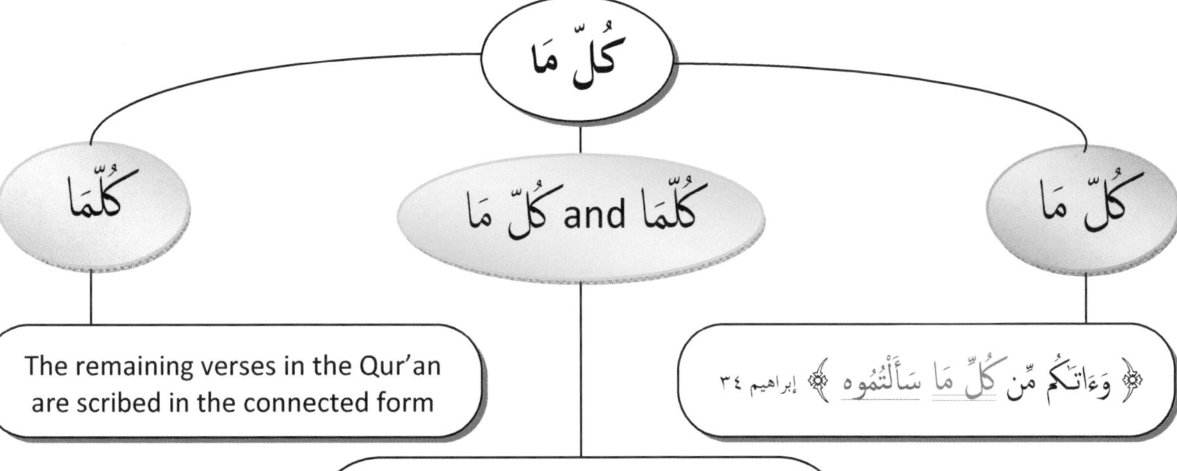

كُلّمَا and كُلّ مَا

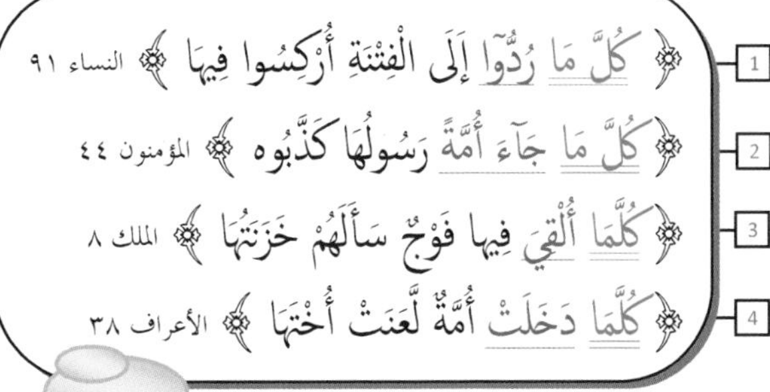

﴿ وَءَاتَاكُم مِّن كُلِّ مَا سَأَلْتُمُوهُ ﴾ إبراهيم ٣٤

1 ﴿ كُلَّ مَا رُدُّوٓا إِلَى الْفِتْنَةِ أُرْكِسُوا فِيهَا ﴾ النساء ٩١
2 ﴿ كُلَّ مَا جَآءَ أُمَّةً رَّسُولُهَا كَذَّبُوهُ ﴾ المؤمنون ٤٤
3 ﴿ كُلَّمَا أُلْقِيَ فِيهَا فَوْجٌ سَأَلَهُمْ خَزَنَتُهَا ﴾ الملك ٨
4 ﴿ كُلَّمَا دَخَلَتْ أُمَّةٌ لَّعَنَتْ أُخْتَهَا ﴾ الأعراف ٣٨

Ibn Al-Jazari only mentions the first of these four ayahs in which (كُلِّ مَا) is scribed both ways in the Othmani copies, but Abu Al-Hasan Ali Al-Mula Al-Qari Al-Harawi (d. 1014 A.H.), in his book *Al-Minah Al-Fikriyah* explaining Al-Jazariyah, wrote a line of poem that precisely captures these three locations:

وَجَاءَ أُمَّةً وَأُلْقِي دَخَلَتْ فِي وَصْلِهَا وَقَطْعِهَا واخْتُلِفَتْ

The Connected and Disconnected

Ibn Al-Jazari says in his poem, *Al-Muqaddimah*

And also scribed both ways is (بِئْسَمَا) that is preceded by "قُلْ", and connected with the following words; "خَلَفْتُمُونِي" and "اشْتَرَوْا"...	... ... وَاخْتُلِفْ ...، كَذَا قُلْ بِئْسَمَا وَالْوَصْلَ صِفْ	86
	[1] خَلَفْتُمُونِي [2] وَاشْتَرَوْا ...	87

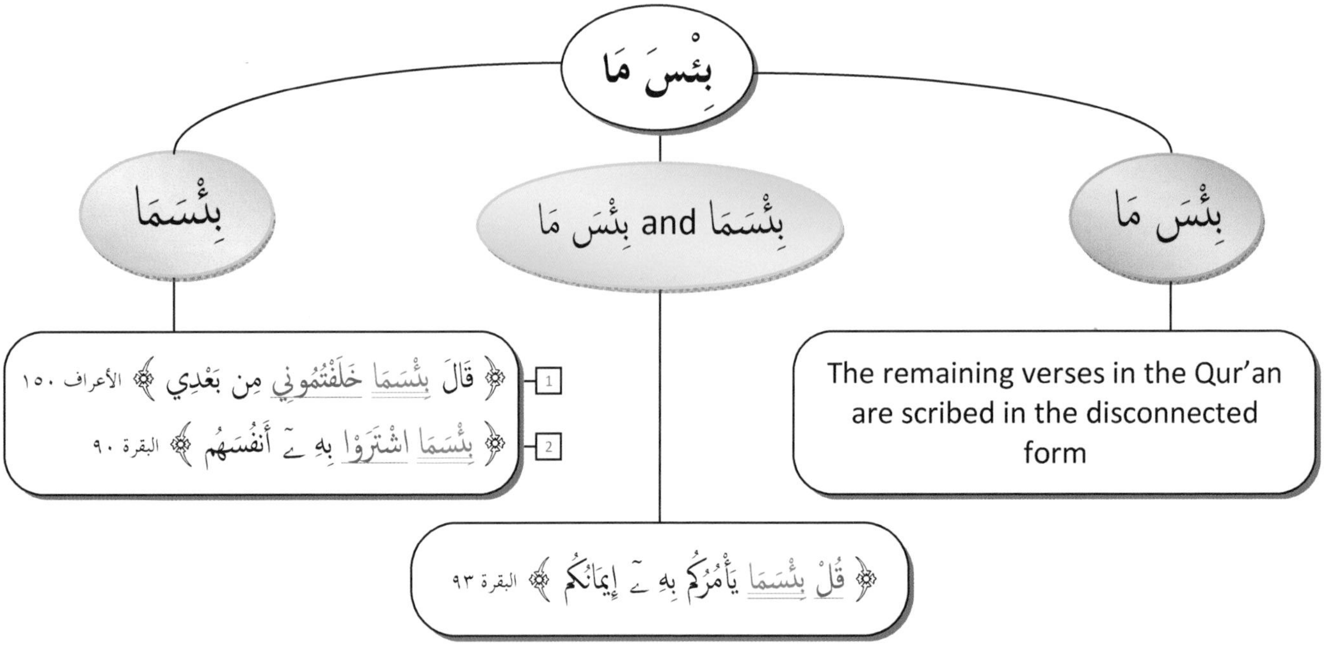

بِئْسَ مَا

- بِئْسَمَا
  - [1] ﴿قَالَ بِئْسَمَا خَلَفْتُمُونِي مِن بَعْدِي﴾ الأعراف ١٥٠
  - [2] ﴿بِئْسَمَا اشْتَرَوْا بِهِۦٓ أَنفُسَهُمْ﴾ البقرة ٩٠
- بِئْسَمَا and بِئْسَ مَا
  - ﴿قُلْ بِئْسَمَا يَأْمُرُكُم بِهِۦٓ إِيمَانُكُم﴾ البقرة ٩٣
- بِئْسَ مَا
  - The remaining verses in the Qur'an are scribed in the disconnected form

The Connected and Disconnected

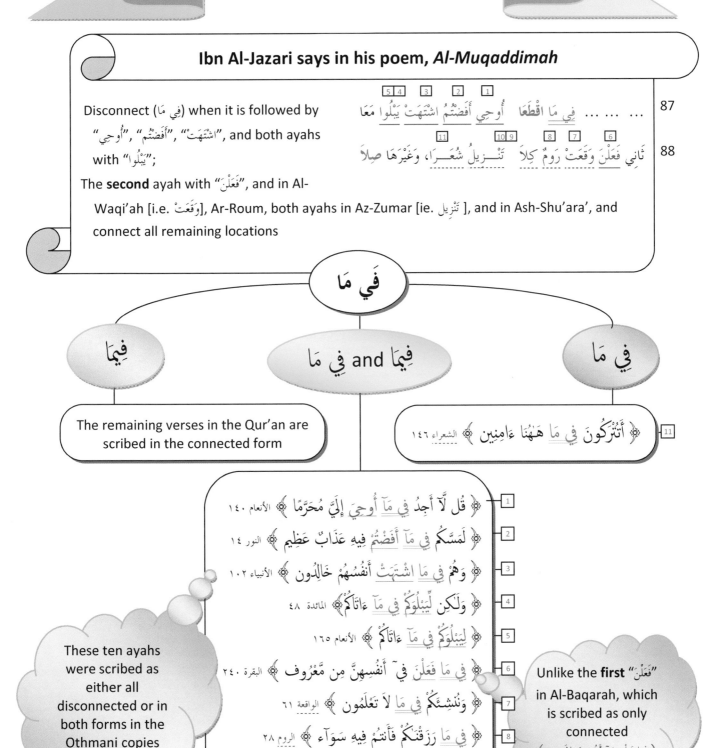

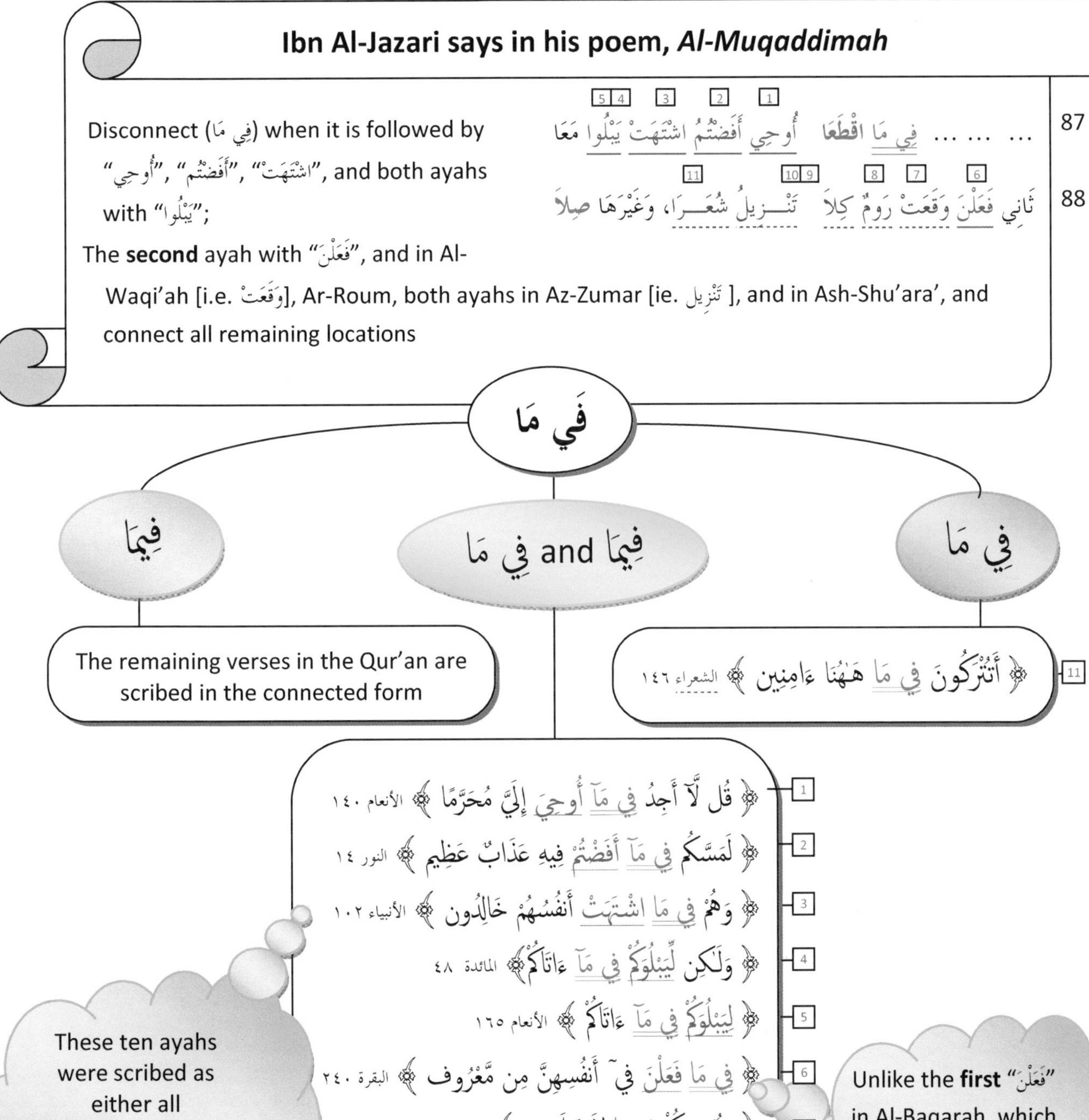

Ibn Al-Jazari says in his poem, *Al-Muqaddimah*
5 4 3 2 1
... ... فِي مَا اقْطَعَا أُوحِي أَفَضْتُمُ اشْتَهَتْ يَبْلُوا مَعَا 87
11 10 9 8 7 6
ثَانِي فَعَلْنَ وَقَعَتْ رُومٌ كِلاَ تَنْـزِيلُ شُعَـرَا، وَغَيْرَهَا صِلاَ 88
Disconnect (فِي مَا) when it is followed by "أُوحِي", "أَفَضْتُم", "اشْتَهَتْ", and both ayahs with "يَبْلُوا";
The **second** ayah with "فَعَلْنَ", and in Al-Waqi'ah [i.e. وَقَعَتْ], Ar-Roum, both ayahs in Az-Zumar [ie. تَنْزِيل], and in Ash-Shu'ara', and connect all remaining locations
فِي مَا
فِيمَا
فِيمَا and فِي مَا
فِي مَا
The remaining verses in the Qur'an are scribed in the connected form
11 ﴿أَتُتْرَكُونَ فِي مَا هَاهُنَا ءَامِنِينَ﴾ الشعراء ١٤٦
1 ﴿قُل لَّآ أَجِدُ فِي مَآ أُوحِيَ إِلَيَّ مُحَرَّمًا﴾ الأنعام ١٤٥
2 ﴿لَمَسَّكُمْ فِي مَآ أَفَضْتُمْ فِيهِ عَذَابٌ عَظِيمٌ﴾ النور ١٤
3 ﴿وَهُمْ فِي مَا اشْتَهَتْ أَنفُسُهُمْ خَالِدُونَ﴾ الأنبياء ١٠٢
4 ﴿وَلَكِن لِّيَبْلُوَكُمْ فِي مَآ ءَاتَاكُمْ﴾ المائدة ٤٨
5 ﴿لِيَبْلُوَكُمْ فِي مَآ ءَاتَاكُمْ﴾ الأنعام ١٦٥
6 ﴿فِي مَا فَعَلْنَ فِيٓ أَنفُسِهِنَّ مِن مَّعْرُوفٍ﴾ البقرة ٢٤٠
7 ﴿وَنُنشِئَكُمْ فِي مَا لَا تَعْلَمُونَ﴾ الواقعة ٦١
8 ﴿فِي مَا رَزَقْنَاكُمْ فَأَنتُمْ فِيهِ سَوَآءٌ﴾ الروم ٢٨
9 ﴿فِي مَا هُمْ فِيهِ يَخْتَلِفُونَ﴾ الزمر ٣
10 ﴿فِي مَا كَانُوا فِيهِ يَخْتَلِفُونَ﴾ الزمر ٤٦
These ten ayahs were scribed as either all disconnected or in both forms in the Othmani copies
Unlike the **first** "فَعَلْنَ" in Al-Baqarah, which is scribed as only connected
﴿فِيمَا فَعَلْنَ فِيٓ أَنفُسِهِنَّ بِالْمَعْرُوفِ﴾ البقرة ٢٣٤

The Connected and Disconnected

Ibn Al-Jazari says in his poem, *Al-Muqaddimah*

89	فَأَيْنَمَا [1] كَالنَّحْلِ [2] صِلْ، وَمُخْتَلِفْ فِي الشُّعَرَا [1] الأَحْزَابِ [2] وَالنِّسَا [3] وُصِفْ	And connect (أَيْنَ مَا) in the word "فَأَيْنَمَا" and in An-Nahl, and it was described to be both ways in Ash-Shu'ara', Al-Ahzab, and An-Nisa';
90	وَصِلْ فَإِلَّمْ هُودَ … …	And connect (إِن لَّمْ) in Houd ...

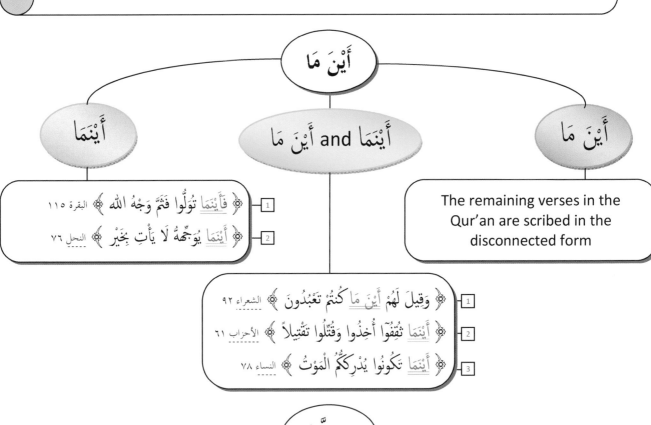

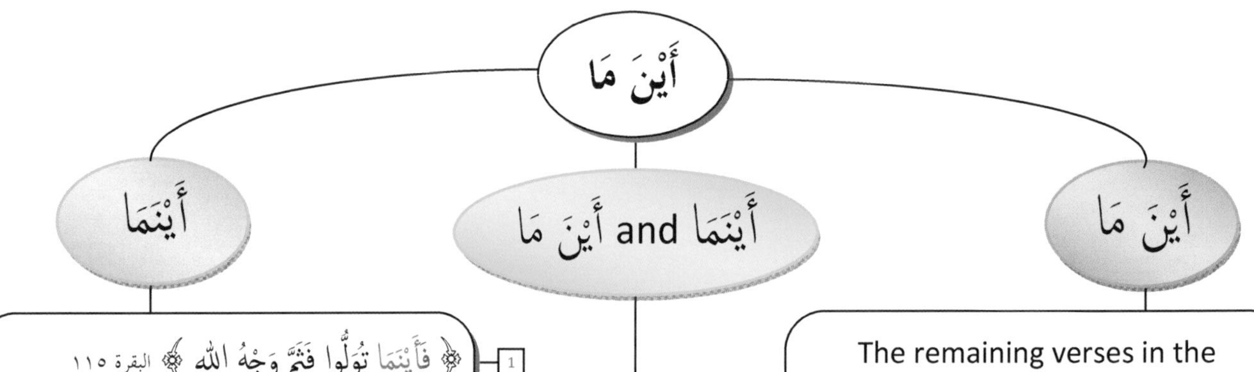

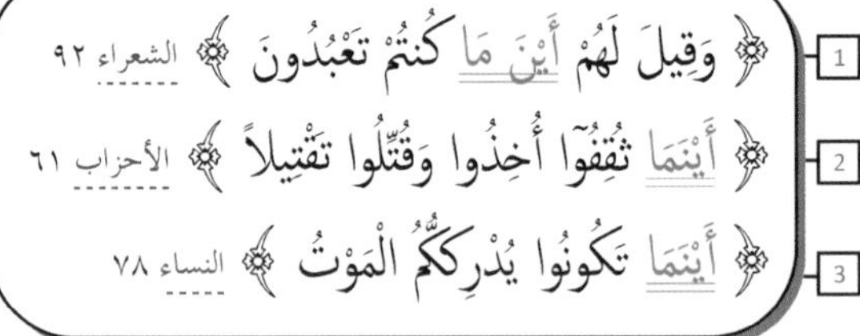

1 ﴿وَقِيلَ لَهُمْ أَيْنَ مَا كُنتُمْ تَعْبُدُونَ﴾ الشعراء ٩٢
2 ﴿أَيْنَمَا ثُقِفُوٓا أُخِذُوا وَقُتِّلُوا تَقْتِيلاً﴾ الأحزاب ٦١
3 ﴿أَيْنَمَا تَكُونُوا يُدْرِككُّمُ الْمَوْتُ﴾ النساء ٧٨

إِن لَّمْ

إِلَّمْ

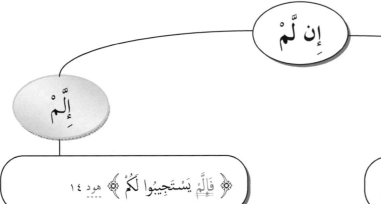

﴿فَإِلَّمْ يَسْتَجِيبُوا لَكُمْ﴾ هود ١٤

إِن لَّمْ

1 ﴿فَأَيْنَمَا تُوَلُّوا فَثَمَّ وَجْهُ اللهِ﴾ البقرة ١١٥
2 ﴿أَيْنَمَا يُوَجِّههُّ لَا يَأْتِ بِخَيْرٍ﴾ النحل ٧٦
The remaining verses in the Qur'an are scribed in the disconnected form

The Connected and Disconnected

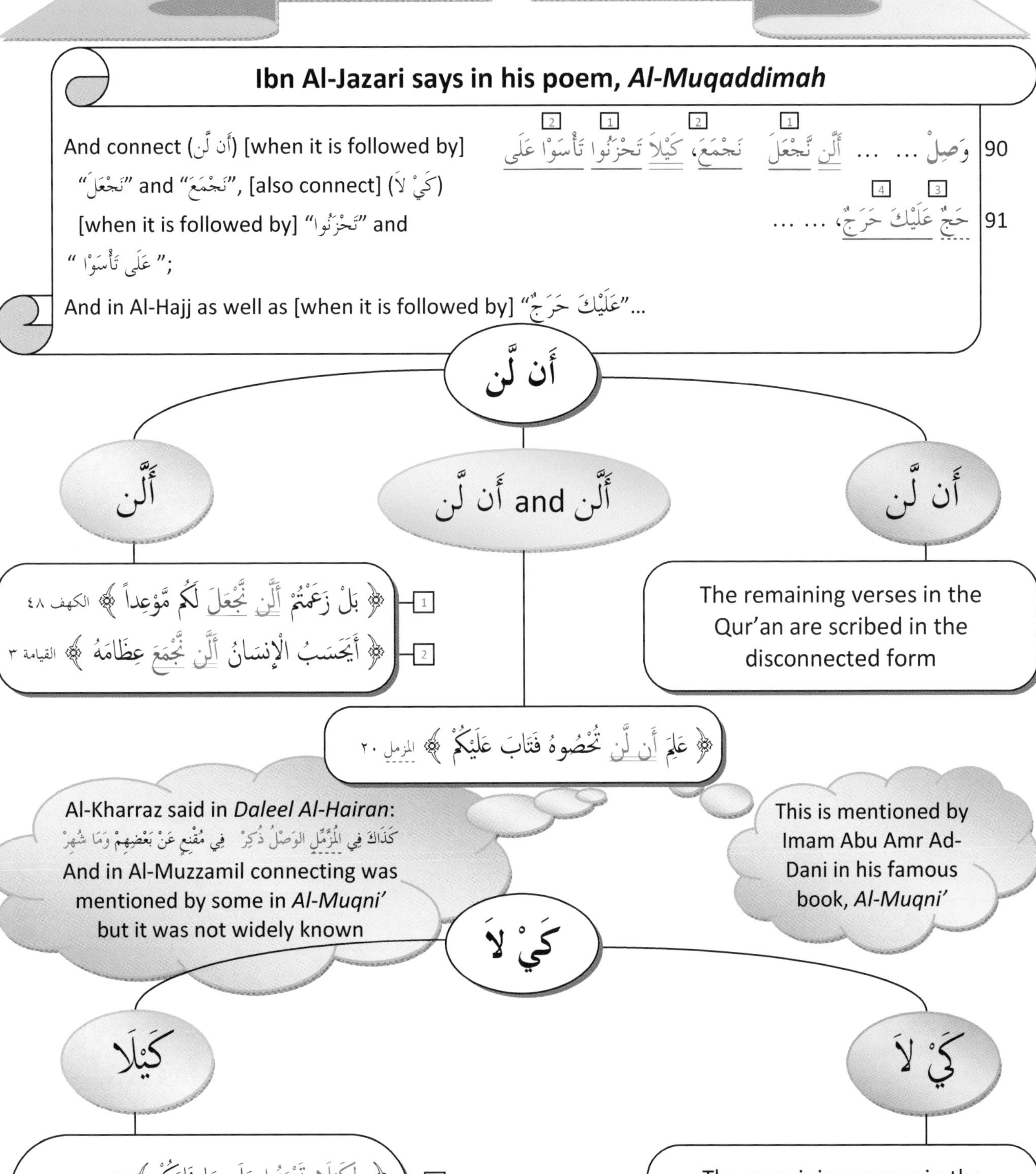

Ibn Al-Jazari says in his poem, *Al-Muqaddimah*
90 وَصِلْ ... ... أَلَّن نَّجْعَلَ نَجْمَعَ، كَيْلاَ تحزَنُوا تَأْسَوْا عَلَى
91 حَجٌّ عَلَيْكَ حَرَجٌ، ... ...
And connect (أَن لَّن) [when it is followed by] "نَّجْعَلَ" and "نَّجْمَعَ", [also connect] (كَيْ لاَ) [when it is followed by] "تَحْزَنُوا" and "عَلَى تَأْسَوْا";
And in Al-Hajj as well as [when it is followed by] "عَلَيْكَ حَرَجٌ"...
أَن لَّن
أَلَّن
أَلَّن and أَن لَّن
أَن لَّن
﴿ بَلْ زَعَمْتُمْ أَلَّن نَّجْعَلَ لَكُم مَّوْعِداً ﴾ الكهف ٤٨
﴿ أَيَحْسَبُ الإنسَانُ أَلَّن نَّجْمَعَ عِظَامَهُ ﴾ القيامة ٣
The remaining verses in the Qur'an are scribed in the disconnected form
﴿ عَلِمَ أَن لَّن تُحْصُوهُ فَتَابَ عَلَيْكُمْ ﴾ المزمل ٢٠
Al-Kharraz said in *Daleel Al-Hairan*:
كَذَاكَ فِي الْمُزَّمِّلِ الوَصْلُ ذُكِرْ فِي مُقْنِعٍ عَنْ بَعْضِهِمْ وَمَا شُهِرْ
And in Al-Muzzamil connecting was mentioned by some in *Al-Muqni'* but it was not widely known
This is mentioned by Imam Abu Amr Ad-Dani in his famous book, *Al-Muqni'*
كَيْ لاَ
كَيْلَا
كَيْ لاَ

1. ﴿ لِكَيْلَا تَحْزَنُوا عَلَى مَا فَاتَكُمْ ﴾ آل عمران ١٥٣
2. ﴿ لِكَيْلَا تَأْسَوْا عَلَى مَا فَاتَكُمْ ﴾ الحديد ٢٣
3. ﴿ لِكَيْلَا يَعْلَمَ مِن بَعْدِ عِلْمٍ شَيْئاً ﴾ الحج ٥
4. ﴿ لِكَيْلَا يَكُونَ عَلَيْكَ حَرَجٌ ﴾ الأحزاب ٥٠

The remaining verses in the Qur'an are scribed in the disconnected form

The Connected and Disconnected

Ibn Al-Jazari says in his poem, *Al-Muqaddimah*

And they disconnect (عَن مَّن) that is followed by "يَشَاءُ" and by "تَوَلَّى", [and also disconnect] (يَوْمَ هُمْ)

… … … … وَقَطْعُهُمْ عَن مَّن يَشَاءُ مَن تَوَلَّى يَوْمَ هُمْ 91

عَن مَّن

All verses in the Qur'an are scribed in the disconnected form, and there are only two of them

1. ﴿وَيَصْرِفُهُ عَن مَّن يَشَاءُ﴾ النور ٤٣
2. ﴿فَأَعْرِضْ عَن مَّن تَوَلَّى عَن ذِكْرِنَا﴾ النجم ٢٩

يَوْمَ هُم

يَوْمَ هُم

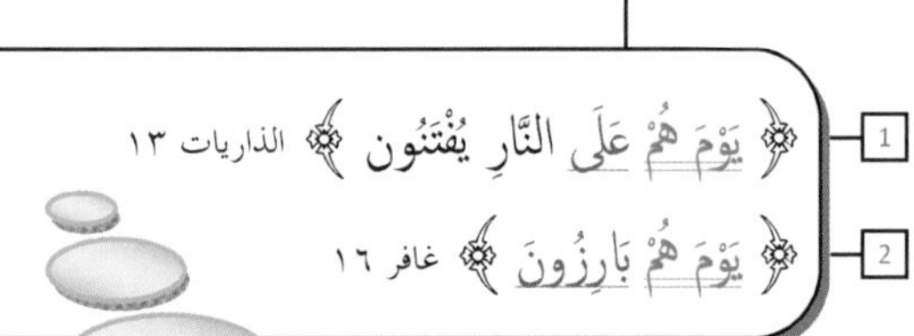

1 ﴿يَوْمَ هُمْ عَلَى النَّارِ يُفْتَنُونَ﴾ الذاريات ١٣
2 ﴿يَوْمَ هُم بَارِزُونَ﴾ غافر ١٦

As-Samannoudi made it easy for us to remember these two ayahs by saying in his poem, *La'ali' Al-Bayan*:

وَقَطْعُ حَيْثُ مَا مَعًا وَيَوْمَ هُمْ عَلَى وَبَارِزُونَ عَكْسُ يَنْتَوِمْ

يَوْمَهُمُ | يَوْمِهِمُ

The remaining verses in the Qur'an are scribed in the connected form

In the recital of Hafs, the remaining ayahs differ from يَوْمَ هُمْ by either having a kasrah under the first Meem, or an incidental dammah on the second

The Connected and Disconnected

Ibn Al-Jazari says in his poem, *Al-Muqaddimah*

91	وَقَطْعُهُمْ	And they disconnect (مَا لِ) that is followed by "هَذَا" , "الَّذِينَ", and "هَـؤُلاَ",
92	وَمَالِ هَـٰذَا وَالَّذِينَ هَـؤُلاَ، تَحِينَ فِي الإِمَامِ صِلْ وَوُهِّلاَ	(تَحِينَ) was found connected in the private copy of Othman ﷺ in Medina, but not all scholars agree with that

مَا لِ ...

مَا لِ ...

1. ﴿مَا لِ هَـٰذَا الْكِتَـٰبِ﴾ الكهف ٤٩
2. ﴿وَقَالُوا مَا لِ هَـٰذَا الرَّسُولِ﴾ الفرقان ٧
3. ﴿فَمَا لِ الَّذِينَ كَفَرُوا قِبَلَكَ مُهْطِعِينَ﴾ المعارج ٣٦
4. ﴿فَمَا لِ هَـٰؤُلَاءِ الْقَوْمِ﴾ النساء ٧٨

In the case of a forced or teaching stop, one can do so on (مَا) or on (مَالْ)

مَا لِـــ

The remaining verses in the Qur'an are scribed with Laam connected to the following word

تَ حِينَ

وَلاَ تَحِينَ and وَلاَتَ حِينَ

﴿فَنَادَوا وَّلَاتَ حِينَ مَنَاصٍ﴾ ص ٣

It was scribed (تَحِينَ) only in one copy of the original Othmani ones, which is his private copy, and thus most scholars did not have access to it and dismiss its legitimacy

Because of the scholars' disagreement, in the case of a forced or teaching stop, one can only do so on (وَلاَتْ) but not on (وَلاَ)

THE CONNECTED AND DISCONNECTED

Ibn Al-Jazari says in his poem, *Al-Muqaddimah*

And connect (وَزَنُوهُمُ) and (كَالُوهُمْ), and also connect (الْ), (يَـ), and (هَـ) to whatever follows them	وَوَزَنُوهُمُ وَكَالُوهُمْ صِلِ كَذَا مِنَ الْ وَيَـ وَهَـ لاَ تَفْصِلِ	93

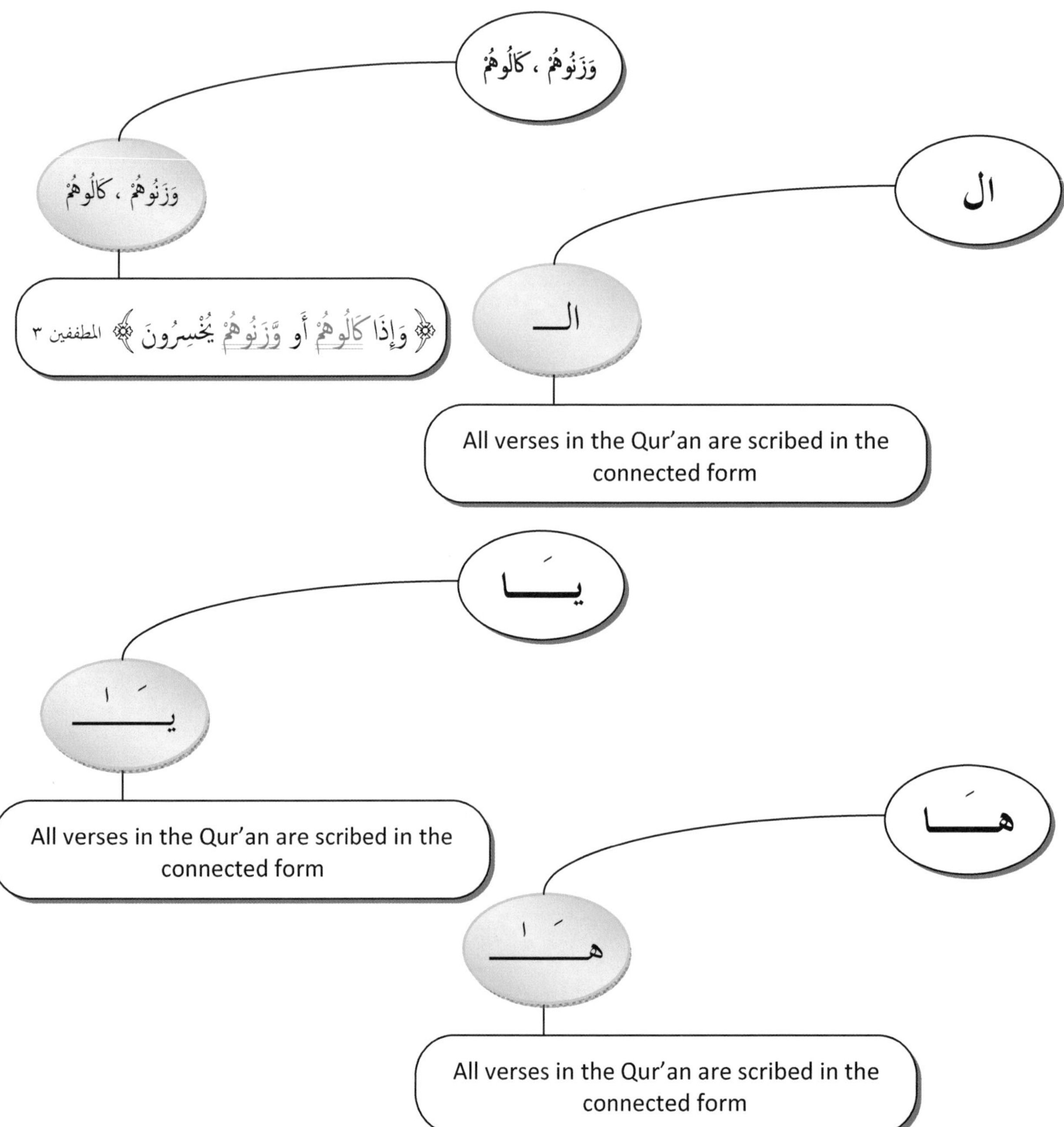

وَزَنُوهُمْ ، كَالُوهُمْ
وَزَنُوهُمْ ، كَالُوهُمْ
﴿وَإِذَا كَالُوهُمْ أَو وَّزَنُوهُمْ يُخْسِرُونَ﴾ المطففين ٣
ال
الـــ
All verses in the Qur'an are scribed in the connected form
يَـــا
يَــــا
All verses in the Qur'an are scribed in the connected form
هَـــا
هَــــا
All verses in the Qur'an are scribed in the connected form

FROM *LA'ALI' AL-BAYAN*

By the imam and scholar Ibrahim Ali Shahatah As-Samannoudi (d. 1429 A.H.)

١٣٥ تُقْـطَعُ أَنْ عَنْ كُلِّ لَمْ وَلَوْ نَـشَا ... كَانُوا يَشَا وَالْخُلْـفُ فِي الْجِنِّ فَشَا

١٣٦ وَقَطْـعُ أَنْ لَنْ غَيـرَ أَلَّنْ نَجْعَـلا ... نَجْمَعَ وَالْخُلْـفُ بِتُحْصُوهُ انْجَلَى

١٣٧ وَنُـونَ أَنْ لا يَدْخُلَنَّـهَا افْصِـلا ... يُشْرِكْنَ مَعْ مَلْجَأً مَعْ تَعْـلُوا عَلَى

١٣٨ تُشْـرِكْ أَقُولَ مَعْ يَقُولُوا تَعْبُـدُوا ... يـس وَالأُخْرَى بِهُـودٍ قَيِّـدُوا

١٣٩ كَـذَا بِهَا أَنْ لا إِلَـهَ وَاخْتُلِـفْ ... فِي الأَنْبِيَا وَوَصْلَ إِلا الكُلِّ صِفْ

١٤٠ كَنُـونِ إِلَّمْ هُودَ وَافْـصِلْ إِنْ مَا ... بِالرَّعْـدِ ثُمَّ صِـلْ جَمِيـعَ أَمَّا

١٤١ وَقُطِـعَتْ أَمْ مَنْ بِذِبْـحٍ وَالنِّـسَا ... وَفُصِّـلَتْ أَيْضًا وَأَمْ مَنْ أَسَّـسَا

١٤٢ وَأَنَّ مَا يَدْعُـونَ الاثْنَيْنِ افْـصِلا ... وَخُلْـفُ أَنَّمَا غَنِمْـتُمْ حَصَـلا

١٤٣ مَعْ إِنَّمَا عِنْدَ لَـدَى النَّحْلِ وَقَـعْ ... وَقَبْلَ تُوعَـدُونَ الأَنْعَامَ انْقَـطَعْ

١٤٤ وَصِـلْ فَأَيْـنَمَا كَنَـحْلٍ وَجَرَى ... خُلْـفٌ بِالاَحْزَابِ النِّسَا وَالشُّعَرَا

١٤٥ وَقَطْعُ حَيْـثُ مَا مَـعًا وَيَوْمَ هُمْ ... عَلَى وَبَـارِزُونَ عَكْـسُ يَبْـنَؤُمّْ

١٤٦ وَفِي النِّسَا مِنْ مَا بِقَطْـعِهِ وُصِفْ ... وَفِي الْمُنَافِقُـونَ وَالرُّومِ اخْتُلِـفْ

١٤٧ وَمِمَّ مَعْ مِمَّنْ جَمِيـعِهَا صِـلا ... وَمَوْضِعَيْ عَنْ مَنْ وَمَا نُهُوا افْصِلا

١٤٨ وَعَمَّ صِـلْ وَقَطْعُ مَالِ فِي النِّـسَا ... وَسَالَ وَالفُرقَانِ وَالكَهْـفِ رَسَا

١٤٩ وَوَقْـفُهُ بِـمَا أَوِ اللامِ اعْـلَـمَا ... كَوَقْـفِ أَيَّـامًّا بِأَيًّـا أَوْ بِمَـا

١٥٠ وَكُـلِّ مَا سَأَلْـتُمُـوهُ فُصِلَـتْ ... وَخُلْفُ جَا رُدُّوا وَأُلْقِي دَخَلَـتْ

١٥١ وَبِئْسَمَا اشْتَرَوْا فَصِلْ وَالْخُلْـفُ فِي ... خَلَفْتُمُـونِي مَعَ يَأْمُـرْكُمْ قُفِي

١٥٢ وَقَطْعُ كَي لا أَوَّلَ الأَحْزَابِ مَـعْ ... نَحْـلٍ وَحَشْـرٍ وَبِعِمْرَانَ وَقَعْ

١٥٣ خُلْـفٌ كَفِي مَا الرُّومِ هَـهُنَا كِلا ... تَنْزِيـلَ ءَاتَاكُمْ مَـعًا أُوحِي وَلا

١٥٤ فَعَلْنَ فِي الأُخْرَى أَفَضْتُمْ وَاشْتَهَـتْ ... أَوْ وَصْلُهَا مَعْ قَطْعِ هَـهُنَا ثَبَتْ

١٥٥ أَوْ هِيَ وَاشْتَـهَتْ أَوِ الْكُلُّ فُصِـلْ ... وَفِيمَ صِلْ وَلاتَ حِيـنَ مُنْفَصِلْ

١٥٦ وَقِيـلَ وَصْلُهُ وَهَـا وَيَـا وَالْ ... كَالُـوهُمُ أَوْ وَزَنُـوهُمُ اتَّصَـلْ

١٥٧ كَرُبَـمَا مَهْـمَا نِعِـمَّا يَوْمَئِـذْ ... كَأَنَّـمَا وَوَيْـكَأَنَّ حِينَئِذْ

١٥٨ وَجَـاءَ إِلْ يَـاسِينَ بِانْفِصَالِ ... وَصَـحَّ وَقْـفُ مَنْ تَلاهَـا آلِ

The Connected and Disconnected

Not mentioned in *Al-Jazariyyah*

As-Samannoudi says in his poem, *La'ali' Al-Bayan*

135 تُقْطَعُ أَنْ عَنْ كُلِّ لَمْ وَلَوْ نَشَا [1] كَانُوا [2] يَشَا [3] وَالخُلْفُ فِي الجِنِّ فَشَا

Disconnect (أَن لَّوْ) when it is followed by "نَشَا", "كَانُوا", and "يَشَا", and it is scribed both ways in Al-Jinn

(أَن لَّمْ) was addressed by Ibn Al-Jazari in previous lessons

أَن لَّوْ

أَن لَّو

[1] ﴿أَن لَّوْ نَشَآءُ أَصَبْنَٰهُم بِذُنُوبِهِمْ﴾ الأعراف ١٠٠

[2] ﴿أَن لَّوْ كَانُوا يَعْلَمُونَ الْغَيْبَ﴾ سبأ ١٤

[3] ﴿أَن لَّوْ يَشَآءُ اللَّهُ لَهَدَى النَّاسَ جَمِيعًا﴾ الرعد ٣١

أَلَّو and أَن لَّو

It was not scribed solely in the connected form

﴿وَأَلَّوِ اسْتَقَٰمُوا عَلَى الطَّرِيقَةِ﴾ الجن ١٤

THE CONNECTED AND DISCONNECTED

Not mentioned in *Al-Jazariyyah*

As-Samannoudi says in his poem, *La'ali' Al-Bayan*

Disconnect … unlike (يَبْنَؤُمّ) ;	وَقَطْعُ … … … … … … … عَكْسُ يَبْنَؤُمّ	145
And stop on (أَيًّامًّا) with either (أيــًّا) or (مَا)	… … … … … كَوَقْفِ أَيًّامًّا بِأيــًّا أَوْ بِمَا	149

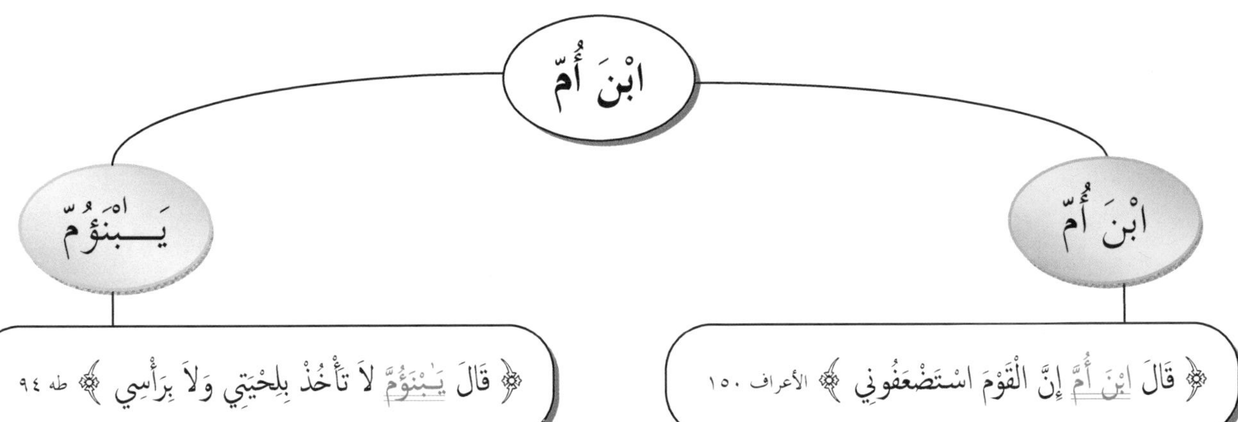

ابْنَ أُمّ
يَــبْنَؤُمَّ
ابْنَ أُمّ
﴿ قَالَ يَـبْنَؤُمَّ لاَ تَأْخُذْ بِلِحْيَتِي وَلاَ بِرَأْسِي ﴾ طه ٩٤
﴿ قَالَ ابْنَ أُمَّ إِنَّ الْقَوْمَ اسْتَضْعَفُونِي ﴾ الأعراف ١٥٠

أَيًّا مَّا

أَيًّا مَّا

﴿ أَيًّا مَّا تَدْعُوا فَلَهُ الْأَسْمَاءُ الْحُسْنَى ﴾ الإسراء ١١٠

There is only one (أَيًّا مَّا) in the Qur'an, and since it is scribed disconnected one may stop on either (أَيًّا) or on (مَا) when forced or tested

The Connected and Disconnected

Not mentioned in *Al-Jazariyyah*

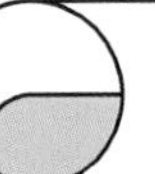

As-Samannoudi says in his poem, *La'ali' Al-Bayan*

Connect (رُبَمَا), (مَهْمَا), (نِعِمَّا), (يومَئِذْ), (كَأَنَّمَا), (وَيْكَأَنَّ), and (حِينَـــئِذْ);	... ... اتَّصَلْ	156
And (إِلْ يَاسِين) was scribed disconnected,	كَرُبَمَا مَهْمَا نِعِمَّا يومَئِذْ كَأَنَّمَا وَوَيْكَأَنَّ حِينَـــئِذْ	157
but stopping on (إل) is correct if your recitation reads it as (آل)	وَجَاءَ إِلْ يَاسِينَ بِانفِصَالْ وَصَحَّ وَقْفُ مَنْ تَلاهَا آلِ	158

These seven words: (رُبَمَا), (مَهْمَا), (نِعِمَّا), (يومَئِذْ), (كَأَنَّمَا), (وَيْكَأَنَّ), and (حِينَـــئِذْ) are all scribed in the connected form in the Qur'an, and thus stopping must occur at the end of each word

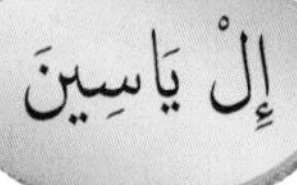

﴿ سَلَٰمٌ عَلَىٰٓ إِلْ يَاسِينَ ﴾ الصافات ١٣٠

This is a unique word because the recital of Hafs, which follows the script when stopping on words, does **not** allow stopping on (إل) although it is scribed disconnected. Conversely, the recitals that read it as (آل) allow stopping on (آل) when forced or in a testing or teaching situation

ت

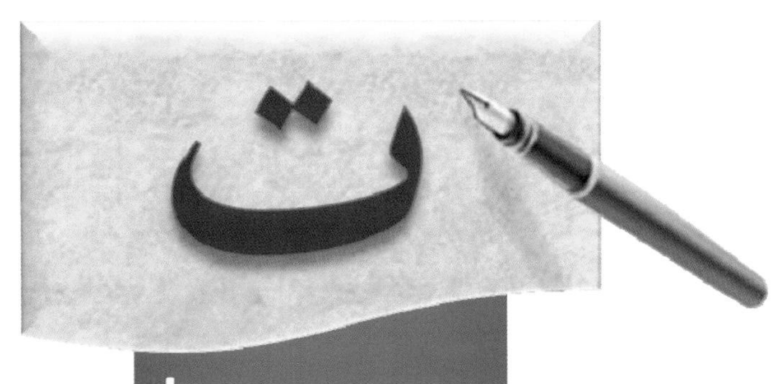

Introduction

Most Arab tribes pronounced the singular Feminine Haa as a Taa when connected and a Haa when they stopped

This resulted in such words being written with a Haa, otherwise known as a *Taa Marboutah*

Reflecting this majority, most singular words ending with a Feminine Haa in the Qur'an were scribed with a Haa

Examples:

﴿رَحْمَة﴾ ﴿نِعْمَة﴾ ﴿لَعْنَة﴾ ﴿جَنَّة﴾ ﴿الشَّجَرَة﴾
﴿غِشَـٰوَة﴾ ﴿الحِجَارَة﴾ ﴿شَفَـٰعَة﴾ ﴿الصَّلَوٰة﴾

All of these words must be pronounced with a Taa when you connect them, and with a Haa when you stop on them

INTRODUCTION

Some tribes, such as Tayyi' and Himyar, ended singular feminine words with a Taa both when connecting and stopping

This resulted in such words being written by these two tribes with a Taa, which is also known as a *Taa Mabsoutah*

Reflecting this minority amongst Arabs, a few singular feminine words in the Qur'an were scribed with a Taa

Examples

﴿رَحْمَت﴾ ﴿نِعْمَت﴾ ﴿لَعْنَت﴾ ﴿جَنَّت﴾

﴿شَجَرَت﴾ ﴿بَقِيَّت﴾ ﴿امْرَأَت﴾ ﴿فِطْرَت﴾

Most recitals stop and connect these special words with a Taa, as with the two tribes of Tayyi' and Himyar

These recitals are brought to us by Nafi', Ibn 'Amir, 'Asim, Hamzah, Abu-Ja'far, and Khalaf

Few recitals stop with a Haa on these words although they are scribed with a Taa, following the majority of Arab tribes

These few recitals are brought to us by Ibn Katheer, Abu-Amr, Al-Kisa'i, and Ya'qoub

Ibn Al-Jazari listed each one of these words in his famous poem, *Al-Muqaddimah*

From *Manthoumah Al-Muqaddimah*

By the imam and scholar Abu-Al-Khair Mohamed Ibn Mohamed Ibn Al-Jazari (d. 833 A.H.)

94	وَرَحْمَتُ الزُّخْرُفِ بِالتَّا زَبَرَهْ الاَعْرَافِ رُومٍ هُودَ كَافَ الْبَـقَرَهْ	Scribed as a Taa is the word (رَحْمَت) in Al-A'raaf, Ar-Roum, Houd, Maryam, and Al-Baqarah;
95	نِعْمَتُهَا ثَلاثُ نَحْـلٍ إِبْـرَهَمْ مَعاً أَخِـيرَاتٌ عُقُـودُ الثَّانِ هَمّْ	Her [i.e. Al-Baqarah] (نِعْمَت) and three in An-Nahl, both words in Ibrahim, all of which are the last ones, and the second in Al-Ma'idah with the word "هَمّ";
96	لُقْـمَانُ ثُمَّ فَـاطِرٌ كَالطُّـورِ عِمْـرَانَ لَعْـنَتَ بِهَا وَالنُّـورِ	In Luqman, Fatir, At-Tour, and Aal-Imran, also (لَعْنَت) is in Aal Imran and in An-Nour;
97	وَامْرَأَتٌ يُوسُفَ عِمْرَانَ الْقَصَصْ تَحْرِيمُ مَعْصِيَتْ بِقَدْ سَمِعْ يُخَصّْ	And [scribed with Taa is] (امْرَأَتٌ) in Yousuf, Aal Imran, Al-Qasas, and At-Tahreem, and (مَعْصِيَتْ) which is only in قَدْ سَمِعَ [i.e. Al-Mujadalah];
98	شَجَرَتَ الدُّخَانِ سُـنَّتْ فَاطِرِ كُلاً وَالاَنْفَـالِ وَأُخْرَى غَـافِرِ	(شَجَرَت) in Ad-Dukhan, (سُنَّت) in Fatir, all of them, and in Al-Anfaal, and the final ayah in Ghafir;
99	قُرَّتُ عَيْنٍ جَنَّتٌ فِي وَقَـعَتْ فِطْرَتْ بَقِيَّتْ وَابْنَتٌ وَكَلِمَتْ	And [scribed with Taa are] (قُرَّتُ) when it is possessed by "عَيْنٍ", and (جَنَّتٌ) in Al-Waqi'ah, (فِطْرَتْ), (بَقِيَّتْ), (ابْنَتٌ), as well as (كَلِمَتْ);
100	أَوْسَطَ الاَعْرَافِ وَكُلُّ مَا اخْتُلِفْ جَمْعًا وَفَـرْدًا فِيهِ بِالتَّاءِ عُرِفْ	In Al-A'raaf, and all words that are singular in some recitals and plural in others are known to be with a Taa;

Introduction

Some feminine words in the Qur'an were taught to our beloved Prophet ﷺ as **singular** words in some recitals

At the same time in different recitals, these feminine words were taught to him as **plurals**

When the scribes of the Qur'an wrote such words down, they did so with a Feminine Taa but with no plural Alif preceding it

This way, both the singular and plural pronunciations could be included in one word using one form

Examples:

﴿ جِمَٰلَتٌ ﴾ ﴿ ءَايَٰتٌ ﴾ ﴿ كَلِمَٰتُ ﴾

﴿ الْغُرُفَٰتِ ﴾ ﴿ بَيِّنَٰتٍ ﴾ ﴿ ثَمَرَٰتٍ ﴾ ﴿ غَيَٰبَٰتِ ﴾

The recital that Hafs transmitted to us reads some of these words in the plural form and some in the singular form

Hafs' recital follows the way these words were scribed, and stops on all of them with a Taa, even the singular words

FROM *AL-LU'LU' AL-MANTHOUM*

By the imam and scholar Mohamed Ibn Ahmed Ibn Abdillah Al-Mutawalli (d. 1313 A.H.)

And all words that are read either singular or plural are known to be with a Taa	وَكُلُّ مَا فِيهِ الْخِلَافُ يَجْرِي جَمْـــعاً وَفَــرْداً فَبِــتَاءٍ فَادْرِ
And they are, Oh lad: (جِمَالَاتٌ) and (ءَايَاتٌ) in Yousuf and Al-'Ankabout;	وَذَا : جِمَالَاتٌ ، وَءَايَاتٌ أَتَى فِي يُوسُفَ وَالعَنْكَبُوتِ يَا فَتَى
And (كَلِمَاتُ) is in "الطول" [i.e. Ghafir] with Al-An'aam and both locations in Younus;	وَكَلِمَاتُ وَهْوَ فِي الطَّوْلِ مَعَ أَنْعَــامِهِ ثُمَّ بِيُــونُسَ مَــعَا
And (الْغُرُفَاتِ) is in Saba', as well as (بَيِّنَتْ) in Fatir, and (ثَمَرَاتٍ) in Fussilat;	وَالغُرُفَاتِ فِي سَبَأْ ، وَبَيِّــنَتْ فِي فَاطِرٍ، وَثَمَرَاتٍ فُصِّــلَتْ
As well as (غَيَابَتِ) when followed by "الْجُبِّ", and it was scribed both ways in the second location in Younus and in "الطول", so understand these meanings;	غَيَابَتِ الْجُبِّ ، وَخُلْفُ ثَانِي يُونُسَ وَالطَّــوْلِ فَعِ الْمَعَانِي

Words Ending with a Feminine Haa

Plural in all Recitals

- The Feminine Haa is scribed as a Taa
- It is pronounced Taa when connecting
- It is pronounced Taa when Stopping

EXAMPLES

﴿ ظُلُمَـٰتِ ﴾

﴿ الصَّـٰلِحَـٰتِ ﴾

Singular in all Recitals

Is possessed by a noun

- The Feminine Haa **may** be scribed as a Taa
- It is pronounced Taa when connecting
- It **may** be pronounced Taa when stopping

EXAMPLES

﴿ رَحْمَتِ اللَّهِ ﴾ الروم ٥٠

﴿ رَحْمَةِ اللَّهِ ﴾ الزمر ٥٣

Is not possessed by a noun

- The Feminine Haa is scribed as a Haa
- It is pronounced Taa when connecting
- It is pronounced Haa when stopping

EXAMPLES

﴿وَرَحْمَةٌ وَأُوْلَـٰٓئِكَ﴾ البقرة ١٥٧

﴿ الصَّلَـوٰةَ ﴾

Singular in Some Recitals, Plural in Others

- The Feminine Haa is scribed as a Taa
- It is pronounced Taa when connecting
- It is pronounced Taa when stopping

EXAMPLES

﴿ جِمَـٰلَتٌ صُفْرٌ ﴾ المرسلات ٣٣

﴿ عَلَىٰ بَيِّنَتٍ مِنْهُ ﴾ فاطر ٤٠

Hafs follows the scripture, so if it is scribed with a Taa he stops as such. Ibn Al-Jazari detailed all such words in the next lessons

Al-Mutawalli detailed these words, and they will be studied in the next unit

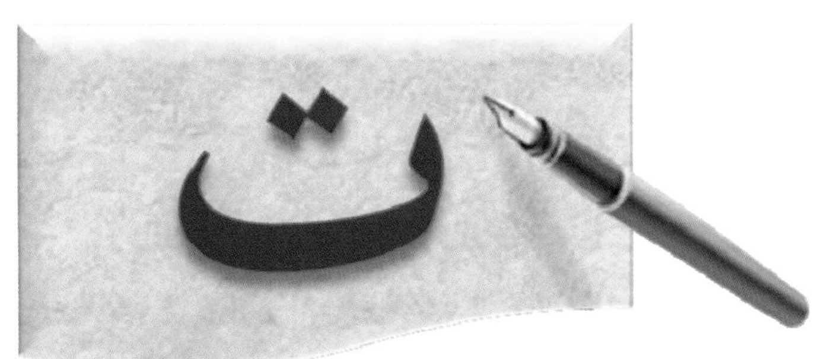

Singular Words which are Possessed by a Noun and Ending with a Feminine Haa

Ibn Al-Jazari says in his poem, *Al-Muqaddimah*

94 وَرَحْمَتُ الزُّخْرُفِ بِالتَّا زَبَرَهْ الاَعْرَافِ رُومٍ هُودَ كَافَ الْبَقَرَهْ

Scribed with a Taa is the word (رَحْمَت) in Al-'Araaf, Ar-Roum, Houd, Maryam, and Al-Baqarah

Abu Dawood mentioned ﴿ فَبِمَا رَحْمَةٍ مِنَ اللهِ ﴾ in Aal-Imran, but Ibn Al-Jazari disagreed. As-Samannoudi summed this up in *La'ali' Al-Bayan*:

وَفِي بِمَا رَحْمَةٍ الْخُلْفُ أَتَى وَنِعْمَتَ الْبَقَرَةِ الأُخْرَى بِتَا

رَحْمَة

- رَحْمَت
  1. ﴿ أَهُمْ يَقْسِمُونَ رَحْمَتَ رَبِّكَ ﴾ الزخرف ٣٢
  2. ﴿ وَرَحْمَتُ رَبِّكَ خَيْرٌ مِّمَّا يَجْمَعُونَ ﴾ الزخرف ٣٢
  3. ﴿ إِنَّ رَحْمَتَ اللهِ قَرِيبٌ مِّنَ الْمُحْسِنِينَ ﴾ الأعراف ٥٦
  4. ﴿ فَانظُرْ إِلَىٰٓ ءَاثَـٰرِ رَحْمَتِ اللهِ ﴾ الروم ٥٠
  5. ﴿ رَحْمَتُ اللهِ وَبَرَكَـٰتُهُۥ عَلَيْكُمْ ﴾ هود ٧٣
  6. ﴿ ذِكْرُ رَحْمَتِ رَبِّكَ عَبْدَهُۥ زَكَرِيَّآ ﴾ مريم ٢
  7. ﴿ أُوْلَـٰٓئِكَ يَرْجُونَ رَحْمَتَ اللهِ ﴾ البقرة ٢١٨
- رَحْمَة
  - The remaining verses in the Qur'an are scribed with a Haa

The words in **green** are possessive nouns, a condition for singular words to be scribed with a Feminine Taa

Singular Words which are Possessed by a Noun and Ending with a Feminine Haa

Ibn Al-Jazari says in his poem, *Al-Muqaddimah*

95	نِعْمَتُهَا ثَلَاثُ نَحْلٍ إِبْرَهَمْ ‏ مَعاً أَخِيرَاتٌ عُقُودُ الثَّانِ هَمّ	Her [i.e. Al-Baqarah] (نِعْمَت) and three in An-Nahl, both words in Ibrahim, all of which are the last ones, and the second in Al-Ma'idah with the word "هَمّ";
96	لُقْمَانُ ثُمَّ فَاطِرٌ كَالطُّورِ ‏ عِمْرَانَ … … … … …	In Luqman, Fatir, At-Tour, and Aal-Imran

نِعْمَة

نِعْمَت

1. ﴿ وَاذْكُرُوا نِعْمَتَ اللَّهِ عَلَيْكُمْ ﴾ البقرة ٢٣١
2. ﴿ وَبِنِعْمَتِ اللَّهِ هُمْ يَكْفُرُونَ ﴾ النحل ٧٢
3. ﴿ يَعْرِفُونَ نِعْمَتَ اللَّهِ ثُمَّ يُنْكِرُونَهَا ﴾ النحل ٨٣
4. ﴿ وَاشْكُرُوا نِعْمَتَ اللَّهِ ﴾ النحل ١١٤
5. ﴿ بَدَّلُوا نِعْمَتَ اللَّهِ كُفْراً ﴾ إبراهيم ٢٨
6. ﴿ وَإِن تَعُدُّوا نِعْمَتَ اللَّهِ لَا تُحْصُوهَا ﴾ إبراهيم ٣٤
7. ﴿ اذْكُرُوا نِعْمَتَ اللَّهِ عَلَيْكُمْ إِذْ هَمَّ قَوْمٌ ﴾ المائدة ١١
8. ﴿ أَنَّ الْفُلْكَ تَجْرِي فِي الْبَحْرِ بِنِعْمَتِ اللَّهِ ﴾ لقمان ٣١
9. ﴿ اذْكُرُوا نِعْمَتَ اللَّهِ عَلَيْكُمْ ﴾ فاطر ٣
10. ﴿ فَمَا أَنتَ بِنِعْمَتِ رَبِّكَ بِكَاهِنٍ وَلَا مَجْنُونٍ ﴾ الطور ٢٩
11. ﴿ وَاذْكُرُوا نِعْمَتَ اللَّهِ عَلَيْكُمْ ﴾ آل عمران ١٠٣

Notice that the locations in Al-Baqarah, An-Nahl, and Ibrahim are the last ones in each

نِعْمَة

The remaining verses in the Qur'an are scribed with a Haa

Abu Dawood also mentioned ﴿ وَلَوْلَا نِعْمَةُ رَبِّي ﴾ in As-Saffaat, but Ibn Al-Jazari disagreed. As-Samannoudi summed this up in *La'ali' Al-Bayan*:

وَالْخُلْفُ فِي نِعْمَةُ رَبِّي وَامْرَأَتْ
مَتَى تُضَفْ لِزَوْجِهَا بِالتَّا أَتَتْ

SINGULAR WORDS WHICH ARE POSSESSED BY A NOUN AND ENDING WITH A FEMININE HAA

Ibn Al-Jazari says in his poem, *Al-Muqaddimah*

[Scribed with Taa] is (لَعْنَت) in Aal-Imran and in An-Nour;	... ... عِمْرَانَ لَعْنَتَ بِهَا وَالنُّورِ	96

لَعْنَة

لَعْنَت

1. ﴿ فَنَجْعَل لَّعْنَتَ اللهِ عَلَى الْكَـٰذِبِينَ ﴾ آل عمران ٦١
2. ﴿ وَالْخَـٰمِسَةُ أَنَّ لَعْنَتَ اللهِ عَلَيْهِ ﴾ النور ٧

لَعْنَة

The remaining verses in the Qur'an are scribed with a Haa

There is another ayah in Aal-Imran
﴿ جَزَآؤُهُمْ أَنَّ عَلَيْهِمْ لَعْنَةَ اللهِ ﴾ آل عمران ٨٧
which is scribed with a Haa, causing confusion between the two locations. As-Samannoudi used better wording in *La'ali' Al-Bayan,* tying the specific location by the word "نجعل":

وَلَعْنَتَ النُّورِ وَنَجْعَلْ لَعْنَتَا   وَابْنَتَ مَعْ قُرَّتُ عَيْنٍ فِطْرَتَا

SINGULAR WORDS WHICH ARE POSSESSED BY A NOUN AND ENDING WITH A FEMININE HAA

Ibn Al-Jazari says in his poem, *Al-Muqaddimah*

And [Scribed with Taa is] (اِمْرَأَتْ) in Yousuf, Aal -Imran, Al-Qasas, and At-Tahreem	‎وَامْرَأَتْ يُوسُفَ عِمْرَانَ الْقَصَصْ تَحْرِيمُ 97

اِمْرَأَة

اِمْرَأَة

اِمْرَأَتْ

The remaining verses in the Qur'an are scribed with a Haa

All of which are not possessed by nouns

1. ‎﴿ وَقَالَ نِسْوَةٌ فِي الْمَدِينَةِ اِمْرَأَتُ الْعَزِيزِ ﴾ يوسف ٣٠
2. ‎﴿ قَالَتِ اِمْرَأَتُ الْعَزِيزِ ﴾ يوسف ٥١
3. ‎﴿ إِذْ قَالَتِ اِمْرَأَتُ عِمْرَٰنَ ﴾ آل عمران ٣٥
4. ‎﴿ وَقَالَتِ اِمْرَأَتُ فِرْعَوْنَ ﴾ القصص ٩
5. ‎﴿ مَثَلاً لِّلَّذِينَ كَفَرُوا اِمْرَأَتَ نُوحٍ ﴾ التحريم ١٠
6. ‎﴿ وَامْرَأَتَ لُوطٍ ﴾ التحريم ١٠
7. ‎﴿ مَثَلاً لِّلَّذِينَ ءَامَنُوا اِمْرَأَتَ فِرْعَوْنَ ﴾ التحريم ١١

98

SINGULAR WORDS WHICH ARE POSSESSED BY A NOUN AND ENDING WITH A FEMININE HAA

Ibn Al-Jazari says in his poem, *Al-Muqaddimah*

97	... ... مَعْصِيَتْ بِقَدْ سَمِعْ يُخَصْ	And [Scribed with Taa is](مَعْصِيَتْ) which is only in قَدْ سَمِع [i.e. Al-Mujadalah];
98	شَجَرَتَ الدُّخَانِ	(شَجَرَت) in Ad-Dukhan ...

مَعْصِيَة

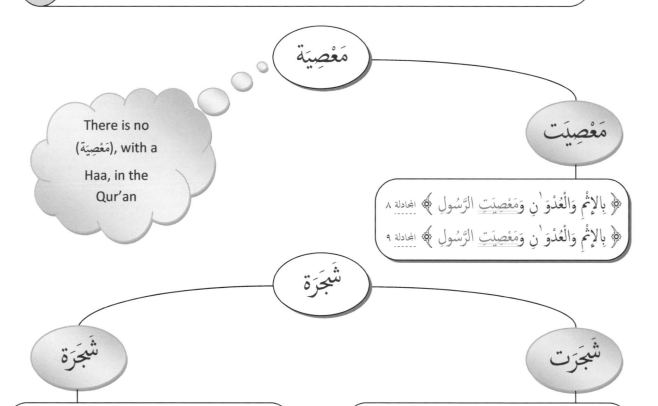

There is no (مَعْصِيَة), with a Haa, in the Qur'an

مَعْصِيَت

﴿ بِالإِثْمِ وَالْعُدْوَانِ وَمَعْصِيَتِ الرَّسُولِ ﴾ المجادلة ٨

﴿ بِالإِثْمِ وَالْعُدْوَانِ وَمَعْصِيَتِ الرَّسُولِ ﴾ المجادلة ٩

شَجَرَة

شَجَرَت

﴿ إِنَّ شَجَرَتَ الزَّقُّومِ ۝٤٣ طَعَامُ الأَثِيمِ ﴾ الدخان ٤٣، ٤٤

شَجَرَة

The remaining verses in the Qur'an are scribed with a Haa

SINGULAR WORDS WHICH ARE POSSESSED BY A NOUN AND ENDING WITH A FEMININE HAA

Ibn Al-Jazari says in his poem, *Al-Muqaddimah*

98	... ... سُنَّتْ فَاطِرٍ [1][2][3] كُلاًّ وَالأَنْفَالِ [4] وَأُخْرَى غَافِرِ [5]	And [scribed with Taa is] (سُنَّت) in Fatir, all of them, and in Al-Anfaal, and the final ayah in Ghafir

سُنَّة

- سُنَّت
  1. ﴿ فَهَلْ يَنظُرُونَ إِلاَّ سُنَّتَ الأَوَّلِينَ ﴾ فاطر ٤٣
  2. ﴿ فَلَن تَجِدَ لِسُنَّتِ اللهِ تَبْدِيلاً ﴾ فاطر ٤٣
  3. ﴿ وَلَن تَجِدَ لِسُنَّتِ اللهِ تَحْوِيلاً ﴾ فاطر ٤٣
  4. ﴿ فَقَدْ مَضَتْ سُنَّتُ الأَوَّلِينَ ﴾ الأنفال ٣٨
  5. ﴿ سُنَّتَ اللهِ الَّتِي قَدْ خَلَتْ فِي عِبَادِهِ ﴾ غافر ٨٥
- سُنَّة
  - The remaining verses in the Qur'an are scribed with a Haa

There is no other (سُنَّة) or (سُنَّت) in Ghafir

SINGULAR WORDS WHICH ARE POSSESSED BY A NOUN AND ENDING WITH A FEMININE HAA

Ibn Al-Jazari says in his poem, *Al-Muqaddimah*

99 | قُرَّتُ عَيْنٍ جَنَّتٌ فِي وَقَعَتْ ... ...

And [scribed with Taa are] (قُرَّتُ) when it is possessed by "عَيْنٍ", and (جَنَّتٌ) in Al-Waqi'ah ...

قُرَّة

قُرَّة

They are possessed by the word "أَعْيُنٍ" not "عَيْنٍ"

قُرَّتُ

The remaining verses in the Qur'an are scribed with a Haa

﴿ وَقَالَتِ امْرَأَتُ فِرْعَوْنَ قُرَّتُ عَيْنٍ لِي وَلَكَ ﴾ القصص ٩

جَنَّة

جَنَّة

جَنَّتُ

The remaining verses in the Qur'an are scribed with a Haa

﴿ فَرَوْحٌ وَرَيْحَانٌ وَجَنَّتُ نَعِيمٍ ﴾ الواقعة ٨٩

101

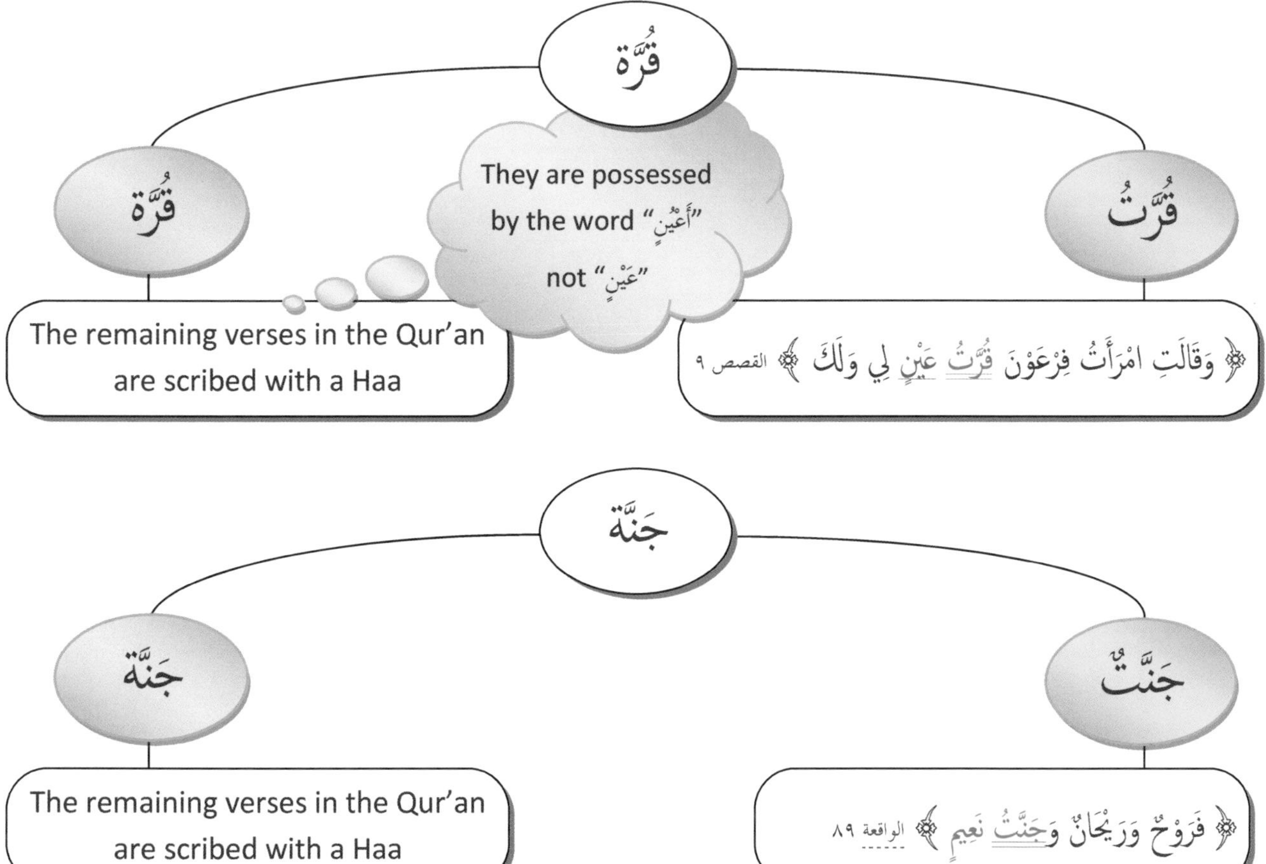

SINGULAR WORDS WHICH ARE POSSESSED BY A NOUN AND ENDING WITH A FEMININE HAA

Ibn Al-Jazari says in his poem, *Al-Muqaddimah*

And [scribed with Taa are] (فِطْرَتْ) and (بَقِيَّتْ)	... فِطْرَتْ بَقِيَّتْ	... ...	99

فِطْرَة

There is no (فِطْرَة), with a Haa, in the Qur'an

فِطْرَت

﴿ فِطْرَتَ اللهِ الَّتِي فَطَرَ النَّاسَ عَلَيْهَا ﴾ الروم ٣٠

بَقِيَّة

بَقِيَّتُ

﴿ بَقِيَّتُ اللهِ خَيْرٌ لَّكُمْ إِن كُنتُم مُّؤْمِنِينَ ﴾ هود ٨٦

بَقِيَّة

The remaining verses in the Qur'an are scribed with a Haa

All of which are not possessed by nouns

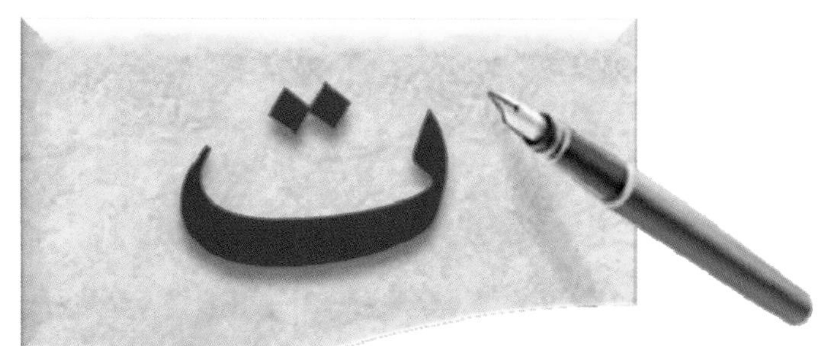

Singular Words which are Possessed by a Noun and Ending with a Feminine Haa

Ibn Al-Jazari says in his poem, *Al-Muqaddimah*

99	... ... وَابْنَتٌ وَكَلِمَتْ	And [scribed with Taa are] (ابْنَتٌ), as well as (كَلِمَتْ) in Al-A'raaf
100	أَوْسَطَ الأَعْرَافِ، ...	

ابْنَة

ابْنَت

There is no (ابْنَة), with a Haa, in the Qur'an

﴿ وَمَرْيَمَ ابْنَتَ عِمْرَانَ ﴾ التحريم ١٢

كَلِمَة

كَلِمَتُ

﴿ وَتَمَّتْ كَلِمَتُ رَبِّكَ الْحُسْنَى ﴾ الأعراف ١٣٧

كَلِمَة

The remaining **singular** words in the Qur'an are scribed with a Haa

This word was scribed with a Taa in the Iraqi mus-haf, but with a Haa in the other Othmani scriptures, and As-Samannoudi indicated this in *La'ali' Al-Bayan:*

كَلِمَتُ الأَعْرَافِ فِي العِرَاقِ تَا وَمَا قُرِي فَرْدًا وَجَمْعًا فَبِتَا

Words which are **Plural** in Some Recitals and **Singular** in Others, Ending with a **Feminine Haa**

Ibn Al-Jazari says in his poem, *Al-Muqaddimah*

And all words that are singular in some recitals and plural in others are known to be with a Taa	... ... وَكُلُّ مَا اخْتُلِفْ جَمْعاً وَفَرْداً فِيهِ بِالتَّاءِ عُرِفْ	100

Al-Mutawalli says in his poem, *Al-Lu'lu' Al-Manthoum*

And all words that are read either singular or plural are known to be with a Taa? And they are: (جمالَاتٌ) ...	وَكُلُّ مَا فِيهِ الخِلَافُ يَجْرِي جَمْعاً وَفَرْداً فَبِتَاءِ فَادْرِ وَذَا جِمَالَاتٌ ... ...

جِمَالَة

There is no (جِمَالَة), with a Haa, in the Qur'an

جِمَـٰلَتٌ | جِمَـٰلَتٌ

﴿كَأَنَّهُ جِمَـٰلَتٌ صُفْرٌ﴾ المرسلات ٣٣

Hafs reads the singular form of this word, and if he stops then it is with a Taa

Note that it is **not** possessed

Words which are **Plural** in Some Recitals and **Singular** in Others, Ending with a **Feminine Haa**

Al-Mutawalli says in his poem, *Al-Lu'lu' Al-Manthoum*

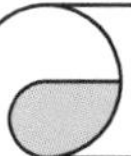

And, oh lad, (ءَايَاتٌ) came in Yousuf and Al-'Ankabout

... وَءَايَاتٌ أَتَى فِي يُوسُفَ وَالعَنْكَبُوتِ يَا فَتَى

ءَايَة

ءَايَة

The remaining **singular** words in the Qur'an are scribed with a Haa

ءَايَـٰتٌ | ءَايَـٰتٌ

﴿ فِي يُوسُفَ وَإِخْوَتِهِۦٓ ءَايَـٰتٌ لِّلسَّآئِلِينَ ﴾ يوسف ٧

﴿ أُنزِلَ عَلَيْهِ ءَايَـٰتٌ مِّن رَّبِّهِۦ ﴾ العنكبوت ٥٠

Hafs reads the plural form in both of these ayahs, and if he stops, then it is with a Taa

Note that neither of these words is possessed

Words which are **Plural** in Some Recitals and **Singular** in Others, Ending with a **Feminine Haa**

Al-Mutawalli says in his poem, *Al-Lu'lu' Al-Manthoum*

And (كَلِمَاتُ) is in "الطول" [i.e. Ghafir] with Al-An'aam and both locations in Younus;

وَكَلِمَاتُ وَهْوَ فِي الطُّوْلِ مَعَ أَنْـعَامِهِ ثُمَّ بِيُـونُسَ مَعَا

… … and it was scribed both ways in the second location in Younus and in "الطول", so understand these meanings

… … وَخُـلْفُ ثَـانِي يُونُسَ وَالطُّوْلِ فَعِ المَعَانِي

كَلِمَة

كَلِمَتُ | كَلِمَـٰتُ

﴿ وَتَمَّتْ كَلِمَتُ رَبِّكَ صِدْقاً وَعَدْلاً ﴾ الأنعام ١١٥

﴿ كَذَٰلِكَ حَقَّتْ كَلِمَتُ رَبِّكَ ﴾ يونس (الموضع الأول) ٣٣

Hafs reads the singular form in both of these ayahs, and if he stops, then it is with a Taa

كَلِمَة and كَلِمَتُ

﴿ حَقَّتْ عَلَيْهِمْ كَلِمَتُ رَبِّكَ ﴾ يونس (الموضع الثاني) ٩٦

﴿ وَكَذَٰلِكَ حَقَّتْ كَلِمَتُ رَبِّكَ ﴾ غافر ٦

Hafs reads the singular form in both of these ayahs, but because these two words were scribed both with a Taa and a Haa in different Othmani scriptures, Hafs stops on them with either a **Haa or a Taa**

كَلِمَة

The remaining **singular** words in the Qur'an are scribed with a Haa excluding the word in Al-A'raaf

WORDS WHICH ARE PLURAL IN SOME RECITALS AND SINGULAR IN OTHERS, ENDING WITH A FEMININE HAA

Al-Mutawalli says in his poem, *Al-Lu'lu' Al-Manthoum*

And (الْغُرُفَات) in Saba', as well as (بَيِّنَت) in Fatir ⬚

وَالْغُرُفَاتِ فِي سَبَأْ وَبَيِّنَتْ فِي فَاطِرٍ ....

الْغُرْفَة

الْغُرْفَة

The remaining **singular** words in the Qur'an are scribed with a Haa

Hafs reads the plural form of this word, and if he stops, then it is with a Taa

الْغُرُفَتِ | الْغُرُفَتِ

﴿ وَهُمْ فِي الْغُرُفَتِ ءَامِنُونَ ﴾ سبأ ٣٧

Note that these words are **not** possessed

بَيِّنَة

بَيِّنَة

The remaining **singular** words in the Qur'an are scribed with a Haa

Hafs reads the singular form of this word, and if he stops, then it is with a Taa

بَيِّنَتٍ | بَيِّنَتِ

﴿ أَمْ ءَاتَيْنَـٰهُمْ كِتَابًا فَهُمْ عَلَى بَيِّنَتٍ مِنْهُ ﴾ فاطر ٤٠

107

Words which are **Plural** in Some Recitals and **Singular** in Others, Ending with a **Feminine Haa**

Al-Mutawalli says in his poem, *Al-Lu'lu' Al-Manthoum*

And (ثَمَرَاتٍ) in Fussilat, as well as (غَيَابَتِ) when followed by "الْجُبِّ"

… … … … … .. وَثَمَرَاتٍ فُصِّلَتْ
غَيَابَتِ الْجُبِّ … …

ثَمَرَة

ثَمَرَتٍ | ثَمَرَٰتٍ

Hafs reads the plural form of this word, and if he stops, then it is with a Taa

﴿وَمَا تَخْرُجُ مِن ثَمَرَٰتٍ مِّنْ أَكْمَامِهَا﴾ فصلت ٤٧

Note that this word is **not** possessed

ثَمَرَة

There is only one remaining **singular** word in the Qur'an and it is scribed with a Haa

غَيَـٰبَة

غَيَـٰبَتِ | غَيَـٰبَـٰتِ

﴿لَا تَقْتُلُوا يُوسُفَ وَأَلْقُوهُ فِي غَيَـٰبَتِ الْجُبِّ﴾ يوسف ١٠
﴿وَأَجْمَعُوٓا أَن يَجْعَلُوهُ فِي غَيَـٰبَتِ الْجُبِّ﴾ يوسف ١٥

Hafs reads both of these words in the singular form, and if he stops, then it is with a Taa

There is no (غَيَـٰبَة), with a Haa, in the Qur'an

FROM *LA'ALI' AL-BAYAN*

By the imam and scholar Ibrahim Ali Shahatah As-Samannoudi (d. 1429 A.H.)

١٥٩ تَا رَحْمَتَ الْبِكْرِ مَعَ الأَعْرَافِ ... وَزُخْرُفٍ وَالرُّومِ هُودٍ كَافِ

١٦٠ وَفِي بِمَا رَحْمَةٍ الخُلْفُ أَتَى ... وَنِعْمَتَ البَقَرَةِ الأُخْرَى بِتَا

١٦١ كَذَا بِإِبْرَاهِيمَ أُخْرَيَيْنِ مَعْ ... ثَلاثَةِ النَّحْلِ أَخِيرَاتٍ تَقَعْ

١٦٢ مَعْ فَاطِرٍ وَفِي العُقُودِ الثَّانِي ... وَالطُّورِ مَعْ عِمْرَانَ مَعْ لُقْمَانِ

١٦٣ وَالخُلْفُ فِي نِعْمَةُ رَبِّي وَامْرَأَتْ ... مَتَى تُضَفْ لِزَوْجِهَا بِالتَّا أَتَتْ

١٦٤ كَاللاتَ مَعْ هَيْهَاتَ ذَاتَ يَا أَبَتْ ... وَلاتَ مَعْ مَرْضَاتَ إِنَّ شَجَرَتْ

١٦٥ وَسُنَّتَ الثَّلاثِ عِنْدَ فَاطِرِ ... وَمَوْضِعَيْ الانفالِ ثُمَّ غَافِرِ

١٦٦ وَلَعْنَتَ النُّورِ وَنَجْعَلْ لَعْنَتَا ... وَابْنَتَ مَعْ قُرَّتُ عَيْنٍ فِطْرَتَا

١٦٧ بَقِيَّتُ اللهِ وَأَيْضًا مَعْصِيَتْ ... مَعًا وَجَنَّتُ نَعِيمٍ وَقَعَتْ

١٦٨ كَلِمَتُ الأَعْرَافِ فِي العِرَاقِ تَا ... وَمَا قُرِي فَرْدًا وَجَمْعًا فَبِتَا

١٦٩ وَهْوَ جِمَالَتُ وَءَايَاتٌ أَتَتْ ... بِالعَنكَبُوتِ فِي الَّتِي تَأَخَّرَتْ

١٧٠ مَعْ يُوسُفٍ وَهُمْ عَلَى بَيِّنَتِ ... وَالغُرُفَاتِ وَكِلا غَيَابَتِ

١٧١ وَثَمَرَاتِ فُصِّلَتْ وَكَلِمَتْ ... يُونُسَ وَالأَنعَامِ وَالطَّوْلِ بَدَتْ

١٧٢ لَكِنْ بِثَانِي يُونُسٍ مَعْ غَافِر ... فِي الفَرْدِ هَا وَالجَمْعِ تَا كَمَا قُرِي

Special Words Ending with a Feminine Haa, Not Mentioned in *Al-Muqaddimah*

As-Samanoudi says in his poem, *La'ali' Al-Bayan*

And scribed with a Taa are (اللَّاتَ) with (هَيْهَاتَ), (ذَاتَ),	... ... بالتَّا أَتَتْ	... ...	163
(يَا أَبَتْ), (وَلَاتَ) with (مَرْضَاتَ) and (شَجَرَتْ) preceded by "إِنَّ"	وَلَاتَ مَعْ مَرْضَاتَ إِنَّ شَجَرَتْ	كَاللَّاتَ مَعْ هَيْهَاتَ ذَاتَ يَا أَبَتْ	164

﴿ هَيْهَاتَ هَيْهَاتَ لِمَا تُوعَدُونَ ﴾ المؤمنون ٣٦

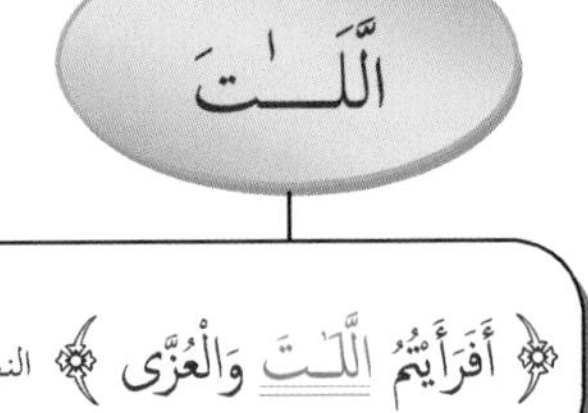

﴿ أَفَرَأَيْتُمُ اللَّـٰتَ وَالْعُزَّىٰ ﴾ النجم ١٩

There are multiple occurrences of this word, all of which are scribed with a Taa

There are multiple occurrences of this word, all of which are scribed with a Taa

There are multiple occurrences of this word, all of which are scribed with a Taa

Hafs stops on each one of these five words with a Taa, since all are scribed with a Taa in the Qur'an. There are **no** similar words scribed with a Haa

Stopping on Words Ending with Consonants

When Two Sukouns Meet

In the Recital of Hafs

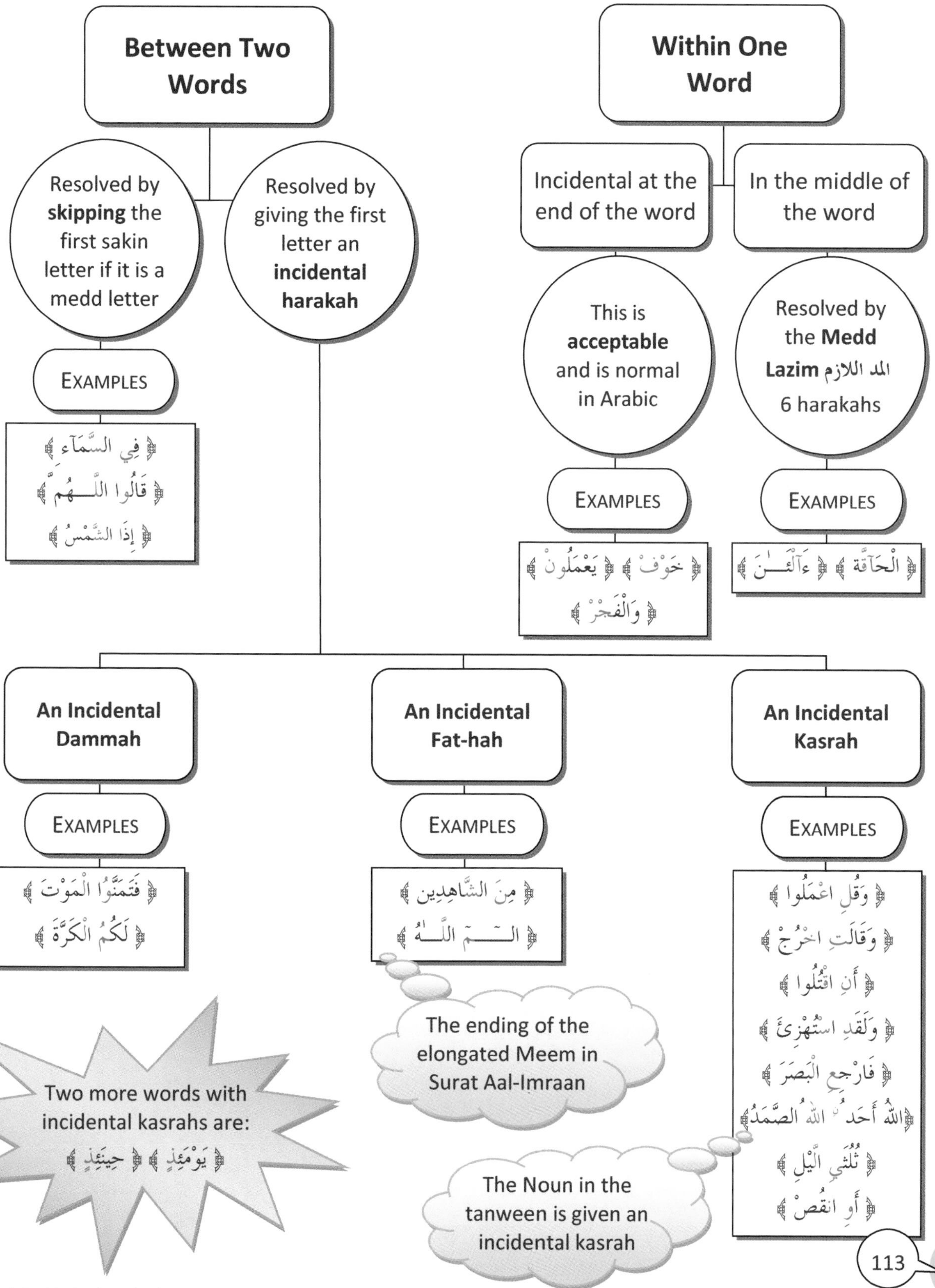

Between Two Words

Resolved by **skipping** the first sakin letter if it is a medd letter

Examples

﴿ فِي السَّمَاءِ ﴾
﴿ قَالُوا اللَّهُمَّ ﴾
﴿ إِذَا الشَّمْسُ ﴾

Resolved by giving the first letter an **incidental harakah**

An Incidental Dammah

Examples

﴿ فَتَمَنَّوُا الْمَوْتَ ﴾
﴿ لَكُمُ الْكَرَّةَ ﴾

An Incidental Fat-hah

Examples

﴿ مِنَ الشَّاهِدِينَ ﴾
﴿ الٓمٓ اللَّهُ ﴾

The ending of the elongated Meem in Surat Aal-Imraan

An Incidental Kasrah

Examples

﴿ وَقُلِ اعْمَلُوا ﴾
﴿ وَقَالَتِ اخْرُجْ ﴾
﴿ أَنِ اقْتُلُوا ﴾
﴿ وَلَقَدِ اسْتُهْزِئَ ﴾
﴿ فَارْجِعِ الْبَصَرَ ﴾
﴿ اللَّهُ أَحَدٌ ۝ اللَّهُ الصَّمَدُ ﴾
﴿ ثُلُثَيِ اللَّيْلِ ﴾
﴿ أَوِ انقُصْ ﴾

The Noun in the tanween is given an incidental kasrah

Two more words with incidental kasrahs are:
﴿ يَوْمَئِذٍ ﴾ ﴿ حِينَئِذٍ ﴾

Within One Word

Incidental at the end of the word

This is **acceptable** and is normal in Arabic

Examples

﴿ خَوْفْ ﴾ ﴿ يَعْمَلُونْ ﴾
﴿ وَالْفَجْرْ ﴾

In the middle of the word

Resolved by the **Medd Lazim** المد اللازم 6 harakahs

Examples

﴿ الْحَاقَّةُ ﴾ ﴿ ءَآلْـَٰٔنَ ﴾

Stopping on Words Ending with Consonants *

In the recital of Hafs from ‘Asim by the way of *Shatibiyyah*

Stopping with Ishmaam

May be applied when:

The word ends with an original dammah e.g. ﴿ الْحَمْدُ لِلَّهِ ﴾

Ishmaam is rounding the lips as if they are pronouncing a dammah, without actually producing the sound of a dammah, and it is given the rules of stopping with a pure sukoun such as:

- The elongated cases of Incidental Medd (المد العارض للسكون) are applied e.g. ﴿ وَإِيَّاكَ نَسْتَعِينُ ﴾ can be read with 2, 4, or 6 harakahs
- The elongated cases of Medd Leen (مد اللين) are applied e.g. ﴿ فِرْعَوْنُ ﴾ can be read with less than 2, 4, or 6 harakahs
- The rules of Raa must be that of a Raa sakinah e.g. ﴿ سِحْرُ ﴾ is light while ﴿ الْقَمَرُ ﴾ is heavy
- Qalqalah is applied e.g. ﴿ قُلْ هُوَ اللَّهُ أَحَدُ ﴾

Stopping with Rowm

May be applied when:

- The word ends with an original kasrah e.g. ﴿ الْحَمْدُ لِلَّهِ ﴾
- The word ends with an original dammah e.g. ﴿ الْحَمْدُ لِلَّهِ ﴾

Since *rowm* is giving a partial kasrah or dammah, up to one-third of the normal length and sound intensity, it is given the rules of connecting, and that includes:

- The elongated cases of Incidental Medd (المد العارض للسكون) do not apply. It is read with only 2 harakahs: e.g. ﴿ الرَّحِيمِ ﴾
- The elongated cases of Medd Leen (مد اللين) do not apply. It is read with less than 2 harakahs: e.g. ﴿ مِنْ خَوْفٍ ﴾ ﴿ فِرْعَوْنَ ﴾
- The rules of Raa must follow that of a vowelled Raa e.g. ﴿ سِحْرٌ ﴾ is heavy while ﴿ وَالْفَجْرِ ﴾ is light
- Qalqalah does not apply e.g. ﴿ مِن مَّسَدٍ ﴾ ﴿ أَحَدٌ ﴾

Stopping with a Pure Sukoun

Must be applied when:

- The word ends with a sukoun at all times e.g. ﴿ قُمْ فَأَنذِرْ ﴾
- The word ends with an incidental harakah of any kind e.g. ﴿ أَنذِرِ النَّاسَ ﴾ ﴿ جَآءَهُمُ الْعِلْمُ ﴾ ﴿ حِينَئِذٍ ﴾ ﴿ مِنَ الشَّاهِدِينَ ﴾
- The word ends with an original fat-hah without tanween e.g. ﴿ وَتَبَّ ﴾ ﴿ الصِّرَاطَ الْمُسْتَقِيمَ ﴾

May be applied when:

- The word ends with an original kasrah e.g. ﴿ وَالْفَجْرِ ﴾
- The word ends with an original dammah e.g. ﴿ وَانشَقَّ الْقَمَرُ ﴾

* Words ending with a **Pronoun Haa** or a **Feminine Haa** have differing rules and will be examined in the following lessons

Stopping on Words Ending with a Feminine Haa

In the recital of Hafs from 'Asim by the way of *Shatibiyyah*

Written as a **Haa Marboutah** ة ، ـــة

Must stop with a pure sukoun only

Examples

﴿ مِنَ الْجَنَّـــةِ ﴾

﴿ هُمَزَةٍ لُمَزَةٍ ﴾

﴿ مُؤْصَدَةٌ ﴾

﴿ الزَّبَانِيَـــةَ ﴾

When we stop with a pure sukoun on the Haa Marboutah, we must pronounce it with a Haa sound, replacing the Taa sound

Written as a **Taa Mabsoutah** in some masahif, and as a **Haa Marboutah** in others

May stop with a pure sukoun, rowm, or ishmaam

Only Two Examples

﴿ كَلِمَتُ رَبِّكَ ﴾ (غافر ٦)

﴿ كَلِمَتُ رَبِّكَ ﴾ (يونس ٩٦)

Both can be read:

a) As a Taa with a pure sukoun, rowm, or ishmaam

or

b) As a Haa with only a pure sukoun

Written as **Taa Mabsoutah** ت

May stop with a pure sukoun, rowm, or ishmaam

Examples

﴿ بَقِيَّتُ اللهِ ﴾ can be read with a pure sukoun, rowm, or ishmaam

﴿ بِنِعْمَتِ اللهِ ﴾ can be read with a pure sukoun or rowm

﴿ امْرَأَتَ نُوحٍ ﴾ should be read with a pure sukoun only

Hafs pronounces the letters as they are written, thus these Feminine Haas are all read with a Taa sound

Ibn Al-Jazari says in his poem, *Al-Muqaddimah*

وَحَاذِرِ الْوَقْفَ بِكُلِّ الحَرَكَةْ   إِلاَّ إِذَا رُمْتَ فَبَعْضُ الحَرَكَةْ

إِلاَّ بِفَتْحٍ أَوْ بِنَصْبٍ وَأَشِـــمْ   إِشَارَةً بِالضَّمِّ فِي رَفْعٍ وَضَمْ

And beware of stopping with full vowels, unless you give rowm as a partial vowel;
Except in the case of fat-h or nasb, and signal a dammah by ishmaam in the case of raf' or damm

Ash-Shatibi says in his poem, *Hirz Al-Amani*

وَرَوْمُـــكَ إِسْمَاعُ الْمُحَرَّكِ وَاقِفًا   بِصَوْتٍ خَفِيٍّ كُلَّ دَانٍ تَنَـــوَّلاَ

وَالإِشْمَامُ إِطْبَاقُ الشِّفَاهِ بُعَيْدَ مَا   يُسَكَّنُ لاَ صَوْتٌ هُنَاكَ فَيَصْحَلاَ

وَفِي **هَاءِ تَأْنِيثٍ** وَمِيمِ الجَمِيعِ قُلْ   وَعَارِضِ شَكْلٍ لَمْ يَكُونَا لِيَدْخُلاَ

And your rowm is to give a low sound to the vowelled when you stop, so low is the sound that only the attentive, near listener can hear it;
And ishmaam is to round your lips immediately after silencing the letter, without producing any sound, not even rasping;
And in the **Feminine Haa**, the plural Meem, and the incidental harakah, rowm and ishmaam should not be applied

Stopping on Words Ending with a Pronoun Haa

In the recital of Hafs from 'Asim by the way of *Shatibiyyah*

~ The **Connecting Medd** مد الصلة is always omitted upon stopping ~

All Stopping is Allowed

Examples

﴿ قُلْتُهُ ﴾ ﴿ حَرِّقُوهُ ﴾

﴿ رَأَوْهُ ﴾ ﴿ عَلِمْتَهُ ﴾

﴿ وَعَلَّمْنَـٰهُ ﴾ ﴿ فَلْيَصُمْهُ ﴾

All of which may be read with a pure sukoun, rowm, or ishmaam

﴿ أَهْلِهِ ﴾ ﴿ أَرْضِعِيهِ ﴾

﴿ لِوَٰلِدَيْهِ ﴾

may be read with a pure sukoun or rowm

This method considers the Pronoun Haa to be a normal consonant treated like any other letter, applying the regular rules for rowm and ishmaam

Stopping with Rowm or Ishmaam is Conditional

The Haa must NOT be preceded by a dammah nor a kasrah, a Waw sakinah nor a Yaa sakinah

Examples

﴿ عَلِمْتَهُ ﴾

﴿ وَعَلَّمْنَـٰهُ ﴾ ﴿ فَلْيَصُمْهُ ﴾

may all be read with a pure sukoun, rowm, or ishmaam

﴿ قُلْتُهُ ﴾ ﴿ أَهْلِهِ ﴾

﴿ حَرِّقُوهُ ﴾ ﴿ رَأَوْهُ ﴾

﴿ أَرْضِعِيهِ ﴾ ﴿ لِوَٰلِدَيْهِ ﴾

may only be read with a pure sukoun

Ibn Al-Jazari prefers this approach

Only Pure Sukoun is Allowed

Examples

﴿ قُلْتُهُ ﴾

﴿ أَهْلِهِ ﴾

﴿ حَرِّقُوهُ ﴾

﴿ رَأَوْهُ ﴾

﴿ أَرْضِعِيهِ ﴾

﴿ لِوَٰلِدَيْهِ ﴾

﴿ عَلِمْتَهُ ﴾

﴿ وَعَلَّمْنَـٰهُ ﴾

﴿ فَلْيَصُمْهُ ﴾

This method is based on the similarity in appearance between the Pronoun Haa and the Feminine Haa, resulting in the same method of stopping by pure sukoun

Ash-Shatibi says in his poem, *Hirz Al-Amani*

وَرَوْمُـــكَ إِسْمَاعُ الْمُحَرَّكِ وَاقِفًا ... بِصَوْتٍ خَفِيٍّ كُلُّ دَانٍ تَنَـــوَّلاَ

وَالاِشْمَامُ إِطْبَاقُ الشِّفَاهِ بُعَيْدَ مَا ... يُسَكَّنُ لاَ صَوْتٌ هُنَاكَ فَيَصْحَلاَ

وَفِي هَاءِ تَأْنِيثٍ وَمِيمِ الجَمِيعِ قُلْ ... وَعَارِضِ شَكْلٍ لَمْ يَكُونَا لِيَدْخُلاَ

وَفِي الهَاءِ لِلإِضْمَارِ قَوْمٌ أَبَوْهُمَا ... وَمِنْ قَبْلِهِ ضَـــمٌّ أَوِ الْكَسْرُ مُثِّلاَ

أَوُ امَّاهُمَا وَاوٌ وَيَاءٌ وَبَعْضُـــهُمْ ... يُرَى لَهُمَا فِي كُلِّ حَالٍ مُحَلِّلاَ

And your rowm is to give a low sound to the vowelled when you stop, so low is the sound that only the attentive, near listener can hear it;

And ishmaam is to round your lips immediately after silencing the letter, without producing any sound, not even rasping;

And in the Feminine Haa, the plural Meem, and the incidental harakah, rowm and ishmaam should not be applied; And in the **Pronoun Haa** some have prevented rowm and ishmaam, and if this Haa is preceded by a dammah or a kasrah; Or if it is preceded by their mothers, the Waw and Yaa, and some are seen to allow rowm and ishmaam always without conditions

Stopping on Words Ending with Tanween

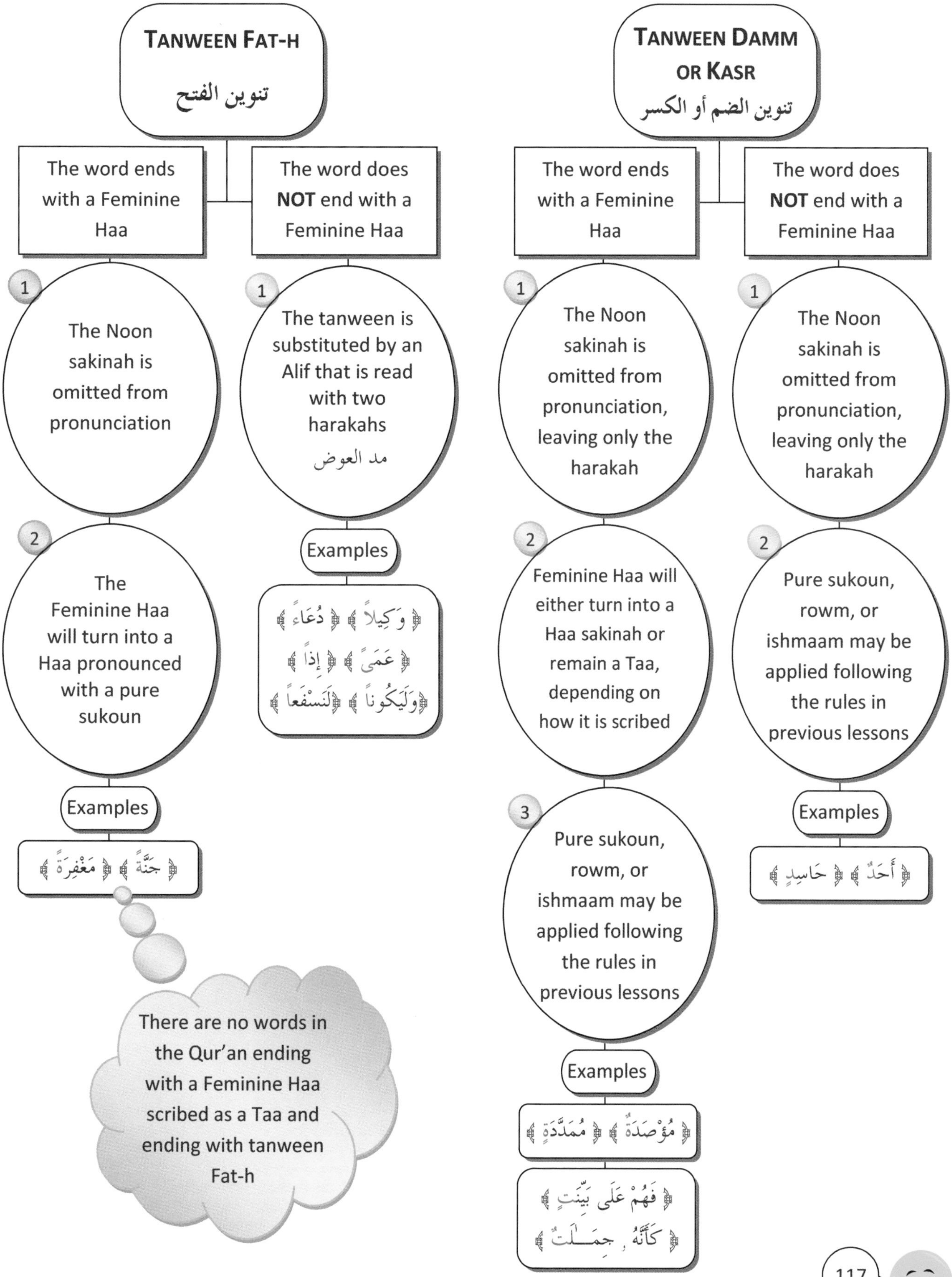

Tanween Fat-h
تنوين الفتح

The word ends with a Feminine Haa

1. The Noon sakinah is omitted from pronunciation

2. The Feminine Haa will turn into a Haa pronounced with a pure sukoun

Examples

﴿ جَنَّةً ﴾ ﴿ مَغْفِرَةً ﴾

There are no words in the Qur'an ending with a Feminine Haa scribed as a Taa and ending with tanween Fat-h

The word does **NOT** end with a Feminine Haa

1. The tanween is substituted by an Alif that is read with two harakahs
مد العوض

Examples

﴿ وَكِيلاً ﴾ ﴿ دُعَاءً ﴾
﴿ عَمًى ﴾ ﴿ إِذًا ﴾
﴿ وَلَيَكُوناً ﴾ ﴿ لَنَسْفَعاً ﴾

Tanween Damm or Kasr
تنوين الضم أو الكسر

The word ends with a Feminine Haa

1. The Noon sakinah is omitted from pronunciation, leaving only the harakah

2. Feminine Haa will either turn into a Haa sakinah or remain a Taa, depending on how it is scribed

3. Pure sukoun, rowm, or ishmaam may be applied following the rules in previous lessons

Examples

﴿ مُؤْصَدَةٌ ﴾ ﴿ مُمَدَّدَةٍ ﴾

﴿ فَهُمْ عَلَى بَيِّنَتٍ ﴾
﴿ كَأَنَّهُ, جِمَـٰلَتٌ ﴾

The word does **NOT** end with a Feminine Haa

1. The Noon sakinah is omitted from pronunciation, leaving only the harakah

2. Pure sukoun, rowm, or ishmaam may be applied following the rules in previous lessons

Examples

﴿ أَحَدٌ ﴾ ﴿ حَاسِدٍ ﴾

An Advanced Study of Medd

AN ADVANCED STUDY OF MEDD

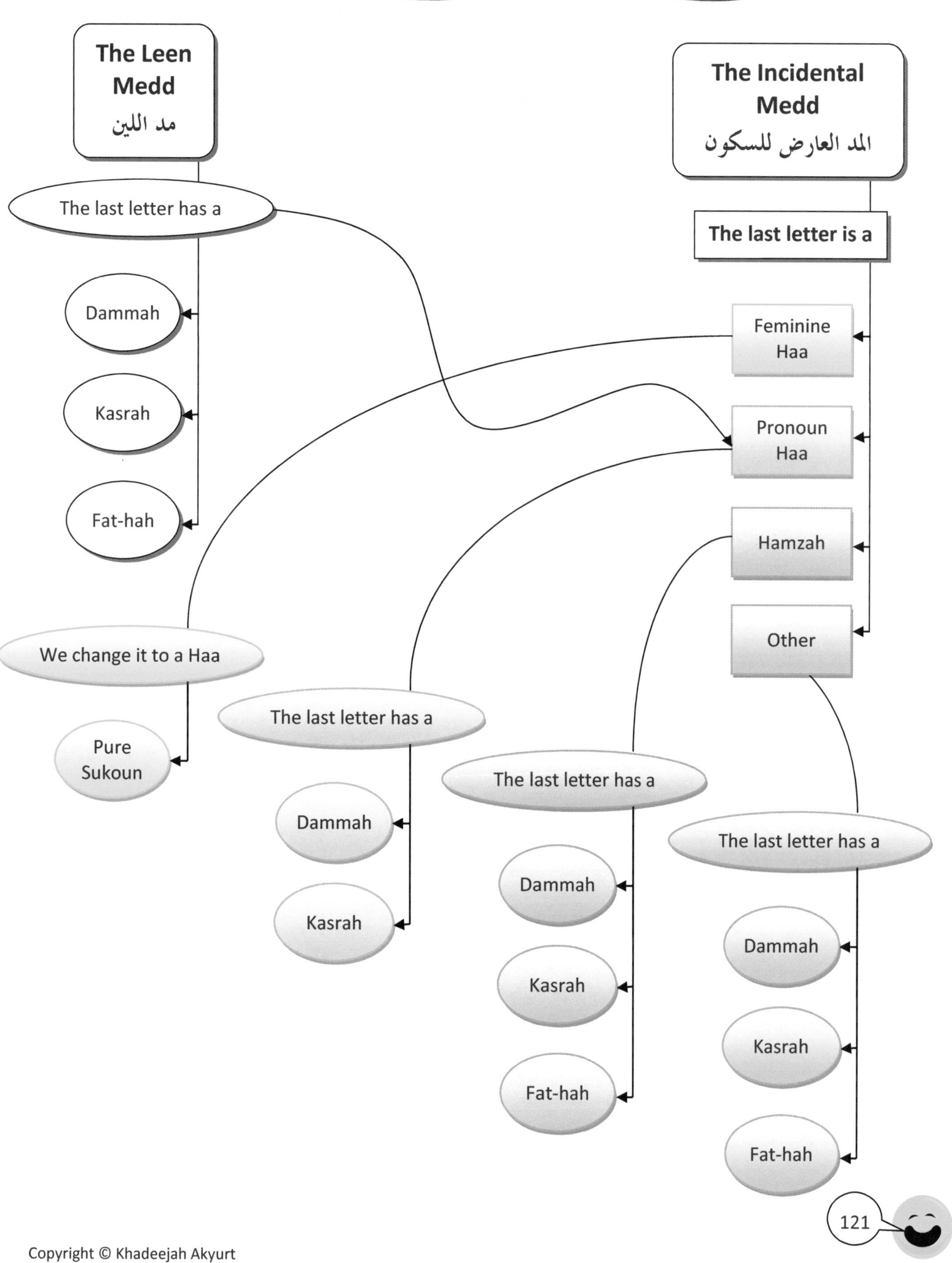

An Advanced Study of Medd Leen

The last letter is preceded by a Waw or Yaa of Leen

The last letter has a...

Dammah	Kasrah	Fat-hah
Examples	Examples	Examples
﴿ وَلَا خَوْفٌ ﴾ ﴿ لَيْسَ كَمِثْلِهِۦ شَيْءٌ ﴾	﴿ وَءَامَنَهُم مِّنْ خَوْفٍ ﴾ ﴿ هَذَا الْبَيْتِ ﴾	﴿ فَلَا فَوْتَ ﴾ ﴿ وَتَوَدُّونَ أَنَّ غَيْرَ ﴾
Pure Sukoun: Less than 2, 4, or 6 harakahs	**Pure Sukoun**: Less than 2, 4, or 6 harakahs	**Pure Sukoun**: Less than 2, 4, or 6 harakahs
Rowm: Less than 2 harakahs	**Rowm**: Less than 2 harakahs	
Ishmaam: Less than 2, 4, or 6 harakahs		

AN ADVANCED STUDY OF INCIDENTAL MEDD

The last letter is preceded by an Alif, Waw or Yaa of Medd

The last letter has a...

Dammah	**Kasrah**	**Fat-hah**
EXAMPLES	EXAMPLES	EXAMPLES
﴿ الرَّحْمَـٰنُ ﴾ ﴿ يَـٰهُودُ ﴾ ﴿ نَسْتَعِينُ ﴾	﴿ يَسْجُدَانِ ﴾ ﴿ نَبَأَ نُوحٍ ﴾ ﴿ الرَّحْمَـٰنِ الرَّحِيمِ ﴾	﴿ فَاتَّقُوا اللَّـهَ ﴾ ﴿ يَعْمَلُونَ ﴾ ﴿ الْمُسْتَقِيمَ ﴾
Pure Sukoun: 2, 4 or 6 harakahs	**Pure Sukoun**: 2, 4 or 6 harakahs	**Pure Sukoun**: 2, 4 or 6 harakahs
Rowm: 2 harakahs	**Rowm**: 2 harakahs	
Ishmaam: 2, 4, or 6 harakahs		

AN ADVANCED STUDY OF INCIDENTAL MEDD

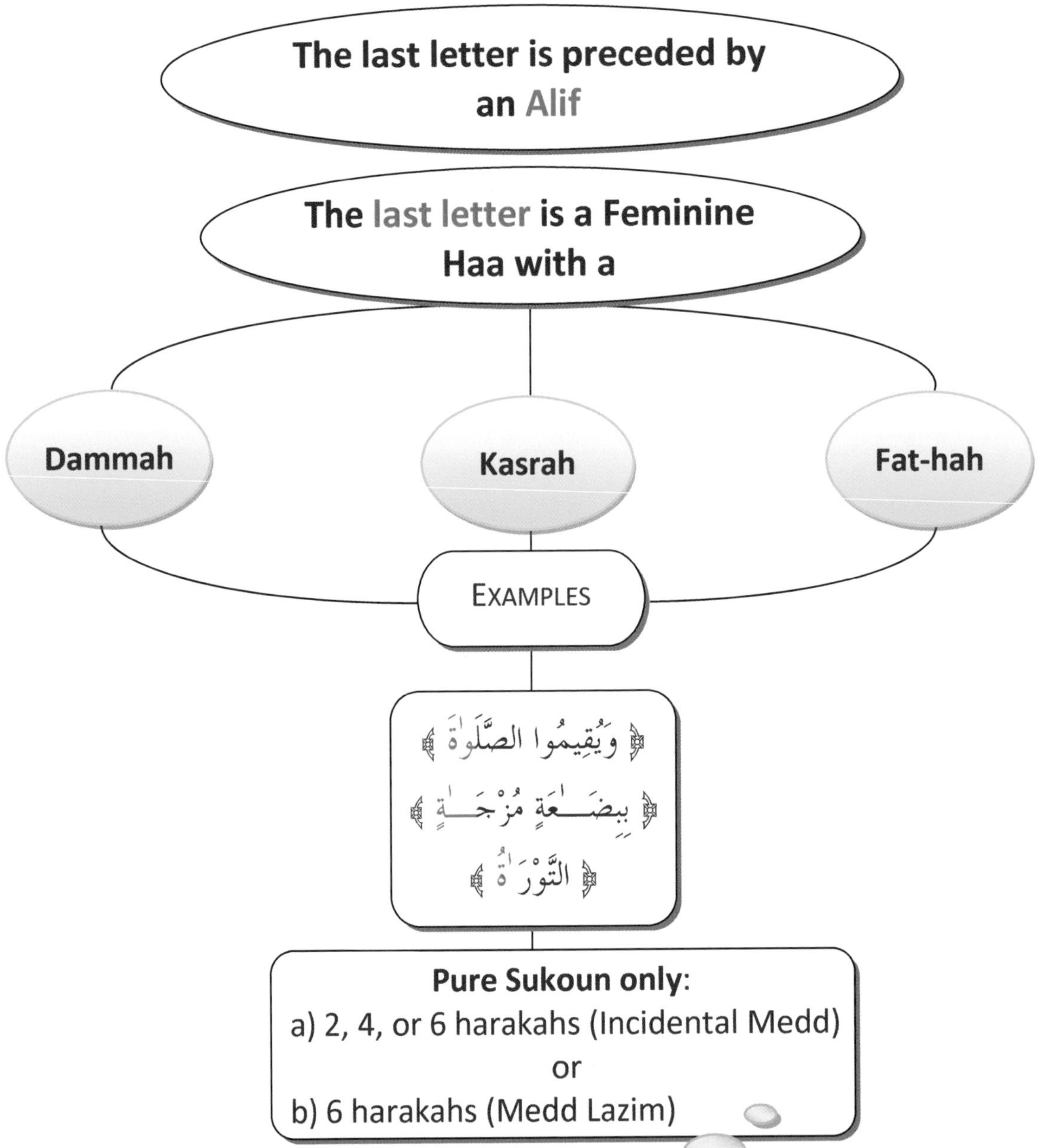

The last letter is preceded by an Alif

The last letter is a Feminine Haa with a

Dammah

Kasrah

Fat-hah

EXAMPLES

﴿ وَيُقِيمُوا الصَّلَوٰةَ ﴾

﴿ بِبِضَـٰعَةٍ مُزْجَـٰةٍ ﴾

﴿ التَّوْرَىٰةُ ﴾

Pure Sukoun only:
a) 2, 4, or 6 harakahs (Incidental Medd)
or
b) 6 harakahs (Medd Lazim)

Remember, if the Feminine Haa is scribed as a Haa, it is pronounced as a pure Haa when stopping, and that rowm and ishmaam are not applied

AN ADVANCED STUDY OF INCIDENTAL AND LEEN MEDDS

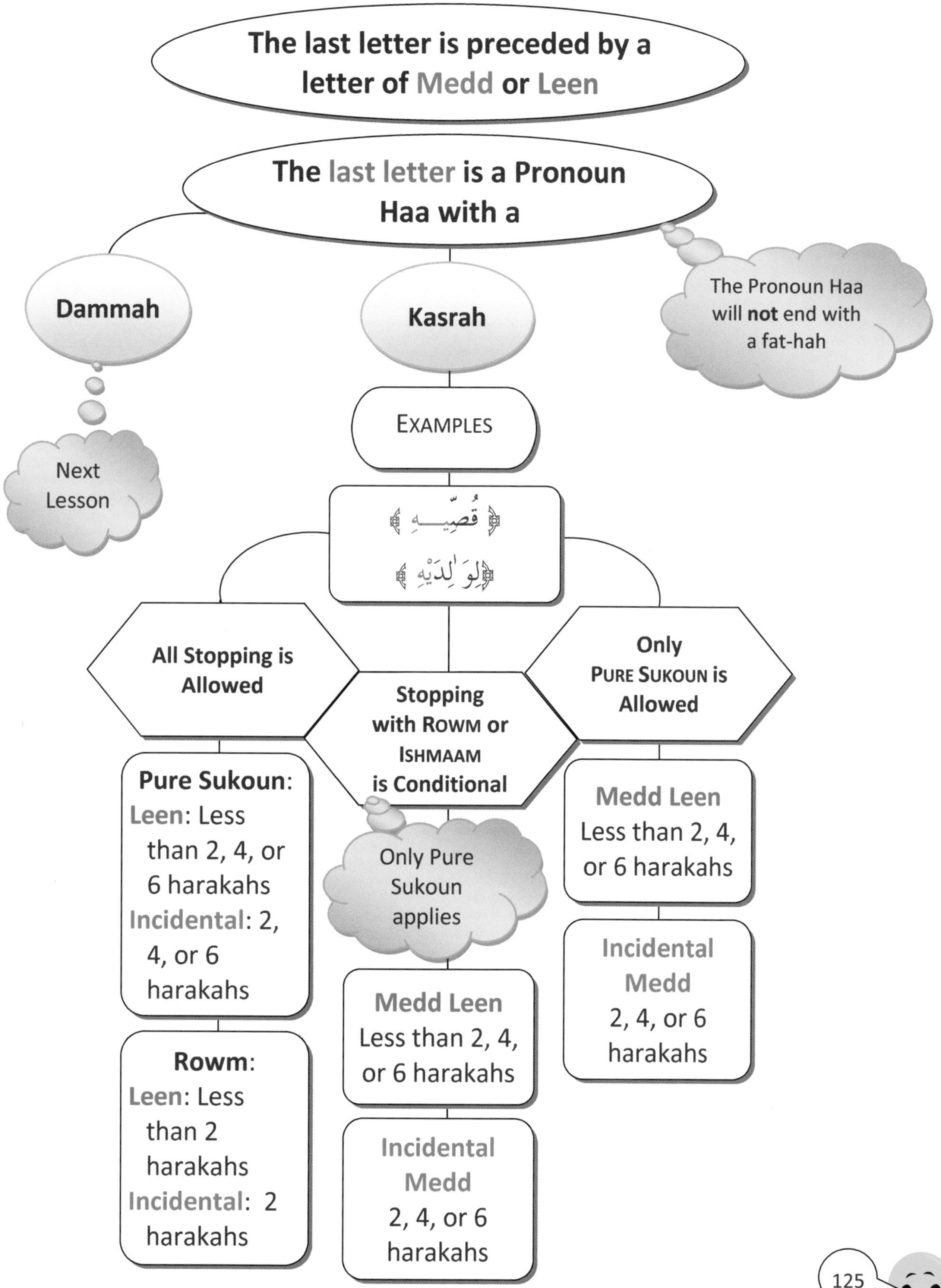

The last letter is preceded by a letter of Medd or Leen

The last letter is a Pronoun Haa with a

The Pronoun Haa will **not** end with a fat-hah

Dammah

Next Lesson

Kasrah

EXAMPLES

﴿ قُصِّيهِ ﴾

﴿ لِوَٰلِدَيْهِ ﴾

All Stopping is Allowed

Pure Sukoun:
Leen: Less than 2, 4, or 6 harakahs
Incidental: 2, 4, or 6 harakahs

Rowm:
Leen: Less than 2 harakahs
Incidental: 2 harakahs

Stopping with ROWM or ISHMAAM is Conditional

Only Pure Sukoun applies

Medd Leen
Less than 2, 4, or 6 harakahs

Incidental Medd
2, 4, or 6 harakahs

Only PURE SUKOUN is Allowed

Medd Leen
Less than 2, 4, or 6 harakahs

Incidental Medd
2, 4, or 6 harakahs

An Advanced Study of Incidental and Leen Medds

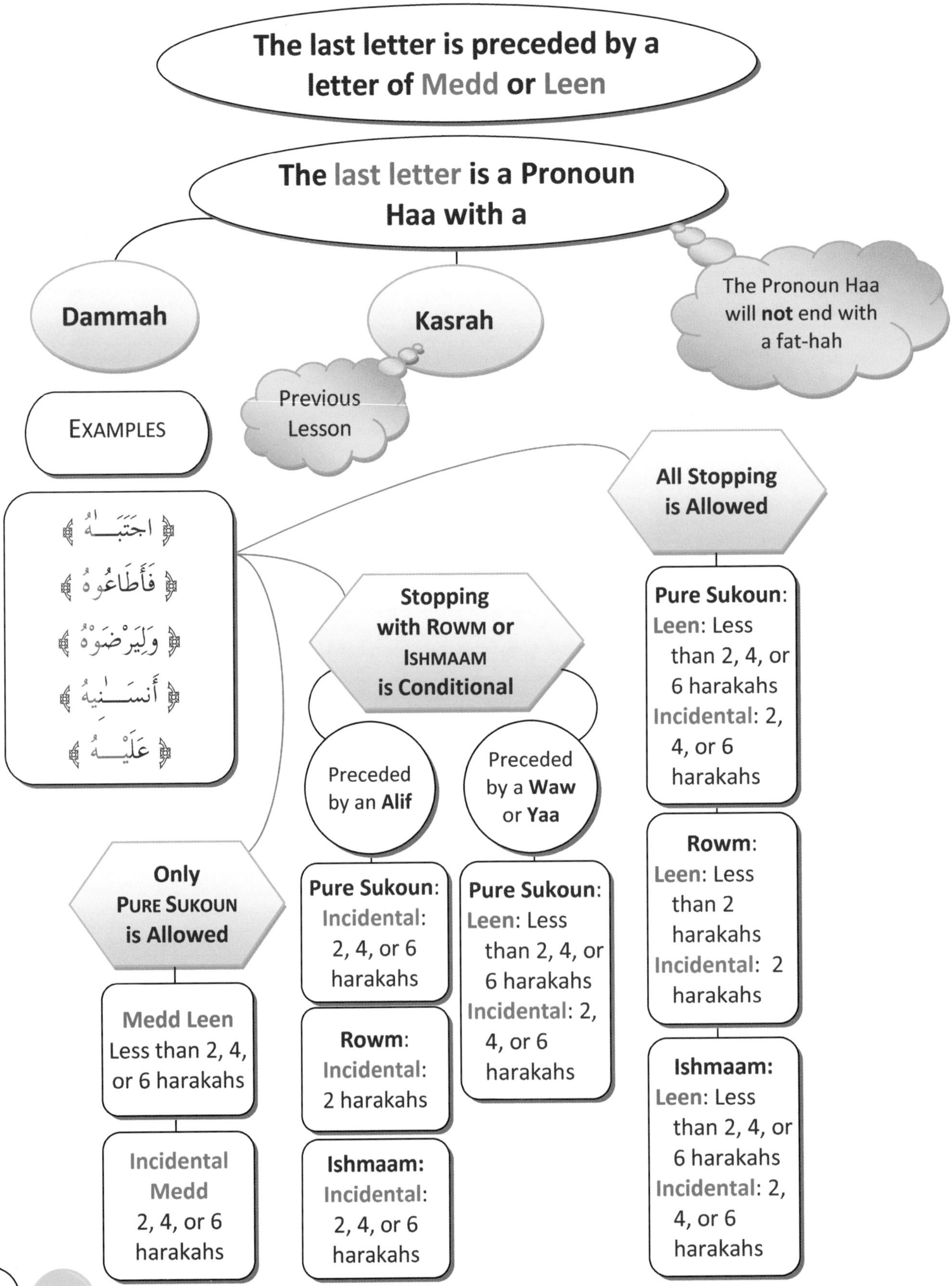

The last letter is preceded by a letter of Medd or Leen

The last letter is a Pronoun Haa with a

Dammah

Kasrah

The Pronoun Haa will **not** end with a fat-hah

Previous Lesson

Examples

﴿ اجْتَبَـٰهُ ﴾

﴿ فَأَطَاعُوهُ ﴾

﴿ وَلِيَرْضَوْهُ ﴾

﴿ أَنسَـٰنِيهُ ﴾

﴿ عَلَيْـهُ ﴾

Only Pure Sukoun is Allowed

Medd Leen
Less than 2, 4, or 6 harakahs

Incidental Medd
2, 4, or 6 harakahs

Stopping with Rowm or Ishmaam is Conditional

Preceded by an **Alif**

Pure Sukoun: **Incidental**: 2, 4, or 6 harakahs

Rowm: **Incidental**: 2 harakahs

Ishmaam: **Incidental**: 2, 4, or 6 harakahs

Preceded by a **Waw** or **Yaa**

Pure Sukoun: **Leen**: Less than 2, 4, or 6 harakahs **Incidental**: 2, 4, or 6 harakahs

All Stopping is Allowed

Pure Sukoun: **Leen**: Less than 2, 4, or 6 harakahs **Incidental**: 2, 4, or 6 harakahs

Rowm: **Leen**: Less than 2 harakahs **Incidental**: 2 harakahs

Ishmaam: **Leen**: Less than 2, 4, or 6 harakahs **Incidental**: 2, 4, or 6 harakahs

An Advanced Study of Incidental Medd

The last letter is preceded by an Alif, Waw or Yaa of Medd

The last letter is a Hamzah and has a...

Dammah

EXAMPLES

﴿ مَن يَشَآءُ ﴾
﴿ لَهُم سُوٓءُ ﴾
﴿ بَرِيٓءٌ ﴾

Pure Sukoun: 4, 5 or 6 harakahs

Rowm: 4 or 5 harakahs

Ishmaam: 4, 5, or 6 harakahs

Kasrah

EXAMPLES

﴿ لِلْفُقَرَآءِ ﴾
﴿ ثَلَـٰثَةَ قُرُوٓءٍ ﴾

Pure Sukoun: 4, 5 or 6 harakahs

Rowm: 4 or 5 harakahs

Fat-hah

EXAMPLES

﴿ نَسُوقُ الْمَآءَ ﴾
﴿ يَعْمَلُونَ السُّوٓءَ ﴾
﴿ وَجِيٓءَ ﴾

Pure Sukoun: 4, 5 or 6 harakahs

Stopping on Words Ending with Vowels

Stopping on Words Ending with Vowels

In the recital of Hafs from 'Asim by the way of *Shatibiyyah*

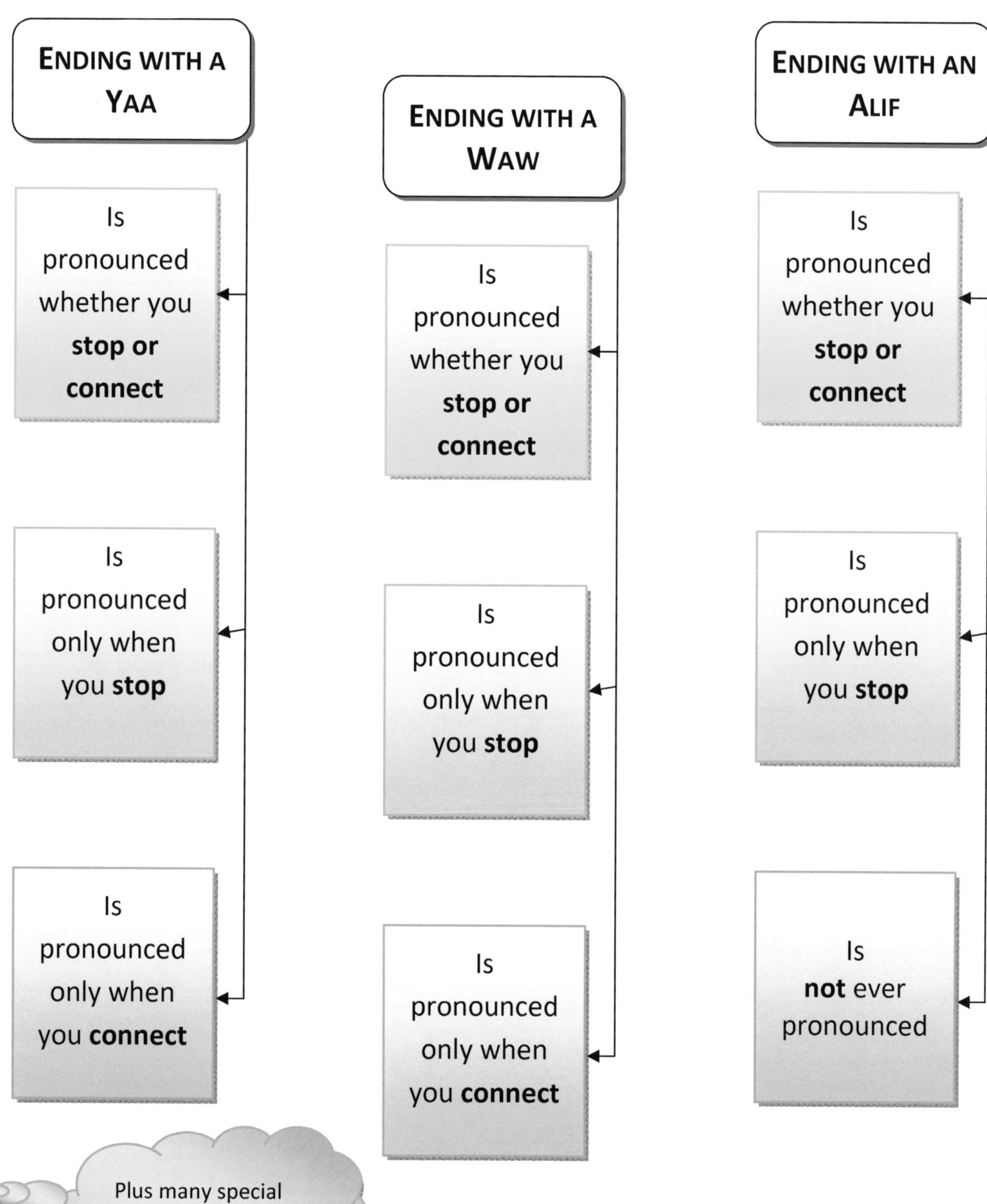

Plus many special cases for each letter

Stopping on Words Ending with an Alif

In the recital of Hafs from 'Asim by the way of *Shatibiyyah*

Is pronounced whether you **stop or connect**

If the Alif is **void** of tashkeel, and is **not** followed by a sakin

EXAMPLES

﴿ الَّذِي نَجَا مِنْهُمَا ﴾

﴿ يَكَادُ سَنَا بَرْقِهِ ﴾

﴿ مَعَكُمَآ أَسْمَعُ ﴾

Pronounced

(الَّذِي نَجَا)

(يَكَادُ سَنَا)

(مَعَكُمَا)

Is pronounced only when you **stop**

If the Alif is followed by a sakin

If the Alif has an **Oval Sukoun** on it

If the Alif is a result of stopping on **Tanween**

Details are on the next page

Is **not** ever pronounced

If the Alif has a **Rounded Sukoun** on it

EXAMPLES

﴿ أَلَا إِنَّ ثَمُودَاْ ﴾

﴿ قَوَارِيرَاْ مِن فِضَّةٍ ﴾

﴿ قَالُواْ ﴾

Pronounced

(أَلَا إِنَّ ثَمُودْ)

(قَوَارِيرْ)

(قَالُو)

Stopping on Words Ending with an Alif

In the recital of Hafs from 'Asim by the way of *Shatibiyyah*

Details were on the previous page

Details were on the previous page

Is pronounced whether you **stop or connect**

Is pronounced only when you **stop**

Is **not** ever pronounced

If the Alif is a result of stopping on **Tanween**

EXAMPLES

﴿ فِي قُرًى مُحَصَّنَةٍ ﴾

﴿ رُكَّعاً سُجَّداً ﴾

﴿ وَلَيَكُوناً مِّنَ ﴾

Pronounced

(فِي قُرى)

(رُكَّعا)

(وَلَيَكُونا)

If the Alif has an **Oval Sukoun** on it

Seven Words

﴿ أنا ﴾ All locations

﴿ لَـٰكِنَّا هُوَ اللَّهُ ﴾ الكهف 38

﴿ وَتَظُنُّونَ بِاللَّهِ الظُّنُونَا ﴾ الأحزاب 10

﴿ وَأَطَعْنَا الرَّسُولَا ﴾ الأحزاب 66

﴿ فَأَضَلُّونَا السَّبِيلَا ﴾ الأحزاب 67

﴿ وَأَكْوَابٍ كَانَتْ قَوَارِيرَا ﴾ الإنسان 15

﴿ لِلْكَافِرِينَ سَلَاسِلَا وَأَغْلَالًا ﴾ الإنسان 4

Pronounced

If the Alif is followed by a sakin

EXAMPLES

﴿ قُلْنَا اهْبِطُوا ﴾

﴿ ذِكْرَى الدَّارِ ﴾

﴿ يَـٰٓأَيُّهَا النَّاسُ ﴾

Pronounced

(قُلْنَا)

(ذِكْرَى)

(يَـٰٓأَيُّهَا)*

Two ways for stopping

(أنا) (لَـٰكِنَّا) (وَتَظُنُّونَ بِاللَّهِ الظُّنُونَا)

(وَأَطَعْنَا الرَّسُولَا) (فَأَضَلُّونَا السَّبِيلَا) (وَأَكْوَابٍ كَانَتْ قَوَارِيرَا)

(لِلْكَافِرِينَ سَلَاسِلَا) and (لِلْكَافِرِينَ سَلَاسِل)

* For special cases that look similar, yet are different, please go to the "Special Cases" lesson

STOPPING ON WORDS ENDING WITH A
WAW OF MEDD
In the recital of Hafs from 'Asim by the way of *Shatibiyyah*

Is pronounced whether you **stop or connect**	Is pronounced only when you **stop**	Is pronounced only when you **connect**
If the Waw is **not** followed by a sakin	If the Waw is followed by a sakin	If the Waw is the result of **Connecting Medd**
EXAMPLES	EXAMPLES	EXAMPLES
﴿ وَأَوْفُوا بِالْعَهْدِ ﴾ ﴿ ءَامَنُوا وَهَاجَرُوا ﴾ ﴿ وَجَاءُو عَلَى ﴾	﴿ مُلَـٰقُوا اللَّهِ ﴾ ﴿ وَأَوْفُوا الْكَيْلَ ﴾ ﴿ وَأَقِيمُوا الصَّلَوٰةَ ﴾	﴿ لَهُ ۥ مُلْكُ ﴾ ﴿ يَرَهُ ۥ أَحَدْ ﴾ ﴿ رزْقَهُ ۥ فَيَقُولُ ﴾
Pronounced	Pronounced	Pronounced
(وَأَوْفُو) (ءَامَنُو) (وَجَاءُو)	(مُلَـٰقُو) (وَأَوْفُو) (وَأَقِيمُو)	(لَهْ) (يَرَهْ) (رزْقَهْ)

STOPPING ON WORDS ENDING WITH A
YAA OF MEDD
In the recital of Hafs from 'Asim by the way of *Shatibiyyah*

Is pronounced whether you **stop or connect**	Is pronounced only when you **stop**	Is pronounced only when you **connect**
If the Yaa is **not** followed by a sakin	If the Yaa is followed by a sakin	If the Yaa is the result of **Connecting Medd**
EXAMPLES	EXAMPLES	EXAMPLES
﴿ يَعْصِمُنِي مِنَ ﴾ ﴿ يَقْضِي بِالْحَقّ ﴾ ﴿ إِنِّي تُبْتُ ﴾	﴿ يُؤْتِي الْحِكْمَةَ ﴾ ﴿ مِن بَعْدِي اسْمُهُ ﴾ ﴿ إِنِّي اصْطَفَيْتُكَ ﴾	﴿ وَكُتُبِهِ وَرُسُلِهِ ﴾ ﴿ هَـٰذِهِ بِضَاعَتُنَا ﴾ ﴿ فِيهِ مُهَانًا ﴾
Pronounced	Pronounced	Pronounced
(يَعْصِمُنِي) (يَقْضِي) (إِنِّي)	(يُؤْتِي) (مِن بَعْدِي) (إِنِّي)	(وَكُتُبِهْ) (هَـٰذِهْ) (فِيهْ)

There is a singular ayah in Surat An-Naml, in which the Yaa is pronounced when you connect, and has two ways for stopping: with and without the Yaa

﴿ فَمَآ ءَاتَـٰنِ ۦَ اللَّهُ ﴾ النمل 36

When stopping, can be read with a Yaa: (فَمَآ ءَاتَـٰنِي)

or without the Yaa: with pure sukoun or rowm (فَمَآ ءَاتَـٰنْ)

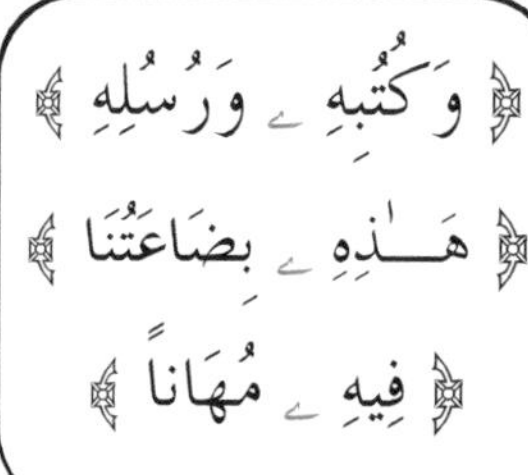

STOPPING ON WORDS ENDING WITH VOWELS

SPECIAL CASES

In the recital of Hafs, the literal scripture is followed when stopping on words, even though it might be surprising to some of us. For example, ﴿ أَيُّهَ الْمُؤْمِنُونَ ﴾ is (أَيُّهْ) when you stop.

Similarly, you have ﴿ أَيُّهَ الثَّقَلَانِ ﴾ and ﴿ يَـٰٓأَيُّهَ السَّاحِرُ ﴾, and other cases such as

﴿ فَمَا تُغْنِ النُّذُرُ ﴾, and ﴿ وَيَمْحُ اللَّهُ ﴾, ﴿ وَيَدْعُ الإِنسَانُ ﴾

AN EXCEPTIONAL CASE

Although Yaa is not written, it **must** be pronounced when you **stop**

EXAMPLES

﴿ تُحْيِ الْمَوْتَى ﴾

﴿ وَيُحْيِ الأَرْضَ ﴾

﴿ نَحْنُ نُحْيِ الْمَوْتَى ﴾

Pronounced

(تُحْيِي)

(وَيُحْيِي)

(نَحْنُ نُحْيِي)

SPECIAL CASES

SPECIAL CASES

that have not yet been addressed

In the recital of Hafs from 'Asim by the way of *Shatibiyyah*

ءَاْعْجَمِيٌّ سورة فصلت ٤٤	This is pronounced with a Hamzah Qat' maftouhah, followed by a Hamzah Musahhalah maftouhah, which is pronounced between a Hamzah and an Alif
 سورة هود ٤١	The Alif is pronounced with full *imalah*, which is between an Alif and a Yaa, but is closer to the sound of the Yaa, and can be accomplished by opening the lips horizontally instead of vertically
ضَعْف سورة الروم ٥٤	The Daad can be read with a fat-hah or with a dammah in all three of these words in this ayah, and both ways of reading are equally correct
 سورة البقرة ٢٤٥	The Saad is pronounced as a Seen in this particular word in this ayah. There are no other acceptable ways to read this word in the recital of Hafs from 'Asim by the way of *Shatibiyyah*
 سورة الأعراف ٦٩	The Saad is pronounced as a Seen in this particular word in this ayah. There are no other acceptable ways to read this word in the recital of Hafs from 'Asim by the way of *Shatibiyyah*
 سورة الطور ٣٧	The Saad is pronounced as either a Saad or a Seen in this particular word in this ayah. Both ways are equally correct
 سورة الغاشية ٢٢	The Saad is pronounced as a Saad in this particular word in this ayah. There are no other acceptable ways to read this word in the recital of Hafs from 'Asim by the way of *Shatibiyyah*
 سورة مريم ١ سورة الشورى ١	The Ain in both ayahs can be read with either 4 or 6 harakahs, because the center letter is a leen letter, thus it differs from the medd letters. The way of 6 harakahs is preferred, as Imam Shatibi states in *Hirz Al-Amani*: " وَفِي عَيْنِ الْوَجْهَانِ وَالطُّولُ فُضِّلاَ "

SPECIAL CASES

Continued

In the recital of Hafs from 'Asim by the way of *Shatibiyyah*

When connecting the Meem with "Allah", giving Meem an incidental fat-hah, there are two ways to read the medd in Meem: 2 or 6 harakahs, and both ways are equally correct

الٓمٓ ۗ اللَّهُ

سورة آل عمران ١، ٢

There is a Lesser Connecting Medd in this ayah, even though the conditions for such a medd are not fulfilled because the Pronoun Haa is preceded by a sukoun

وَيَخْلُدْ فِيهِۦ مُهَانًا

سورة الفرقان ٦٩

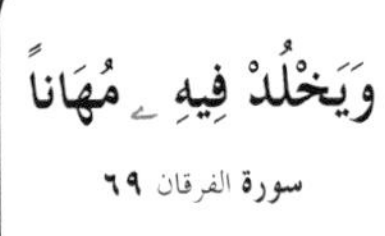

There is no Lesser Connecting Medd in this ayah, even though all the conditions for such a medd are fulfilled

يَرْضَهُ لَكُمْ

سورة الروم ٥٤

SAKTAHS

Pausing without a Breath

The reader may stop fully with a breath, or shortly without a breath on both of these words, but may **not** connect them with the following words

عِوَجًا ۜ

سورة الكهف ١

مَرْقَدِنَا ۜ

سورة يس ٥٢

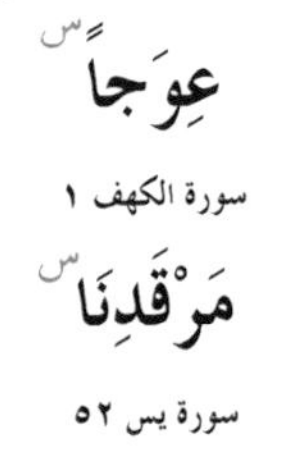

The reader **must** stop shortly without a breath on both of these words. Choosing to stop fully is incorrect, as is connecting them

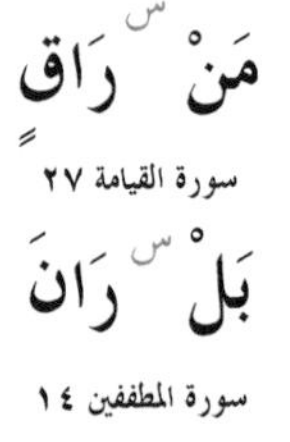

مَنْ ۜ رَاقٍ

سورة القيامة ٢٧

بَلْ ۜ رَانَ

سورة المطففين ١٤

The reader may stop fully with a breath, shortly without a breath, or connect both of these words with the following words. When connecting them, Idghaam must be applied in Al-Haaqqah, and Iqlaab is applied between Al-Anfaal and At-Tawbah

مَالِيَهْ ۜ هَلَكَ

سورة الحاقة ٢٨

عَلِيمٌ ۜ بَرَآءَةٌ

سورة الأنفال ٧٥ – التوبة ١

SPECIAL CASES

Continued

In the recital of Hafs from 'Asim by the
way of *Shatibiyyah*

When starting with the second word, the Laam is given an incidental kasrah to prevent starting with a sukoun, and the word is pronounced لِيَقْطَعْ

ثُمَّ لْيَقْطَعْ
سورة الحج ١٥

When starting with the second word, a Hamzah Wasl with a fat-hah is added to prevent starting with a sukoun, and the word is pronounced أَلْـئَيْكَةِ

أَصْحَـٰبُ لْـَٔيْكَةِ
سورة الشعراء ١٧٦
ص ١٣

141

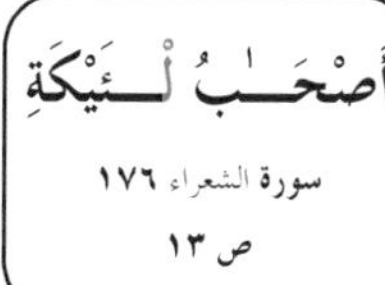

CHAINS OF NARRATION

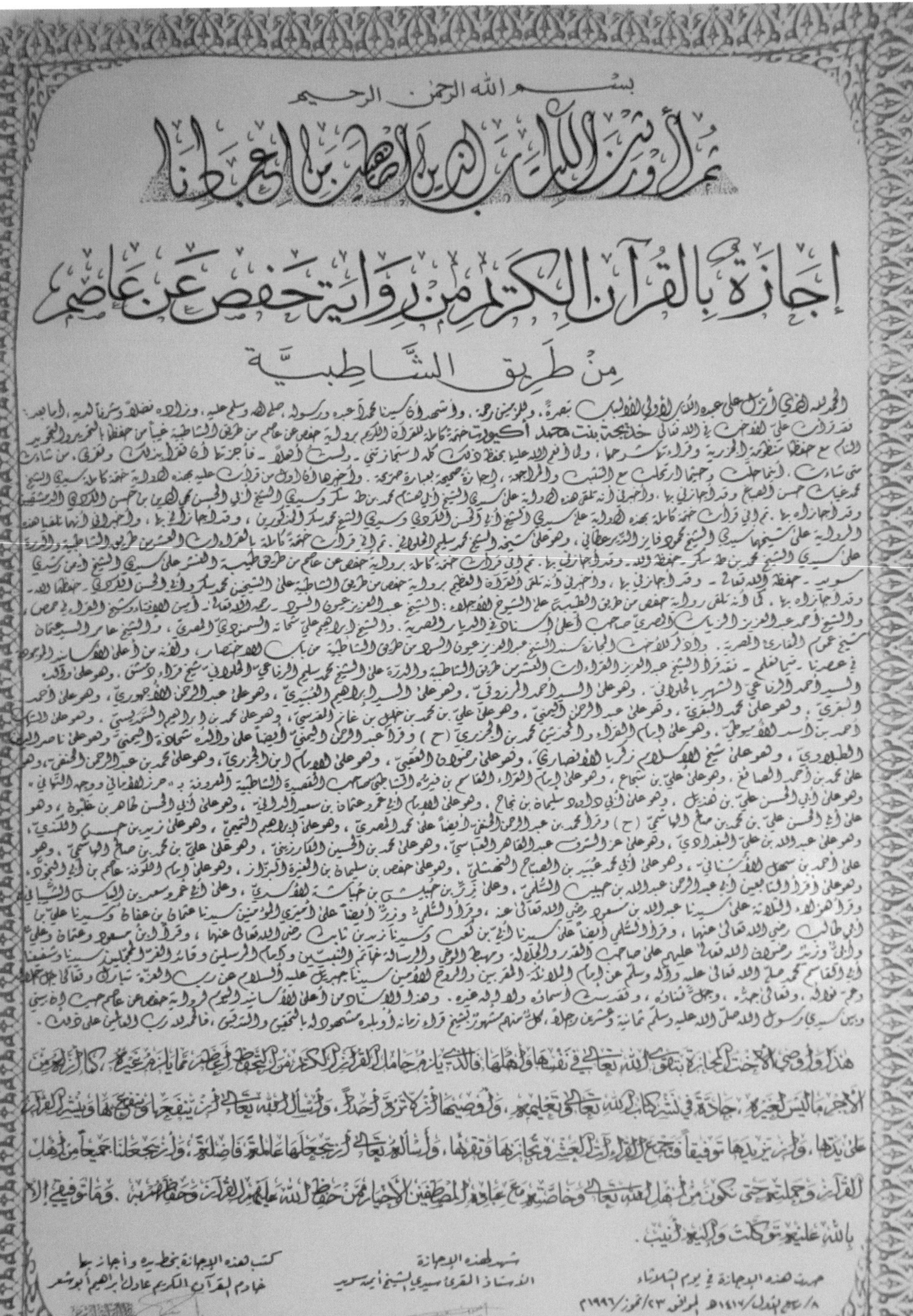

بسم الله الرحمن الرحيم

ثم أورثنا الكتاب الذين اصطفينا من عبادنا

إجازة بالقرآن الكريم من رواية حفص عن عاصم

من طريق الشاطبية

الحمد لله الذي أنزل على عبده الكتاب لأولي الألباب تبصرة، وللمؤمنين رحمة. وأشهد أن سيدنا محمداً عبده ورسوله، صلى الله وسلم عليه، وزاده فضلاً وشرفاً لديه، أما بعد:

فقد قرأت عليّ الأخت في الله تعالى خديجة بنت محمد أكيورت ختمة كاملة للقرآن الكريم برواية حفص عن عاصم من طريق الشاطبية غيباً من حفظها بالتحرير والتجويد التام مع حفظها منظومة الجزرية وقراءتها شرحها، ولما أتم الله عليها بحفظ ذلك كله استجازتني. ولست أهلاً. فأجزتها أن تقرأ بذلك وتقرئ من شاءت متى شاءت، أينما حلّت وحيثما ارتحلت مع التثبت والمراجعة، إجازة صحيحة بعبارة صريحة. وأخبرها أني أول من قرأت عليه بهذه الرواية ختمة كاملة سيدي الشيخ محمد غياث حسن الصباغ وقد أجازني بها. وأخبرني أنه تلقى هذه الرواية على سيدي الشيخ أبي هشام محمد بن طه سكر وسيدي الشيخ أبي الحسن محي الدين بن حسن الكردي الدمشقي وقد أجازاه بها. [illegible]

هذا وأوصي الأخت المجازة بتقوى الله تعالى في نفسها وأهلها فالذي يلزم حامل القرآن الكريم من التحفظ أعظم مما يلزم غيره، كما أن له من الأجر ما ليس لغيره، جادة في نشر كتاب الله تعالى وتعليمه، وأوصيها أن لا تنسى أحداً. وأسأل الله تعالى أن ينفعها وينفع بها وينشر القرآن على يدها، وأن يزيدها توفيقاً فتجمع القراءات العشر وتجازها وتقرئها، وأسأله تعالى أن يجعلها عالمة فاضلة، وأن يجعلنا جميعاً من أهل القرآن وحملته حتى نكون من أهل الله تعالى وخاصته مع عباده المصطفين الأخيار ممن حفظ الله عليهم القرآن وحفظهم به. وما توفيقي إلا بالله عليه توكلت وإليه أنيب.

حررت هذه الإجازة في يوم الثلاثاء ٨/ربيع الأول/١٤١٧هـ الموافق ٢٣/تموز/١٩٩٦م	شهد لهذه الإجازة الأستاذ المقرئ سيدي الشيخ أيمن سويد	كتب هذه الإجازة بخط يده وأجازها خادم القرآن الكريم عادل إبراهيم أبو شعر

الرقم المتسلسل ٥٠١

Prophet Mohamed, may the peace and blessings of Allah be on him

Ubay Ibn Ka'b & Zaid Ibn Thabit & Ali Ibn Abi-Talib & Othman Ibn 'Affan 1

Abdullah Ibn Habeeb As-Sulami (d. 74 A.H.) 2

'Asim Ibn Abi-An-Najoud (d. 127 A.H.) 3

Hafs Ibn Sulaiman Al-Bazzaz Al-Koufi (d. 180 A.H.) 4

'Ubaid Ibn As-Sabbah An-Nahshali (d. 235 A.H.) 5

Ahmad Ibn Sahl Al-Ushnani (d. 307 A.H.) 6

Ali Ibn Mohamed Al-Hashimi (d. 368 A.H.) 7

Tahir Ibn Ghalboun (d. 399 AH) 8

Abu-Amr Othman Ibn Saeed Ad-Dani (d. 444 A.H.) 9

Abu-Dawood Sulaiman Ibn Najah (d. 496 A.H.) 10

Ali Ibn Mohamed Ibn Huthail Al-Andalusi (d. 564 A.H.) 11

Al-Qasim Ibn Ferro Ash-Shatibi (d. 590 A.H.) 12

Ali Ibn Shujaa' Al-Abbasi (d. 661 A.H.) 13

Mohamed Ibn Ahmad As-Sai'gh (d. 725 A.H.) 14

Abdul-Rahman Ibn Ahmad Al-Baghdadi (d. 781 A.H.) 15

Mohamed Ibn Mohamed Al-Jazari (d. 833 A.H.) 16

Ahmad Ibn Asad Al-Umyouti (d. 872 A.H.) 17

Mohamed Ibn Ibrahim As-Samadeesi (d. 932 A.H.) 18

Ali Ibn Mohamed Al-Maqdisi (d. 1004 A.H.) 19

Abdul-Rahman Ibn Shahatha Al-Yamani (d. 1050 A.H.) 20

Mohamed Ibn Qasim Al-Baqari (d. 1111 A.H.) 21

Ahmad Ibn Rajab Al-Baqari (d. 1189 A.H.) 22

Abdul-Rahman Ibn Hasan Al-Ujhouri (d. 1198 A.H.) 23

Ibrahim Ibn Badawi Al-Ubaidi (d. circa 1237A.H.) 24

Ahmad Ibn Ramadan Al-Marzouqi (d. 1262 A.H.) 25

Ahmad Ar-Rifaa'i Al-Halwani (d. 1307 A.H.) 26

Mohamed Saleem Ar-Rifaa'i Al-Halwani (d. 1363 A.H.) 27

Abdul-'Azeez 'Uyoun As-Soud (d. 1399 A.H.) 28

Dr. Ayman Rushdi Suwaid 29

Dr. Adel Ibrahim Abushaar 30

Khadeejah Mehmet Akyurt

Chain of narration for the Ijazah of **Hafs** who learned from **'Asim**, by the way of ***Shatibiyyah***, which was handed down to Khadeejah Mehmet Akyurt

الإسناد الذى أدى إلي هذا المتن عن الناظم رحمه الله

تلقيتُ هذا النظم المبارك، وقرأتُهُ غيباً من حفظي، في مجلس واحد، على سيدي وشيخي العلامة المقرئ عبدالعزيز عيون السود رحمه الله تعالى، أمين الإفتاء وشيخ القراء في مدينة حمص، وأجازني به، وأخبرني أنه تلقاه عن شيخه فريد العصر، وتاج القراء بمصر، الأستاذ الشيخ علي محمد الضباع شيخ القراء وعموم المقارئ بالديار المصرية، رحمه الله تعالى، وهو تلقاه عن الأستاذ الجليل الشيخ عبدالرحمن بن حسين الخطيب الشعار، وهو عن خاتمة القراء المحققين، شمس الملة والدين، الشيخ محمد بن أحمد المتولي شيخ قراء ومقارئ مصر الأسبق، وهو عن شيخه المحقق، العمدة المدقق، السيد أحمد الدّريّ الشهير بالتهامي، وهو عن شيخ قراء وقته العالم العامل الشيخ أحمد بن محمد المعروف بسلمونة، وهو عن شيخه المحقق المدقق السيد إبراهيم العبيدي، كبير المقرئين في وقته، وهو عن الأستاذ الكبير، العلم الشهير، الشيخ عبدالرحمن بن حسن بن عمر الأجهوري، وهو عن العالم العلامة الإمام الفاضل الشيخ أحمد البقري المعروف بأبي السماح، وهو عن العلامة شيخ قراء مصر في وقته شمس الدين محمد بن قاسم البقري، وهو عن شيخ قراء وقته أيضاً الشيخ عبدالرحمن اليمني، وهو عن والده الذي اشتهر صيته في جميع الآفاق، الشيخ شحاذة اليمني، وهو عن شيخ أهل زمانه العلامة ناصر الدين محمد بن سالم الطبلاوي، وهو عن شيخ الإسلام والمسلمين، أبي يحيى زكريا الأنصاري، وهو عن شيخ شيوخ وقته، أبي النُّعيم رضوان ابن محمد العُقْبي، وهو عن ناظمها شيخ القراء والمحدثين، شمس الملة والدين، محمد بن محمد بن محمد الجزري، تغمد الله الجميع برحمته، وأسكنهم فسيح جنته، آمين.

خادم القرآن الكريم

أيمن رشدي سويد الدمشقي

عفا الله عنه

جدة / الخميس / ١٨/ شعبان/ ١٤٠٧هـ

بسم الله الرحمن الرحيم

الحمد لله رب العالمين، وأفضل الصلاة وأتم التسليم على سيدنا ونبينا محمد وعلى آله وصحبه أجمعين أما بعد:

فقد قرأت عليّ الأخت الفاضلة خديجة محمد أكيورت هذا المتن المبارك في مجلس واحد من حفظها لفظ إتقان وحفظ إتقان، وقد أجزتها أن ترويه عني لمن تراه أهلاً لذلك من طالبيه

وأخبرتها أني تلقيت هذا النظم المبارك على سيدي الشيخ أيمن سويد حفظه الله تعالى وهو على شيخه الشيخ عبدالعزيز عيون السود رحمه الله تعالى وهو على الشيخ علي الضباع رحمه الله تعالى - بسنده إلى الناظم رحمه الله تعالى ورضي عنه. وأسأل الله تعالى أن يزيدها توفيقاً، وأن يحفظنا وإياها في السر والعلن، إنه سميع قريب مجيب وصلى الله على سيدنا محمد وعلى آله وصحبه أجمعين

عادل إبراهيم أبو شعر

جدة ٢/رمضان/١٤٣٢هـ

THE AUTHOR'S CHAIN TO IBN AL-JAZARI

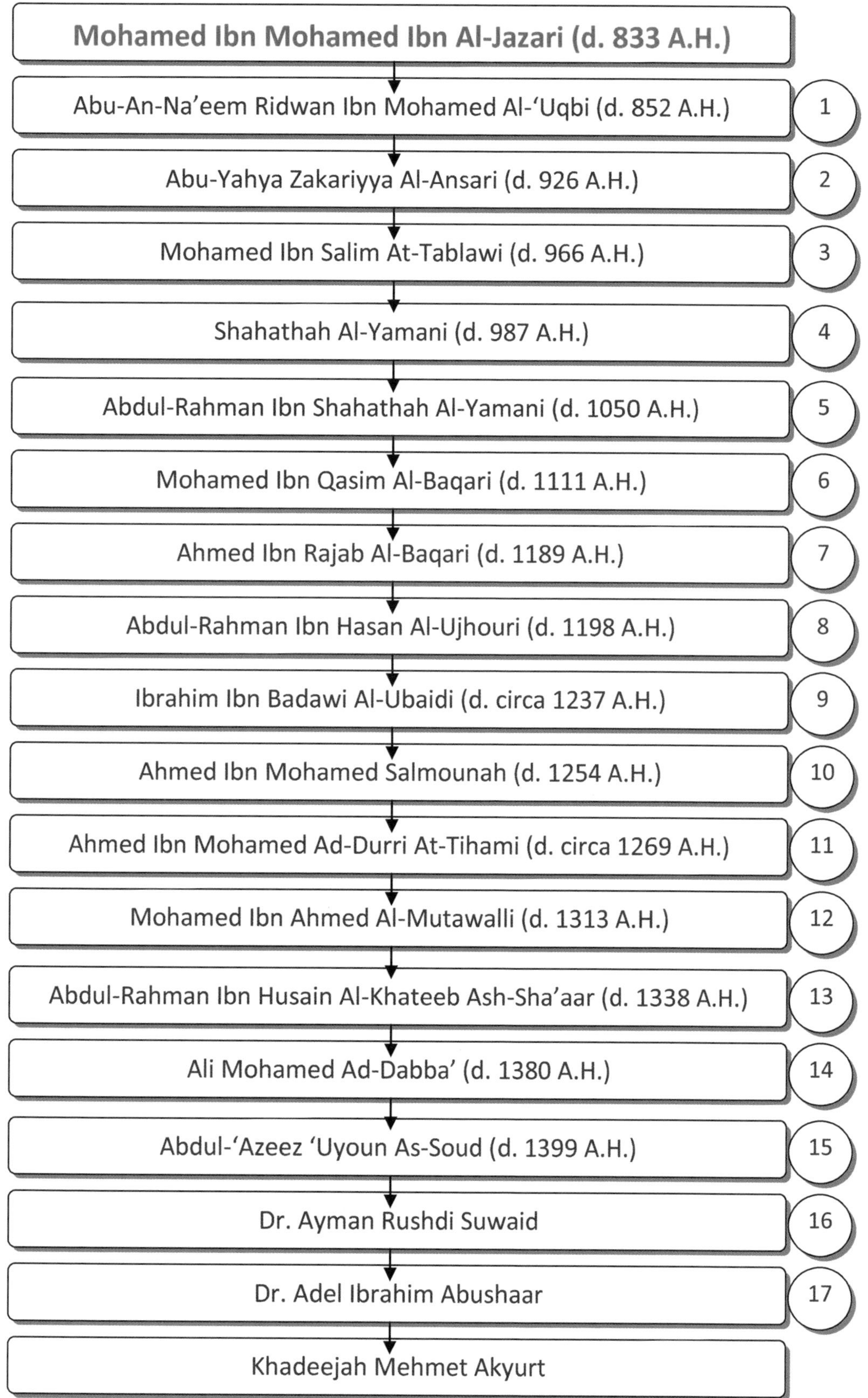

Mohamed Ibn Mohamed Ibn Al-Jazari (d. 833 A.H.)
Abu-An-Na'eem Ridwan Ibn Mohamed Al-'Uqbi (d. 852 A.H.) 1
Abu-Yahya Zakariyya Al-Ansari (d. 926 A.H.) 2
Mohamed Ibn Salim At-Tablawi (d. 966 A.H.) 3
Shahathah Al-Yamani (d. 987 A.H.) 4
Abdul-Rahman Ibn Shahathah Al-Yamani (d. 1050 A.H.) 5
Mohamed Ibn Qasim Al-Baqari (d. 1111 A.H.) 6
Ahmed Ibn Rajab Al-Baqari (d. 1189 A.H.) 7
Abdul-Rahman Ibn Hasan Al-Ujhouri (d. 1198 A.H.) 8
Ibrahim Ibn Badawi Al-Ubaidi (d. circa 1237 A.H.) 9
Ahmed Ibn Mohamed Salmounah (d. 1254 A.H.) 10
Ahmed Ibn Mohamed Ad-Durri At-Tihami (d. circa 1269 A.H.) 11
Mohamed Ibn Ahmed Al-Mutawalli (d. 1313 A.H.) 12
Abdul-Rahman Ibn Husain Al-Khateeb Ash-Sha'aar (d. 1338 A.H.) 13
Ali Mohamed Ad-Dabba' (d. 1380 A.H.) 14
Abdul-'Azeez 'Uyoun As-Soud (d. 1399 A.H.) 15
Dr. Ayman Rushdi Suwaid 16
Dr. Adel Ibrahim Abushaar 17
Khadeejah Mehmet Akyurt

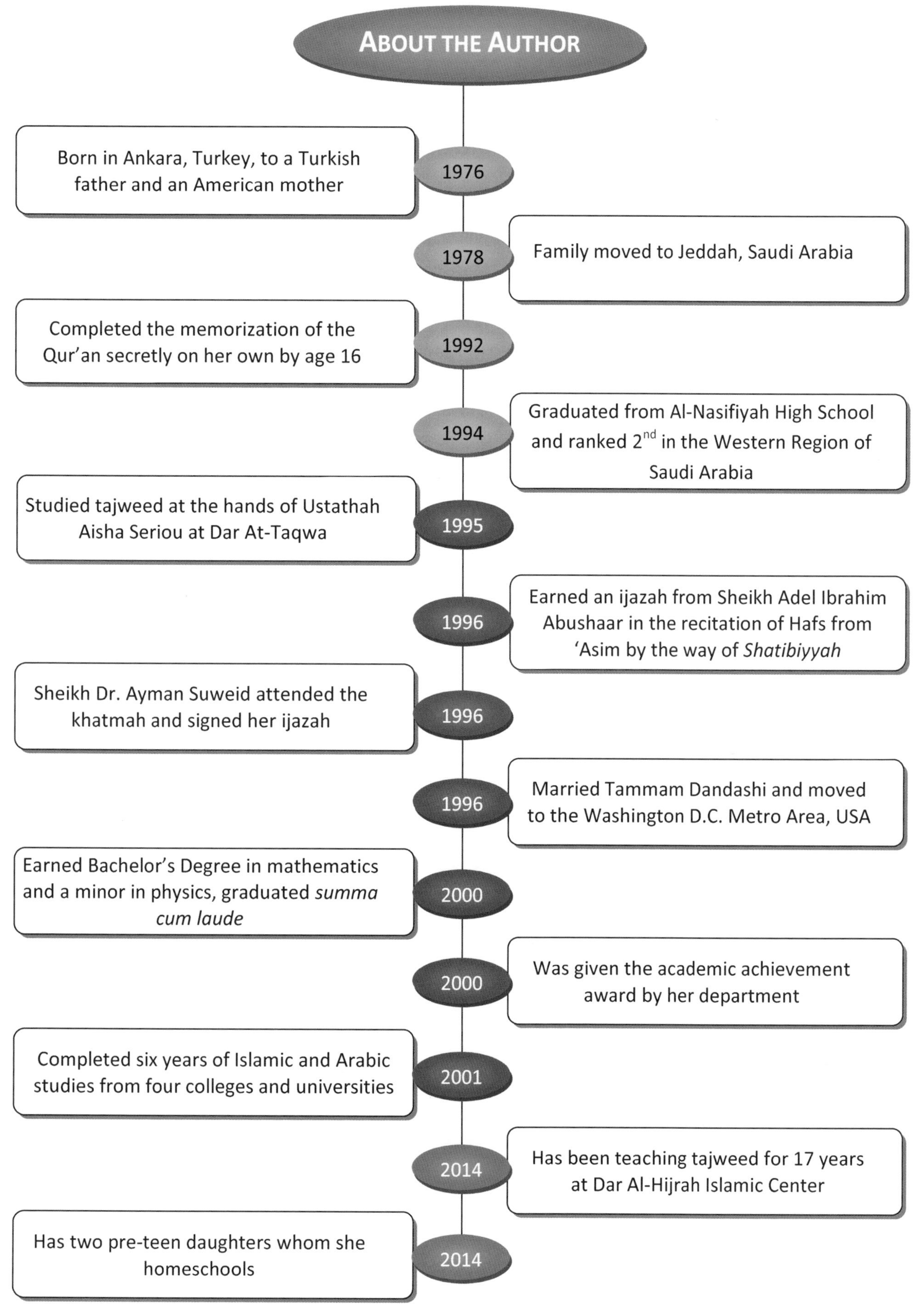
About the Author
1976
Born in Ankara, Turkey, to a Turkish father and an American mother
1978
Family moved to Jeddah, Saudi Arabia
1992
Completed the memorization of the Qur'an secretly on her own by age 16
1994
Graduated from Al-Nasifiyah High School and ranked 2nd in the Western Region of Saudi Arabia
1995
Studied tajweed at the hands of Ustathah Aisha Seriou at Dar At-Taqwa
1996
Earned an ijazah from Sheikh Adel Ibrahim Abushaar in the recitation of Hafs from 'Asim by the way of Shatibiyyah
1996
Sheikh Dr. Ayman Suweid attended the khatmah and signed her ijazah
1996
Married Tammam Dandashi and moved to the Washington D.C. Metro Area, USA
2000
Earned Bachelor's Degree in mathematics and a minor in physics, graduated summa cum laude
2000
Was given the academic achievement award by her department
2001
Completed six years of Islamic and Arabic studies from four colleges and universities
2014
Has been teaching tajweed for 17 years at Dar Al-Hijrah Islamic Center
2014
Has two pre-teen daughters whom she homeschools

REFERENCES

The Holy Qur'an. Medina: King Fahd Complex for the Printing of the Holy Qur'an, 1406 A.H. Print.

Abushaar, Adel Ibrahim (Dr.Adel Abushaar). Facebook. Web. 30 January 2014.

Ad-Dabba', Ali Mohamed (d. 1380 A.H.). Sareeh An-Nass fi Al-Kalimaat Al-Mukhtalaf Feeha 'an Hafs. Egypt: Mustafa Al-Babi Al-Halabi, 1930 C.E. PDF file.

Ad-Dabba', Ali Mohamed (d. 1380 A.H.). Sameer At-Talibeen fi Rassm wa Dabt Al-Kitaab Al-Mubeen. 1357 A.H. PDF file.

Ad-Dani, Abu-'Amr Othman Ibn Sa'eed (d. 444 A.H.). Al-Muqni' fi Rasm Masahif Al-Amsaar , Kitaab An-Naqt. Ed. Mohamed As-Sadiq Qamhawi. Cairo: Maktabah Al-Kulliyyat Al-Azhariyyah, 1978 C.E. PDF file.

Al-Ansari, Abu-Yahya Zakariyya (d. 926 A.H.). Sharh Al-Muqaddimah Al-Jazariyyah. Ed. Mohamed Ghayyath As-Sabbagh. Jeddah: Al- Jama'ah Al-Khairiyyah Litahfeeth Al-Qur'an Al-Kareem, 1412 A.H. Print.

Al-Jazari, Mohamed Ibn Mohamed (d. 833 A.H.). An-Nashr fi Al-Qira'aat Al-'Ashr. Ed. Ali Mohamed Ad-Dabba'. Dar Al-Kitaab Al-Arabi. Print.

Al-Jazari, Mohamed Ibn Mohamed (d. 833 A.H.). Manthoumah Al-Muqaddimah. Ed. Ayman Rushdi Suweid. Jeddah: Lina, 1407 A.H. Print.

Al-Mutawalli, Mohamed Ibn Ahmed Ibn Abdillah (d. 1313 A.H.). Al-Lu'lu' Al-Manthoum, Ar-Raheeq Al-Makhtoum. Ed. Hasan Ibn Khalaf Al-Husaini. Cairo: Al-Maktabah Al-Azhariyyah Lit-Turath, 2003 C.E. PDF file.

Al-Qadi, Abdul-Fattah Abdul-Ghani (d. 1403 A.H.). Al-Wafi fi Sharh Ash-Shatibiyyah fi Al-Qira'aat As-Sab'. Jeddah: Maktabah As-Sawaadi, 1414 A.H. Print.

Al-Qari, Abul-Hasan Ali Al-Mulla Al-Harawi (d. 1014 A.H.). Al-Minah Al-Fikriyyah fi Sharh Al-Muqaddimah Al-Jazariyyah. Egypt: Mustafa Al-Babi Al-Halabi, 1948 C.E. Print.

Al-Qattan, Manna' Khaleel (d. 1420 A.H.). Mabahith fi 'Uloum Al-Qur'an. Beirut: Mo'assasah Ar-Risalah, 1411 A.H. Print.

Ash-Shatibi, Al-Qasim Ibn Ferro (d. 590 A.H.). Hirz Al-Amani wa Wajh At-Tahani. Ed. Mohamed Tameem Az-Zu'bi. Jeddah: Dar Al-Matbou'aat Al-Hadeethah, 1410 A.H. Print.

As-Samannoudi, Ibrahim Ali Shahatah (d. 1429 A.H.). La'ali' Al-Bayan fi Tajweed Al-Qur'an. PDF file.

As-Soud, Abdul-'Aziz 'Uyoun (d. 1399 A.H.). Manthoumah Talkhees Sareeh An-Nass fi Al-Kalimaat Al-Mukhtalaf Feeha 'an Hafs. Ed. Ayman Rushdi Suweid. PDF file.

As-Suyouti, Abdul-Rahman Ibn Abi-Bakr (d. 911 A.H.). Al-Itqaan fi 'Uloum Al-Qur'an. Ed. Center for Qur'anic Studies. Medina: King Fahd Complex for the Printing of the Holy Qur'an, 1426 A.H. PDF file.

Nasr, 'Atiyyah Qabil. Ghayah Al-Mureed fi 'Ilm At-Tajweed. Ar-Ri'asah Al-'Aammah Li'idarah Al-Buhouth Al-'Ilmiyah, 1414 A.H. Print.

Nasr, Mohamed Makki (d. 1325 A.H.). Nihayah Al-Qawl Al-Mufeed fi 'Ilm At-Tajweed. Ed. Ali Mohamed Ad-Dabba'. Egypt: Mostafa Al-Babi Al-Halabi, 1349 A.H. Print.

Gharabah, Rawiyah Hamdi. Minhaj At-Tilawah. Jeddah: Dar Al-'Ilm Lit-Tiba'ah wa An-Nashr, 1413 A.H. Print.

Suweid, Ayman Rushdi. Al-Itqaan Litilawah Al-Qur'an. IQRA, 2010-2013. YouTube. Web. 30 January 2014.

Made in the USA
Columbia, SC
30 October 2017